THE NETHERLANDS IN COURT

Essays in Honour of Johan G. Lammers

Johan G. Lammers during the hearings in the Case Concerning Legality of Use of Force (Yugoslavia *v.* the Netherlands) before the International Court of Justice, Peace Palace, April 2004 (photo: PE Studio, Wassenaar).

THE NETHERLANDS IN COURT

ESSAYS IN HONOUR OF JOHAN G. LAMMERS

Edited by

NIELS BLOKKER
RENÉ LEFEBER
LIESBETH LIJNZAAD
INEKE VAN BLADEL

MARTINUS NIJHOFF PUBLISHERS
LEIDEN / BOSTON

A C.I.P. Catalogue record for this book is available from the Library of Congress.

Printed on acid-free paper.

Layout and camera-ready copy:
Anne-Marie Krens – Oegstgeest – The Netherlands

ISBN 10 90 04 14705 0
ISBN 13 978 90 04 15705 7

http://www.brill.nl

Printed and bound in the Netherlands

TABLE OF CONTENTS

PREFACE

Pieter H. Kooijmans

Johan Lammers had been a member of the staff of the Department of International Law of Leyden University for a number of years when I was appointed Professor of Public International Law. I knew him superficially but very soon I learned to appreciate how lucky I was to have the assistance of a person of his calibre. He was an experienced teacher but I was struck most of all by his keen scholarly mind. From 1971 on he had regularly published on the legal aspects of the pollution of international watercourses – highly topical at that time because of the heavily polluted water of the Rhine –, a subject which was then relatively new. His research in this field culminated in 1984 in the completion of a doctor's thesis on this subject which – significantly – had as subtitle: 'a search for substantive rules and principles of law'. A search indeed for, in particular with regard to the issue of State responsibility for the pollution of international watercourses, he had to walk virtually untrodden paths. The result of this search was a seminal and rich book the importance of which was widely recognized. Deservedly he obtained the doctor's degree with the qualification *cum laude.*

I told Johan that he now should get some practical experience since I felt that an academic career is enriched by a personal knowledge of the practice of international law. Although he felt a slight hesitation to leave the academic sphere, he applied for the function of assistant legal adviser at the Ministry of Foreign Affairs. Evidently he never regretted that decision since he has served the Netherlands Government uninterruptedly from 1984 until the day of his retirement. Although he undoubtedly could have returned to a full time academic profession, he preferred to combine university with practice. By doing so, he followed the example of his illustrious predecessors as legal adviser, Professors Francois and Riphagen.

In his case this choice is fully understandable. It surely must have been both challenging and rewarding to participate actively at the negotiating table in the realization and materialization of the ideas he had developed during his 'search for substantive rules and principles'. He has attended virtually all law-making conferences in the field of the preservation and protection of the environment, both at the universal and the regional level, and sometimes was able to contribute personally in a meaningful way to a positive result.

At the same time he passed on his knowledge and practical experience to a new generation of lawyers, first as Professor of general international law and, since 1990, as Professor of International Environmental Law at the University of Amsterdam. He did so – and does so – at a time when the threat to the environment is steadily increasing and the need for conservatory and protective measures is therefore evermore urgent. The future needs well-informed and well-trained lawyers and Johan has contributed his bit towards their education.

I have also had the pleasure of meeting Johan Lammers at the other side of the bar when he was agent for the Netherlands Government in proceedings before the International Court of Justice and the Permanent Court of Arbitration. As is observed in the introductory chapter of this book, his term as legal adviser is also characterized by the involvement of the Netherlands in litigation before a number of international tribunals. Fully in line with his personality his interventions were always brief and to the point and brought in a sober and businesslike way, without the ornate style and flamboyant phraseology which so often characterizes legal pleading in international proceedings.

For what typifies Johan Lammers is his matter of factness and his straightforwardness. As I write these words former US Vice-President Al Gore is crusading in Europe for the preservation and the protection of the environment. His appeal is urgent and his language dramatic; his movie 'An Inconvenient Truth' is based on a doomsday scenario. The last what can be said of Johan Lammers is that he is an activist warning for the dangers of the future in dramatic words. But in a quiet yet tenacious manner Johan Lammers has contributed to the establishment of a legal framework directed to an effective control of the behaviour of international actors in order to protect the environment. He thus acted as the trustee of future generations.

INTRODUCTION

Niels Blokker, René Lefeber,
Liesbeth Lijnzaad & Ineke van Bladel

The contributions to this book have been written by colleagues and former colleagues of Johan Lammers, Legal Adviser of the Ministry of Foreign Affairs of the Kingdom of the Netherlands and head of its International Law Division, on the occasion of his retirement from the Ministry. It marks their respect and friendship for him and his unique qualities as an academic and a legal practitioner.

The work of legal practitioners in the field of international law, particularly when working in a ministry of foreign affairs, takes place at the crossroads of international relations and international law. The legal advisers of ministries of foreign affairs provide advice on the content of international law, and how it should be interpreted and applied in a particular situation. There are few places where international law is more law in action than at a ministry of foreign affairs. In every day legal practice, questions are never hypothetical but concrete, direct and formulated with the urgency of contemporary international relations. While all having solid academic backgrounds, the staff of the International Law Division of the Ministry of Foreign Affairs of the Kingdom of the Netherlands rarely have the time for philosophical or theoretical discussions as they are constantly pushed to deal with real legal questions in an international environment, which require practical answers. Yet this constant stream of issues arising should not detract from the important responsibility of promoting that the Netherlands acts in conformity with international law. At the same time, the International Law Division also fully uses opportunities to contribute to the codification and progressive development of international law, be it through treaty negotiations or through its participation in the formation of customary law. In addition, the International Law Division is responsible for acting as agent for the Netherlands when cases are brought by or against the Netherlands before international courts or arbitral tribunals.

Johan Lammers joined the Ministry in 1984, the same year in which he defended his authoritative dissertation on 'Pollution of International Watercourses – A Search for Substantive Rules and Principles of law'. On behalf of the Netherlands, he continued his search for the rules and principles of law on international watercourses and actively participated in the negotiations on treaties in this field at the regional and global level. The culmination of this search was undoubtedly the preparation and adoption of the 1997 United Nations Convention on the Law of the Non-navigational Uses of International Watercourses to which he made significant contributions, notably as the chairman of the drafting committee. In the early years of his diplomatic career, he furthermore had the opportunity to contribute to the development of international environmental law in particular. International environmental lawyers around the world still remember him for his performance at the United Nations Conference on Environment and Development that took place in Rio de Janeiro in 1992. Johan would explain a legal issue and identify corresponding interests and positions before he would engage in negotiations to pursue his own instructions. He has not only served the national interest, but also promoted the common interest of the international community as a whole.

Johan Lammers was appointed as Legal Adviser in 1999. We are grateful for having worked for and with him during his tenure, both as our head of the division and as our mentor. In particular, his approach to the sometimes complex and thorny questions facing the International Law Division is noteworthy. In complex political issues with demanding deadlines, Johan was a master in identifying the salient aspects of public international law. A draft opinion that had been considered and worked on by a member of staff for considerable time would usually be the start of a thorough and fundamental discussion on the precise state of the law and its application in the case at hand. These were inspiring debates, because of his broad insights, and would frequently stimulate further thinking in order to improve the advice.

Since Johan Lammers became Legal Adviser, the Netherlands – quite unexpectedly – was increasingly facing situations in which it would become involved in litigation concerning international law. The Netherlands was brought before the International Court of Justice in a case directly related to the conflict in the former Yugoslavia. During that period the Netherlands was already party in two arbitration cases, one involving France and the other involving Belgium, conducted within the framework of the Permanent Court of Arbitration. The caseload before the European Court of Human Rights grew substantially and the Netherlands was also faced with procedures before other human rights bodies. And, while up until then, domestic courts rarely dealt with international law, a variety of non-governmental organizations and individuals began bringing injunction cases against the government of the Netherlands claiming that it had violated rules of international law.

Consequently, it is only fitting that this collection of essays focuses on the Netherlands in court in cases specifically dealing with international law. It commences with essays that deal with actual or potential interstate disputes involving the Netherlands before international courts and arbitral tribunals. They are followed by essays with respect to international courts and other international bodies before which individuals may appear as applicant or defendant. The final set of essays deal with the increasing number of cases in which international law is invoked in national court proceedings.

Now that Johan Lammers has come to the end of his career as a government lawyer, we hope that this book serves to highlight a part of our work that has become of growing importance during his tenure: defending 'the Netherlands in Court'. Most of the essays describe and analyze recent cases in which staff of the International Law Division have been involved. As such the contributions may provide insight into the role of the international legal practitioner working for the government of the Netherlands. We hope that both our colleagues in other foreign ministries and other lawyers will enjoy this reflection on the law in action.

A publication like this would not have been possible without the participation of many. The editors are in particular grateful for the assistance of Fedelma Claire Smith and Nienke van den Berg who have been of great help in turning the different contributions into a book. We are also indebted to Pieter H. Kooijmans, dissertation supervisor of Johan Lammers, former Professor of International Law at Leiden University, former Minister of Foreign Affairs and former Judge at the International Court of Justice, for his willingness to contribute to this Liber Amicorum by writing the Preface. In addition, we would like to thank Anne-Marie Krens for preparing the camera-ready text and Annebeth Rosenboom from Martinus Nijhoff Publishers for publishing this book.

1

THE IRON RHINE CASE AND THE ART OF TREATY INTERPRETATION

The Application of Nineteenth Century Obligations in the Twenty-first Century

Ineke van Bladel *

The Iron Rhine is a railway linking the port of Antwerp to the Rhine basin in Germany across Dutch territory. Belgium acquired the right of transit over Dutch territory in a treaty from 1839 and requested a reactivation of the railway in 1998. As they failed to come to an understanding in negotiations, the Netherlands and Belgium decided to submit the case to arbitration. The Arbitral Tribunal they set up in 2003 under the auspices of the Permanent Court of Arbitration in The Hague faced the problem of the application of a nineteenth-century treaty in the twenty-first century.[1] The way in which the Tribunal dealt with this problem is the subject of this contribution.

1 THE IRON RHINE: ITS HISTORY AND ITS LEGAL FATE

At the Congress of Vienna of 1815, Great Britain, Prussia, Austria and Russia decided to unite the region known before the Napoleonic era as the Austrian

* Legal counsel at the International Law Division of the Ministry of Foreign Affairs of the Kingdom of the Netherlands. The author acted as co-agent in the Iron Rhine case. The opinions in this essay are solely the author's and do not necessarily represent those of the Kingdom of the Netherlands.

1 Arbitration Regarding the Iron Rhine ("IJzeren Rijn") Railway (Belgium/Netherlands), Award of 24 May 2005. The Award as well as the Rules of Procedure and the pleadings (Memorial, Counter-Memorial, Reply and Rejoinder) are available at http://www.pca-cpa.org.

N. Blokker, R. Lefeber, L. Lijnzaad & I. van Bladel (eds.), *The Netherlands in Court. Essays in Honour of Johan G. Lammers*, © 2006 Koninklijke Brill NV. Printed in the Netherlands, pp. 1-18.

Netherlands and the former principality of Liège with the former Republic of the United Provinces to form the United Kingdom of the Netherlands. The union failed. On 25 August 1830 the population of Brussels rose in revolt against what it considered the dominance of the north and on 17 October 1830 the four Powers and France announced the convention of what became known as the London Conference. The aim of the Conference was to maintain stability and peace in Europe by orchestrating the separation of the Netherlands and Belgium. On 19 April 1839, the Netherlands and Belgium concluded the Treaty between the Kingdom of the Netherlands and the Kingdom of Belgium relative to the Separation of their Respective Territories (the Treaty of Separation).[2] The delay of eight years in the conclusion of the Treaty was due to the persistent refusal of King William I of the Netherlands to ratify it.

The Treaty of Separation grants Belgium the right of transit on the rivers Scheldt and Maas (Article IX), the use of cross-border canals (Article X) and the right of passage through the Dutch towns Maastricht and Sittard (Article XI). Article XII allows for an extension on Dutch territory of a new road to be constructed or a new canal to be dug on Belgian territory. In 1873 the Netherlands and Belgium implemented Article XII and entered into the Iron Rhine Treaty, which permitted the construction of a railway line – instead of a road or canal – and which specified the present route of what became to be known as the "IJzeren Rijn" (Iron Rhine).[3] The railway links the port of Antwerp to the Rhine basin in Germany and was completed in 1879. On Dutch territory it runs through the municipalities of Budel, Weert and Roermond.

Until 1897 the concession for the exploration and maintenance of the Iron Rhine was in Belgian hands. In that year, the Netherlands and Belgium concluded the Railway Convention, in which the Netherlands purchased the land and other immovable property of the Iron Rhine.[4] The Netherlands rendered a concession for the maintenance and exploitation of the Iron Rhine to a Dutch railway company.

The Iron Rhine was used intensively between 1879 and 1914. After World War I, however, international use declined sharply, as Belgium had access to an alternative route, the Hasselt-Montzen-Aken line. The use of the railway

---

2 88 CTS (1838-1839) at 427.

3 Convention between Belgium and the Netherlands relative to the Payment of the Belgian Debt, the Abolition of the Surtax on Netherlands Spirits, and the Passing of a Railway Line from Antwerp to Germany across Limburg of 13 January 1873, 145 CTS (1872-1873) at 447.

4 Railway Agreement between Belgium and the Netherlands of 23 April 1897, 184 CTS (1896-1897) at 374.

in the twentieth century varied, but it never exceeded more than nine trains per day. On 31 May 1991 Belgium terminated the use for international traffic of the Iron Rhine track.

On 10 July 1998, the Belgian Government asked the Netherlands to re-activate the Iron Rhine. The Netherlands acknowledged the Belgian right of transit, while stating that the reactivation would be subject to Dutch environmental legislation and EC legislation on the conservation of natural habitats.[5] The parties agreed that the Iron Rhine should be modernized to achieve a capacity of 43 freight trains each 24 hours in 2020, which should be allowed to have a length of 700 metres and to travel at 100 kph.

The main point of discussion during the negotiations on the reactivation became whether or not Belgium would be required on the basis of Article XII of the Treaty of Separation to pay the costs ensuing from the application of Dutch environmental legislation. When the negotiations stalled in December 2002, the Belgian Prime Minister asked his Dutch counterpart to agree to arbitration. On 23 July 2003 the Netherlands and Belgium concluded a treaty (the Arbitration Agreement), in which they acknowledged that Belgium had the right to the use, restoration, adaptation and modernization of the Iron Rhine railway.[6] In very short terms, the Arbitration Agreement asked the Arbitral Tribunal to answer the question to what extent Dutch legislation was applicable to the reactivation and how the costs of the reactivation, estimated at € 500 million, should be allocated. The Netherlands and Belgium had offered to pay € 180 million and € 100 million respectively. The Agreement required the Arbitral Tribunal to decide on the basis of international law.[7] The Tribunal rendered its Award on 24 May 2005.[8]

5 *See* Memorial, para. 28 and Counter-Memorial, para. 2.10.

6 Trb. 2003, 138; 2005, 177.

7 The Tribunal was requested to include European law "if necessary, while taking into account the Parties obligations under 292 of the EC-Treaty". *See* I. van Bladel, *The Iron Rhine Arbitration Case: On the Right Legal Track? An Analysis of the Award and of its Relation to the Law of the European Community*, in 18 Hague Yearbook of International Law 3 (2005).

8 The Tribunal consisted of Professor Alfred H. Soons, Professor Guy Schrans, International Court of Justice Judges Bruno Simma and Peter Tomka and Judge (now President) of the International Court of Justice Rosalyn Higgins as President. Ms Anne Joyce, Deputy General Counsel of the Permanent Court of Arbitration served as Registrar.

2 The Intertemporal Rule

Faced with the application of an 1839 Treaty in the twenty-first century, there is no surprise that the Tribunal found the problem of intertemporality of great importance. The intertemporal rule entails that regard should be had to the international law in force at the time of the conclusion of a treaty. In the Iron Rhine case this means, in the words of the Tribunal, that "regard should be had in interpreting Article XII to juridical facts as they stood in 1839".[9]

Other than that it is considered a rule of international law as referred to in Article 31, paragraph 3, under (c) of the 1969 Vienna Convention on the law of treaties (Vienna Convention), the intertemporal rule has no basis in this Convention.[10] A proposal to include a reference to intertemporality in Article 31, paragraph 3, under (c) did not make it, as the International Law Commission observed that "it covered only partially the question of the so-called intertemporal law in its application to the interpretation of treaties and might, in consequence, lead to misunderstanding".[11]

How true these last words were, is clear from the Iron Rhine case. The Tribunal states that the intertemporal rule "does not require the Tribunal to be oblivious either to later facts that bear on the effective application of a treaty, nor indeed to all later legal developments". It refers to the case law of international courts, where conceptual or generic terms in treaties allowed for an application of these treaties in accordance with the facts and the law at the time of their implementation.[12]

In its 56th Session, the International Law Commission revisited the issue of intertemporality.[13] It distinguished two different effects which subsequent developments in international law may have on a treaty:

9 Award, para. 79.

10 1155 UNTS 331.

11 1966 Yearbook of the International Law Commission, Vol. II, at 222.

12 Award, para. 79. Nationality Decrees Issued in Tunis and Morocco, 1923 PCIJ (Ser. B), No. 4, at 24; Legal Consequences for States of the Continued Presence of South Africa in Namibia (South West Africa) notwithstanding Security Council Resolution 276 (1970), Advisory Opinion of 21 June 1971, 1971 ICJ Rep. 16; Aegean Continental Shelf (Greece/Turkey), Jurisdiction, Judgment of 19 December 1978, 1978 ICJ Rep. 3; Appellate Report United States – Import Prohibition of Certain Shrimp and Shrimp Products, adopted 6 November 1998, WT/DS58/AB/R.

13 International Law Commission, Fifty-Sixth Session. Report of the Study Group on Fragmentation of International Law. ILC(LVI)/SG/FIL/CRD.3/Rev.1, (2004) at 17.

(a) they may affect its *application*, since the treaty may have to be applied to a situation created by norms which were not in existence at the time it was concluded. This has been described as the process of *actualisation* or *contemporization*; or

(b) they may affect the *interpretation* of the treaty itself, where the concepts of the treaty are themselves "not static but evolutionary".[14]

The Iron Rhine Tribunal seems to refer to the effect described under (a), where it advances that, in the present case, "it is not a conceptual or generic term that is in issue, but rather new technical developments relating to the operation and capacity of the railway" and decides that "here, too, it seems that an evolutive interpretation, which would ensure an application of the treaty that would be effective in terms of its object and purpose, will be preferred to a strict application of the intertemporal rule". The Tribunal supports its view by referring to the *Case concerning the Gabčikovo-Nagymaros Project*.[15]

Applying Article 31, paragraph 3, under (c) of the Vienna Convention, the Tribunal finds that "international environmental law has relevance to the relations between the Parties".[16] After explaining its importance, it observes that

> "[e]nvironmental law and the law on development stand not as alternatives but as mutually reinforcing, integral concepts, which require that where development may cause significant harm to the environment there is a duty to prevent, or at least mitigate, such harm. [...] This duty, in the opinion of the Tribunal, has now become a principle of general international law. This principle applies not only in autonomous activities but also in activities undertaken in implementation of specific treaties between the Parties."[17]

Thus it seems a foregone conclusion that the principle of general international law formulated by the Tribunal is applicable in the present case. This also means that the Tribunal forsakes, at least in this respect, the intertemporal rule.

When discussing the possible inclusion of the intertemporal rule in the Vienna Convention, the International Law Commission considered that "in any

---

14 *Id.*; *see also* C. McLachlan, *The Principle of Systemic Integration and Article 31(3)(c) of the Vienna Convention*, 54 ICLQ 279 (2005) at 316.

15 Award, para. 80. Case Concerning the Gabčikovo-Nagymaros Project (Hungary/Slovakia), Judgment of 25 September 1997, 1997 ICJ Rep. 7.

16 Award, para. 58.

17 Award, para. 59. Here as well, the Tribunal refers to the Gabčikovo-Nagymaros case; *supra* n. 15.

event, the relevance of rules of international law for the interpretation of treaties in any given case was dependent on the intentions of the parties [...]".[18] This is also the view of authors who relatively recently discussed the problem of intertemporality. Thirlway, for example, wrote that

> "[p]rovided that, where it can be established that it was the intention of the parties that the meaning or scope of a term or expression used in a treaty should follow the development of the law, the treaty must be interpreted so as to give effect to that intention".

He based his opinion on a thorough analysis of the case law of the International Court of Justice, as it then stood.[19] President Higgins[20] concluded that the "intention of the parties, reflected by reference to the objects and purpose [...] guides the law of treaties" and that "the intention of the parties is really the key".[21]

But then, in words borrowed from McLachlan:

> "a safe guide to decision on [the issue of intertemporality] will not be found in the chimera of the imputed intention of the parties alone. Rather, the interpreter must find concrete evidence of the parties' intentions in this regard in the material sources referred to in Articles 31-2, namely: in the terms themselves; the object and purpose of the treaty; the rules of international law; and, where necessary, the *travaux*".[22]

The search of the Iron Rhine Tribunal for the intentions of the parties when they concluded the Treaty of Separation in 1839 is the subject of the following section.

---

18 International Law Commission 1966, *supra* n. 11, at 222.

19 H. Thirlway, *The Law and Procedure of the International Court of Justice 1960-1989, Part Three.* LXII BYIL 1 (1991) at 57.

20 R. Higgins, *Time and the Law: International Perspectives on an Old Problem*, 46 ICLQ 501 (1997) at 519, and by the same author *Some Observations on the Inter-Temporal Rule in International Law, in* J. Makarczyk (ed.), Theory of International Law at the Threshold of the 21st Century: Essays in Honour of Krzysztof Skubiszewski, 173 (1996) at 181.

21 *See also* Award, para. 53 and, for example, I. Sinclair, The Vienna Convention on the Law of Treaties (1984) at 140; A. McNair, Law of Treaties (1961) at 383.

22 McLachlan, *supra* n. 14, at 317.

3 The Intentions of the Parties

Before turning to the Tribunal's findings, the views of the parties on the issue of their intentions should be explained. Both referred to Articles 31 and 32 of the Vienna Convention, which reads:

> Article 31
> General rule of interpretation
> 1. A treaty shall be interpreted in good faith in accordance with the ordinary meaning to be given to the terms of the treaty in their context and in the light of its object and purpose.
> 2. The context for the purpose of the interpretation of a treaty shall comprise, in addition to the text, including its preamble and annexes:
> (a) any agreement relating to the treaty which was made between all the parties in connexion with the conclusion of the treaty;
> (b) any instrument which was made by one or more parties in connexion with the conclusion of the treaty and accepted by the other parties as an instrument related to the treaty.
> 3. There shall be taken into account, together with the context:
> (a) any subsequent agreement between the parties regarding the interpretation of the treaty or the application of its provisions;
> (b) any subsequent practice in the application of the treaty which established the agreement of the parties regarding its interpretation;
> (c) any relevant rules of international law applicable in the relations between the parties.
> 4. A special meaning shall be given to a term if it is established that the parties so intended.

> Article 32
> Supplementary means of interpretation
> Recourse may be had to supplementary means of interpretation, including the preparatory work of the treaty and the circumstances of its conclusion, in order to confirm the meaning resulting from the application of article 31, or to determine the meaning when the interpretation according to article 31:
> (a) leaves the meaning ambiguous or obscure; or
> (b) leads to a result which is manifestly absurd or unreasonable.

The Netherlands and Belgium differed in opinion on the interpretation of several parts of Article XII of the Treaty of Separation. This is the translation of the authentic French text of this Article, as provided by the Tribunal:

> "In the case that in Belgium *a new road* would have been built or *a new canal* dug, which would lead to the Maas facing the Dutch canton of Sittard, then Belgium would be at liberty to ask Holland, which in that hypothesis would not refuse it, that the said road, or the said canal *be extended* in accordance with the same plan, entirely at the cost and expense of Belgium, through the canton of Sittard, up to the borders of Germany. This road or canal, which could be used only for commercial communication, would be constructed, at the choice of Holland, either by engineers and workers whom Belgium would obtain authorization to employ for this purpose in the canton of Sittard, or by engineers and workers whom Holland would supply, and who would execute the agreed works at the expense of Belgium, all without any burden to Holland, and without prejudice to the exclusive rights of sovereignty over the territory which would be crossed by the road or canal in question.
> The two Parties would set, by common agreement, the amount and the method of collection of the duties and tolls which would be levied on the said road or canal."[23] [emphasis added]

The Tribunal considers the terms in italic ("a *'new road'* or a *'new canal'* to *'be extended'*") decisive in answering the question whether or not, and to what extent, the conditions contained in Article XII of the 1839 Treaty would be applicable at present.

Belgium embraced the literal meaning of these terms, emphasizing that its request for reactivation was not a request for a new road, canal or track to be extended, as the track was prolonged on Dutch territory in 1879 and still existed to date. Article XII thus dealt only with the construction of the Iron Rhine.[24] Consequently, Article XII would not be applicable to the reactivation of the railway. Furthermore, Belgium construed the object and purpose of Article XII by placing this Article in the context of Article XI of the Treaty, which laid down the right of transit on roads in Maastricht and Sittard. The relevant part of Article XI reads:

> "The use of these roads [...] which will only be subject to the payment of moderate tolls for the maintenance of these roads, in such a manner that the transit trade will not encounter any obstacles on them and that, in return for the above-mentioned tolls, these roads *will be maintained in good state and prone to facilitating trade*". [emphasis added]

23 Award, para. 32.

24 Reply, para. 104.

Without explaining the link between Article XII and Article XI, which, for that matter, refers to the levying of tolls to pay for maintenance and not to maintenance as such, Belgium concluded that the Iron Rhine, too, should be "maintained in good state and prone to facilitating trade".[25] It contended that the Netherlands had, at its costs, the responsibility to maintain the track of the Iron Rhine in light of what Belgium considered commercially viable in the current circumstances.[26] Additional reasons were, according to Belgium, that the Netherlands had maintained the Iron Rhine for the most part of the twentieth century and that it had concluded an agreement on maintenance and renovation with the Dutch company holding the concession to explore the Iron Rhine on Dutch territory.[27] Given the Belgian position that Article XII only dealt with construction, it was not clear why this practice would be relevant.

The Netherlands argued that the request to reactivate the railway was "new", as considerable adaptation and modernization was necessary to achieve the use desired by Belgium and that, therefore, Article XII, and especially the parts which established its exclusive rights of sovereignty over the territory crossed by the Iron Rhine and the provisions that Belgium would bear the financial burden of its request, was applicable.[28] The Netherlands accepted that it had an obligation to maintain the track, but contested the broad meaning Belgium attached to the words "maintenance and renovation" and denied being responsible for the costs of the adaptation and modernization of the Iron Rhine.[29]

In the opinion of the Tribunal the clauses of Article 31 of the Vienna Convention are not hierarchical. It also observes that there is no doubt that the starting point for treaty interpretation is the ordinary meaning to be given to the terms of a treaty, taking them in context, and having regard also to the object and purpose of the treaty.[30]

25 Reply, para. 105, *et seq.*
26 Reply, para. 122.
27 Reply, para. 117.
28 Counter-Memorial, para. 3.3.4.5. The relevant parts of Article XII are "without prejudice to the exclusive rights of sovereignty over the territory which would be crossed by the road or canal in question" and "the said road, or the said canal [would] be extended [...] entirely at the cost and expense of Belgium" as well as "engineers and workers [...] would execute the agreed works at the expense of Belgium, all without any burden to Holland".
29 Rejoinder, para. 135.
30 Award, para. 47.

In 1839, the word "new" cannot have meant anything else but "not existing before" or "now just made"[31] and it is not unsurprising that the Tribunal did not accept the Dutch interpretation but adopts, as did Belgium, the ordinary meaning of this word. The Tribunal also emphasizes that Article XII in relation to the 1873 Iron Rhine Treaty refers to the construction of a railway and that neither Article XII, nor the Iron Rhine Treaty or the Railway Convention addressed the question of maintenance or modernization.[32] On the other hand, the text of Article XII does not preclude maintenance and modernization after the construction of the road, canal or track.

The object and purpose of the 1839 Treaty of Separation was, according to the Tribunal, "to resolve the many difficult problems complicating a stable separation of Belgium and the Netherlands" and that of Article XII was "to provide for transport links from Belgium to Germany. [...] This object was not for a fixed duration and its purpose was 'commercial communication'".[33]

Where the Tribunal found these objects and purposes can only be established by a process of elimination. To start with, the Treaty of Separation has no preamble, where an object and purpose can usually be found. And while the Tribunal mentions the reference by Belgium to Article XI several times,[34] it stays away from deriving the object and purpose of Article XII from this provision or from any other part of the Treaty. Thus the Tribunal exhausted, as possible sources for the intentions of the parties in 1839, the matters intrinsic to the Treaty, which are generally acknowledged to be a better safeguard to prevent a teleological interpretation from burdening the parties with obligations which they never meant to accept.[35]

In terms of Article 31, paragraph 3, under (a) of the Vienna Convention, the 1873 Iron Rhine Treaty is a "subsequent agreement between the parties regarding the interpretation of the treaty or the application of its provisions". It amended the routing described in Article XII of the Treaty of Separation. When ratifying the Iron Rhine Treaty the parties stated that it "constituted the full and complete execution of Article XII of the Treaty of Separation". The parties agreed that this declaration was not meant to terminate Article XII, but that it referred to the change of the routing and precluded Belgium from asking for another implementation of Article XII. The Tribunal confirms this and

31 The Concise Oxford Dictionary of Current English (1964).

32 Award, para. 84.

33 Award, para. 83.

34 Award, paras. 24, 25, 75 and 212.

35 Sinclair, *supra* n. 21, at 118. D. P. O'Connell, International Law (1970) at 253 *et seq.*

expresses the view that the Iron Rhine Treaty was not intended as a treaty of limited or fixed duration.[36]

As the Tribunal establishes that Article XII deals only with the construction of the railroad, any subsequent practice as referred to in Article 31, paragraph 3, sub (b) Vienna Convention ends when the railroad is finished. The circumstances of the use and the exploitation of the Iron Rhine track are thus not relevant to ascertaining the intentions of the parties. So, whereas the Tribunal did decide that the words "maintenance and renovation" did not cover "the significant upgrading costs now involved in Belgium's request", it also quite rightly excludes the use and exploration of the track from its search for the parties' intentions.[37]

The *travaux préparatoires*, of course, come to mind as an important extrinsic source to explore, but the Tribunal refuses to do so, since the extracts, provided by both parties, of the prolonged diplomatic negotiations on the Treaty of Separation in the London Conference do not have the character of *travaux préparatoires* on which it may safely rely as supplementary means of interpretation under Article 32 of the Vienna Convention, as these extracts "do not serve the purpose of illuminating a common understanding as to the meaning of the various provisions of Article XII".[38]

There remains only one source for the object and purpose of both the Treaty of Separation and its Article XII: the circumstances of the conclusion of the Treaty. And, indeed, the Tribunal mentions that it will remain mindful to these circumstances, as required by Article 32 of the Vienna Convention.[39] In the first place, it seems remarkable that the Tribunal does not elaborate on its reason for reverting to Article 32 Vienna Convention. It does not, in other words, disclose whether it considered its tentative finding based on Article 31 ambiguous, obscure, manifestly absurd or unreasonable. Further, "the circumstances of the conclusion of a treaty" not only forms an extrinsic source for interpretation, but it is also a source open to different assessments. There is no indication whether the Tribunal consulted, for instance, a history book, let alone which one, or whether it perhaps turned to the *travaux* anyway. From the point of view of treaty interpretation the Tribunal, imagining itself in the position of the parties in 1839, finds itself on thin ice.

36 Award, para. 82.
37 Award, para. 76.
38 Award, para. 48.
39 Award, para. 48.

Moreover, it is doubtful that the intentions of the Netherlands and Belgium in 1839 were joint intentions. The solution of what was called "the Belgian question" at that time was decisive for the stability and peace in Europe and the Netherlands and Belgium had to comply with the wishes of the London Conference. There was, for instance, a relation between the allocation of the Grand Duchy (now province) of Limburg to the Netherlands, to which Belgium strongly objected, and the Article XII right of transit for Belgium through Limburg, which was vehemently opposed by the Netherlands. This was just one of the reasons why King William I of the Netherlands held out for eight years before giving his authorization to ratify the Treaty of Separation. While the Netherlands and Belgium concluded the Treaty of Separation and shared its rights and obligations, this hardly reflected a meeting of the minds.

Also, one may wonder whether the object and purpose the Tribunal ascribed to the Treaty of Separation really contains a connotation of long duration. After all, separating the Netherlands and Belgium is no longer an issue nowadays. Moreover, some obligations in the Treaty of Separation, such as those referring to the apportionment of the debts of the United Kingdom of the Netherlands,[40] have been fulfilled a long time ago. This cannot but have consequences for the balance of the rights and obligations of the parties which apparently existed in 1839.

It may be concluded that the concrete evidence of the 1839 intentions of the parties is rather weak and that the Tribunal abstains from a detailed analysis of the presumed intentions. It formulates broad objects and purposes and it is thereby able to state that

> "[i]t necessarily follows, even in the absence of specific wording, that such works, [...] as might from time to time be necessary or desirable for contemporary commerciality, would remain a concomitant of the right of transit that Belgium would be able to request. That being so, the entirety of Article XII, with its careful balance of the rights and obligations of the Parties, remains in principle applicable to the adaptation and modernization by Belgium".[41]

There is yet another step which the Tribunal takes to construe its decision on the interpretation of Article XII: it applies the principle of effectiveness, finding this of particular importance in the Iron Rhine case.[42]

40 Treaty of Separation, Art. XIII.
41 Award, para. 83.
42 Award, para. 49.

4 THE PRINCIPLE OF EFFECTIVENESS

The principle of effectiveness (*ut res magis valeat quam perat*) has, according to the Tribunal, relevance in relation to the object and purpose of a treaty and does not entitle a tribunal to revise a treaty.[43] The Tribunal establishes that

> "an interpretation compatible with the principle of effectiveness leads the Tribunal to determine the continued applicability of Article XII of the 1839 Treaty of Separation to upgrading and improvements [...]".[44]

When discussing the recommendations of the International Law Commission on Article 31 of the Vienna Convention, Sinclair indicated that there might exist a difference between a teleological approach to treaty interpretation and an approach based on effectiveness. The first required, in his opinion, a subjective interpretation of what were the aims of the parties, while the latter was "a matter of necessity based upon the presumed interest of the authors [of a treaty] to make a treaty provision effective rather than ineffective".[45]

The (subjective) interpretation by reference to the object and purpose of the Treaty of Separation and Article XII thereof requires no further attention, but the presumed interest of the parties to make a treaty provision effective needs it all the more. In 2003 the Netherlands and Belgium concluded the Arbitration Agreement. They agreed that Belgium had the right not only to the use and the restoration of the Iron Rhine railway, but also to its adaptation and modernization. It follows from the Arbitration Agreement that, in 2003, both parties implicitly recognized a right of transit "not of fixed duration". Belgium, in its Reply, even explicitly supported a contemporary right of commercial transit by emphasizing the archaic equivalent of this notion, that the Iron Rhine, at the beginning of the twenty-first century, "should be prone to facilitating trade". This being so, there is no reason for either party to object to a "dynamic and evolutive approach to a treaty that was meant to guarantee a right of commercial transit through time".[46]

In the Iron Rhine case, the object and purpose of the 1839 Treaty and of Article XII thereof, expressed in general terms, in connection with the principle of effectiveness, changed a potential "chimera of the imputed intention of the

---

43 Award, para. 49.
44 Award, para. 84.
45 Sinclair, *supra* n. 21, at 118.
46 Award, para. 84.

parties"[47] into a performable situation. The translation of this situation in the answers to the questions of the parties will be discussed in the following Section.

5 The Tribunal's Main Answers to the Parties

While the 1839 intentions of the parties and their interest in the effectiveness of Article XII resulted in an evolutive approach to the interpretation of Article XII, neither the ordinary meaning of the part "a new road or a new canal to be extended" nor the fact that Article XII deals with construction only, were discarded. This is illustrated by the following statement of the Tribunal on the allocation of the costs of the adaptation and modernization:

> "although Article XII was directed towards the construction of, and regime for, the Iron Rhine, the right of transit there provided for also covers the reactivation of the track and its use through time. The specific financial provisions of Article XII were formulated in respect of the construction of a new road, canal or track. The real questions, so far as allocation of costs is concerned, are the following: what elements of Article XII relating to costs are applicable to a reactivation that is not a construction of a new railway but is nonetheless within the ambit of Article XII? [...]"[48]

The Tribunal decides, that neither the Netherlands nor Belgium are to bear the costs of adaptation and modernization solely. These costs, including those for environmental measures, are in principle for Belgium, but the Netherlands has an obligation to pay for the extra costs of a deviation from the route described in the Iron Rhine Treaty and for any quantifiable advantages it derives from the reactivation. Further, the parties are to share, in equal parts, the costs of a tunnel to be build in an area designated as a nature reserve. This, according to the Tribunal, was "attributable to the past conduct of both of the Parties".[49] By this the Tribunal means that the Netherlands, when establishing the nature reserve, ignored the Belgian right of transit, while Belgium terminated its use of the track in 1991 and did not inform the Netherlands in timely fashion of a request for reactivation.[50]

47 McLachlan, *supra* n. 14, at 317.
48 Award, para. 219.
49 Award, para. 243.
50 Award, para. 234.

With regard to the Netherlands' right to territorial sovereignty the Tribunal concluded that

> "[t]he Netherlands has forfeited no more sovereignty than that which is necessary for the track to be built and to operate to allow a commercial connection from Belgium to Germany across Limburg. It thus retains the police power throughout that area, the power to establish health and safety standards for work being done on the rack, and the power to establish environmental standards in that area".[51]

The *dictum* on this issue says that the legislation of the Netherlands is applicable to the reactivation of the Iron Rhine as long as it does not amount to a denial of Belgium's right of transit or renders the exercise by Belgium of its right of transit unreasonably difficult.[52]

6 Concluding Remarks

In the present case the Tribunal decided that Article XII of the 1839 Treaty of Separation refers to the construction of a new road, canal or track to be extended on Dutch territory, and not to modernization. However, the objects and purposes of the Treaty of Separation and Article XII thereof, reflecting the intentions of the parties in 1839, allowed for a decision that

> "the entirety of Article XII, with its careful balance of the rights and obligations of the Parties, remains in principle applicable to the adaptation and modernization requested by Belgium".[53]

The object and purpose of Article XII also embodies the twenty-first century need for this provision to be effective and thus brought the Tribunal to a "dynamic and evolutive approach to a treaty that was meant to guarantee a right of commercial transit through time".[54]

The findings of the Tribunal regarding the 1839 intentions of the parties call the role ascribed to these intentions in the doctrine of intertemporal law into question. This opens the door for the notion that the thread with the past is rather thin and that the need to give effect to a treaty is preponderant. This

---

51 Award, para. 87.
52 Award, para. 239.
53 Award, para. 83.
54 Award, para. 84.

is probably not, or to a lesser extent, true in cases where "the concepts of the treaty are themselves 'not static but evolutionary'".[55] In the opinion of the author, the *Gabčikovo-Nagymaros* case also belongs to this category of cases, given that the International Court of Justice refers to "evolving provisions" in the treaty it interpreted in that case.[56]

The Tribunal refers to three cases of the International Court of Justice in which Articles 31 and 32 of the Vienna Convention had been applied to treaties concluded long before the entering into force of the Vienna Convention.[57] The *Sovereignty over Pulau Ligitan and Pulau Sipadan* case and the *Territorial Dispute* case concerned treaties concluded in 1891 and 1955 respectively. Both cases are immaterial in respect of the intertemporal rule, as the relevant provisions of these treaties refer to the establishment of boundaries, so that the intentions of the parties were effected at the conclusion of the treaties in 1891 and 1955 and not at the time of the interpretation by the International Court of Justice.[58]

The *Kasikili/Sedudu Island* case concerned the determination of the boundary between Botswana and Namibia in the Chobe river.[59] The interpretation of the expression "centre of the main channel" in Article III of the 1890 Anglo-German Treaty was a decisive factor in the analysis of the Court. In her Declaration appended to the Judgment, Judge Higgins commented on this aspect and referred to the general character of the 1890 intentions of the parties: "Rather our task is to decide what general idea the parties had in mind, and then make reality of that general idea through the use of contemporary knowledge".[60] Judge Koroma, in his Declaration, stated:

> "It is inevitable that the Court, in performing its judicial task and applying the provisions of the 1890 Treaty, would choose one of a number of possible interpretations of the Treaty as representing the shared intention of the Parties and in the

---

55 *See* Section 2 and n. 12, *supra*.

56 Award, para. 80; *see* Section 2. Case Concerning the Gabčikovo-Nagymaros Project, *supra* n. 15, para. 111 *et seq*.

57 Award, para. 45.

58 Sovereignty over Pulau Ligitan and Pulau Sipadan (Indonesia/Malaysia), Merits, Judgment of 17 December 2002, 2002 ICJ Rep. 625; Territorial Dispute (Libyan Arab Jamahiriya/Chad), Judgment of 13 February 1994, 1994 ICJ Rep. 6; *see* paras. 72, 76.

59 Case Concerning Kasikili/Sedudu Island (Botswana/Namibia), Judgment of 13 December 1999, 1999, ICJ Rep. 1045.

60 *Id.*, at 1114.

> light of the material before it – both historical and contemporary – to identify and locate the boundary prescribed therein".[61]

The idea that an interpreter not just generalizes the intentions of the parties but also picks and chooses a possible interpretation, brings to mind the view of a school of lawyers which denies the existence of, or the need for, any rules of treaty interpretation. These lawyers argue that an application of the rules of treaty interpretation in any particular case is merely an *ex post facto* rationalisation of a conclusion reached on other grounds.[62] A somewhat less extreme view is voiced by O'Connell, who stated that "[t]he problem of treaty interpretation [...] is one of ascertaining the logic inherent in the treaty, and pretending that this is what the parties desired".[63]

One may wonder whether in the Iron Rhine case the Tribunal did not already have in mind, at the outset of its work, that a request for modernization of the Iron Rhine track would only be exercisable in accordance with the present-day situation and that the reactivation of a right of transit established in 1839 should be correlative with obligations in the twenty-first century, such as those on the protection of the environment. If that would be the case, the circumstantial interpretation on the basis of Articles 31 and 32 of the Vienna Convention might be seen as 'much ado about nothing'. A predetermined aim of the Iron Rhine Tribunal was, however, in view of the different visions of the parties, only one of the possible answers to the questions put to the Tribunal. A detailed substantiation of the Tribunal's answer was therefore inescapable. So, far more in keeping with the work of art of the Iron Rhine Arbitral Tribunal than O'Connell's view, are the words which Sir Gerald Fitzmaurice wrote in 1951: "that in the last resort all interpretation must consist in the exercise of common sense by the judge, applied in good faith and with intelligence".[64]

Since Articles 31 and 32 of the Vienna Convention embody what the International Law Commission regarded "as the comparatively few general principles governing treaty interpretation",[65] there is no getting round the application of these articles in disputes concerning treaty interpretation presented to courts and tribunals, as is also clear from consistent case-law of the International Court

61 *Id.*. at 1111.

62 *See* Sinclair, *supra* n. 21, at p. 114.

63 *See* O'Connell, *supra* n. 35, at 252. *See also*: A. Aust, Modern Treaty Law and Practice (2000) at 185. Aust states that there is still much sense in O'Connell's view.

64 G. Fitzmaurice *The Law and Procedure of the International Court of Justice: Treaty Interpretation and Certain Other Treaty Points* XXVIII BYIL 1 (1951) at 3.

65 Aust, *supra* n. 63, at 185.

of Justice. Also, one should not ignore that Articles 31 and 32 of the Vienna Convention are basically intended for the application by States, who cannot, in their mutual relations, afford to rationalize a conclusion reached on other grounds or to claim the logic inherent to a treaty.

Johan G. Lammers, as the legal adviser of the Ministry of Foreign Affairs of the Kingdom of the Netherlands and the head of the International Law Division of the Ministry, was the agent in the Iron Rhine case.[66] His comments on the author's contributions to the pleadings in the Iron Rhine case, concerning treaty interpretation and otherwise, were, as always, and especially against the background of his formidable knowledge of international law, given from the premise that another view might nevertheless prevail. For this and other reasons, he will be greatly missed.

66 The Agent of the Kingdom of Belgium was Mr Jan Devadder.

2

FROM A DISPUTE ABOUT THE USE OF FORCE TO A NON-DISPUTE ABOUT JURISDICTION

The Case Concerning Legality of Use of Force (Yugoslavia *v.* Netherlands) before the International Court of Justice

*Niels Blokker**

1 INTRODUCTION

This contribution discusses the latest case before the International Court of Justice in which the Netherlands was a party: the case bearing the official title 'Legality of Use of Force (Yugoslavia v. Netherlands)'.

The Netherlands is one of the 64 states that have recognized the compulsory jurisdiction of the Court pursuant to Article 36, paragraph 2, of the Statute of the Court. Of these 64 states, many have included far-reaching conditions upon their acceptance of jurisdiction. The conditions included in the Dutch declaration are limited to the requirement of reciprocity (jurisdiction is accepted only *vis-à-vis* states that have done the same) and to a temporal restriction (the requirement that jurisdiction is accepted only in disputes arising or which may arise after 5 August 1921). Furthermore, jurisdiction is not accepted in relation to disputes in respect of which the parties, excluding the jurisdiction of the ICJ, may have agreed to have recourse to some other method of pacific settlement. This acceptance of jurisdiction is done for a period of five years, which is automatically extended for further periods of five years, unless notice is given not

* Legal counsel at the International Law Division of the Ministry of Foreign Affairs of the Kingdom of the Netherlands. He was co-agent for the Netherlands in the case discussed in this contribution. He is also professor of International Institutional Law (Schermers Chair) at the Leiden University Faculty of Law. The opinions in this essay are solely the author's and do not necessarily represent those of the Kingdom of the Netherlands.

N. Blokker, R. Lefeber, L. Lijnzaad & I. van Bladel (eds.), *The Netherlands in Court. Essays in Honour of Johan G. Lammers*, © 2006 Koninklijke Brill NV. Printed in the Netherlands, pp. 19-49.

less than six months before the expiry of any such period. Compared to other declarations, this is a rather broad unilateral acceptance of the jurisdiction of the Court. It is in line with the constitutional obligation of the Dutch Government to promote the development of the international legal order.[1]

Since the establishment of the Court, the Netherlands has been a party in four contentious proceedings. The first of these concerned a dispute between the Netherlands and Sweden concerning the application of the Convention of 1902 Governing the Guardianship of Infants. The Netherlands lost this case.[2] The second case was submitted to the Court by Belgium and the Netherlands under a Special Agreement concluded in 1957. The Court was asked whether sovereignty over certain frontier land in the Baarle-Hertog and Baarle Nassau area belonged to Belgium or to the Netherlands. This case was lost as well; the Court adjudged that the disputed territory belonged to Belgium.[3] The third case was of a more general nature and related to the delimitation of the continental shelf between Germany and Denmark, and between Germany and the Netherlands. On the basis of the principles for such delimitation indicated by the Court,[4] the three countries came to an agreement. The fourth case is the one discussed in this contribution. In all four cases, the Legal Adviser of the Netherlands' Foreign Ministry acted as Agent before the Court. In the first three cases, this was Willem Riphagen. In the most recent case Johan Lammers, to whom this *liber amicorum* is dedicated, acted as Agent.

This contribution is divided into four parts. Paragraph 2 will briefly summarize relevant facts and events that resulted in the application by Yugoslavia instituting proceedings against the Netherlands. Paragraph 3 will discuss the request by Yugoslavia for the indication of provisional measures, the Dutch position in relation to this request, and the Court's order of 2 June 1999. Paragraph 4 will concentrate on subsequent developments and proceedings

1 Constitution of the Kingdom of the Netherlands, Art. 90. On this obligation, *see* L. F.M. Besselink, *The Constitutional Duty to Promote the Development of the International Legal Order: the Significance and Meaning of Article 90 of the Netherlands Constitution*, 34 NYIL 89 (2003).

2 Case Concerning the Application of the Convention of 1902 Governing the Guardianship of Infants (Netherlands *v*. Sweden), Merits, Judgment of 28 November 1958, 1958 ICJ Rep. 55.

3 Case Concerning Sovereignty over Certain Frontier Land (Belgium/Netherlands), Merits, Judgment of 20 June 1959, 1959 ICJ Rep. 206.

4 North Sea Continental Shelf Cases (Federal Republic of Germany/Denmark; Federal Republic of Germany/Netherlands), Merits, Judgment of 20 February 1969, 1969 ICJ Rep. 3.

before the Court in this case, which resulted in the Judgment of 15 December 2004 in which the Court found that it had no jurisdiction in this case. Paragraph 5 will conclude this contribution by making a few general observations relating to this case.

2 Background to the Dispute

Following the break-up of the Socialist Federal Republic of Yugoslavia (SFRY) it did not take long before armed conflicts emerged between Serbia and Montenegro (the Federal Republic of Yugoslavia (FRY)) on the one hand, and its newly independent neighbours on the other. These armed conflicts came to an end in 1995 after NATO forces intervened and the Dayton Peace Agreement was signed. However, subsequently a new ethnic conflict emerged, now within the borders of the FRY, in the province of Kosovo, between a large majority of ethnic Albanians and a small Serb minority.

When the Kosovo conflict started to escalate, the Security Council adopted Resolution 1160 (31 March 1998), in which it called upon the FRY to work towards "a political solution to the issue of Kosovo". This Resolution also called upon the Kosovar Albanian leadership "to condemn all terrorist action", and "pursue their goals by peaceful means only". An arms embargo was imposed on the two parties. Nevertheless, fighting continued and became more intense. There were numerous civilian casualties. The Secretary-General of the UN reported killings and widespread human rights violations, and estimated that there were over 230,000 displaced persons.[5]

Security Council Resolution 1199, adopted on 23 September 1998, demanded all parties, groups and individuals to immediately cease hostilities and maintain a ceasefire, which would "reduce the risks of a humanitarian catastrophe". In the penultimate operational paragraph of this resolution, the Security Council decided: "should the concrete measures demanded in this resolution and resolution 1160 (1998) not be taken, to consider further action and additional measures to maintain or restore peace and stability in the region".

One month later, the Security Council adopted a further resolution relating to the situation in Kosovo. In this Resolution 1203 the Security Council endorsed agreements concerning the verification of compliance by the FRY and all others concerned in Kosovo with the requirements of Resolution 1199.

---

5 *See* UN Doc. S/1998/834 and Add.1.

It also affirmed that in the event of an emergency, "action may be needed" to ensure the safety and freedom of movement of verification missions as envisaged in the relevant agreements. It furthermore demanded immediate action from the FRY and the Kosovo Albanian leadership "to cooperate with international efforts to improve the humanitarian situation and to avert the impending humanitarian catastrophe".

Resolutions 1160, 1199 and 1203 each explicitly referred to Chapter VII of the UN Charter. No further resolutions were adopted by the Council before NATO on 24 March 1999 launched its attacks on the FRY. The Council only adopted two Presidential Statements, in January 1999, in which it *inter alia* condemned the massacre of Kosovar Albanians in the village of Racak. Two days after the beginning of the NATO military action, a draft resolution was tabled in the Security Council, demanding an immediate cessation of the use of force against the FRY.[6] However, this draft resolution failed to receive the necessary support; it obtained only three votes in favour (China, the Russian Federation and Namibia), and twelve votes against.[7]

It was unquestionable that the 1999 NATO operation against the FRY needed a legal basis. But it has always been a matter of controversy whether there existed one in this case. Governments involved in the operation have put forward two possible legal bases. First of all the operation has been based on the relevant Security Council resolutions, in particular resolutions 1199 and 1203. The main difficulty facing this suggested legal basis is that these resolutions do not explicitly authorize the use of force (or, in the usual Security Council parlance, 'the use of all necessary means' or 'the use of all necessary measures'). Any alleged authorization in this case therefore would have to be implied, and such implication would be controversial. Secondly, it has been claimed that the NATO operation could be considered as an example of humanitarian intervention. The main difficulty facing this possible legal basis is that humanitarian intervention is not a generally recognized exception to the prohibition of the use of force.

In these circumstances the FRY saw merit in defending itself against NATO not only by using military means, but also by taking legal action and bringing a complaint before the ICJ. However, the FRY had not yet accepted the jurisdiction of the Court. For that reason, on 26 April 1999 it deposited with the

6 UN Doc. S/1999/328. In the penultimate preambular paragraph of the draft resolution, the Council determined "that the use of force by NATO against the Federal Republic of Yugoslavia constitutes a threat to international peace and security".

7 UN Doc. S/PV.3989 (1999) at 6.

UN Secretary-General its declaration recognizing the compulsory jurisdiction of the Court pursuant to Article 36, paragraph 2, of the Statute. This declaration contains important conditions. One is of particular relevance to this contribution: the jurisdiction of the Court is accepted "in all disputes arising or which may arise after the signature of the present declaration, with regard to the situations or facts subsequent to this signature". Immediately after it had accepted the jurisdiction of the Court, the FRY initiated proceedings before the Court against ten NATO members who participated in the military operation, "for violation of the obligation not to use force".[8]

3 The Yugoslav Request for the Indication of Provisional Measures

On 29 April 1999, immediately after filing its application, Yugoslavia also requested the Court to order provisional measures pursuant to Article 73 of the Rules of the Court. In making this request, Yugoslavia referred in some detail to the victims and damage as a result of the NATO bombardments, and to "new losses of human life, further physical and mental harm" and other damage that could be expected if the Court would not ask the Netherlands and the other nine defendants to "cease immediately its acts of use of force" and to "refrain from any act of threat or use of force against the Federal Republic of Yugoslavia".[9] Public hearings were held between 10 and 12 May 1999.

In the hearings the FRY claimed as ground for jurisdiction of the Court both the unilateral declaration it had made two weeks earlier and Article IX of the Genocide Convention. Most of the FRY's submissions focused on the facts (victims, damage) and on the merits of the case. Essentially it claimed that the use of force by the ten respondents against Yugoslavia was illegal, as a violation of Article 2, paragraph 4 of the Charter of the UN that could not be justified as self-defence or as measures authorized by the Security Council, nor as humanitarian intervention. The FRY submitted that no right of humanitarian intervention was recognized under international law, and even if it was, the NATO bombardments would not qualify as such, *inter alia* because there was no genuine humanitarian purpose and because of the modalities selected (e.g. the bombing of populated areas of Yugoslavia).

---

8 The FRY's application was filed in the Registry of the Court on 29 April 1999.

9 Case Concerning Legality of Use of Force (Yugoslavia *v.* Netherlands), Provisional Measures, Order of 2 June 1999, 1999 ICJ Rep. 542, at 546, 547.

The Netherlands presented its observations to the Court on Tuesday 11 May. Essentially it submitted that the Court had no jurisdiction in this case, "not even prima facie", and it hardly discussed the merits of the case. This lack of jurisdiction was based mainly on the following arguments. First, the FRY was not a member of the United Nations (UN), and therefore it could not be considered to be *ipso facto* a party to the Statute of the Court by virtue of Article 93, paragraph 1, of the UN Charter. Neither had the FRY become a party to the Statute through the procedure envisaged by Article 93, paragraph 2, of the UN Charter. In addition, the FRY's declaration accepting the jurisdiction of the Court was not based on Security Council Resolution 9 (1946) and did not meet the conditions contained in that Resolution. For these reasons, according to the Netherlands, the FRY's declaration must be considered invalid.

Secondly, even if this declaration were to be considered valid, the FRY in this declaration accepted the compulsory jurisdiction of the Court only in relation to "disputes arising or which may arise after the signature of the present declaration, with regard to the situations or facts subsequent to this signature". Since the dispute between the FRY and the Netherlands had arisen before that date, it was not covered by the declaration.

Thirdly, the FRY also based the jurisdiction of the Court on the 1948 Genocide Convention. While the Netherlands agreed that, in principle, the Court could have jurisdiction on the basis of Article IX of that Convention, it submitted that this could only be the case with regard to disputes relating to the interpretation, application or fulfilment of that Convention. Since the FRY's complaints do not, even prima facie, amount to the crime of genocide, in particular in view of the absence of genocidal intent by the Netherlands, the Court could not have jurisdiction on this basis.

Next to these observations, the Netherlands referred to the discretionary nature of the power of the Court to indicate provisional measures. Should the Court consider that it had jurisdiction in this case, it should nevertheless reject the request for provisional measures, since the FRY has come to the Court "with extremely dirty hands".[10] The FRY had violated Security Council resolutions and had acted in gross violation of universal human rights, which "not only caused a massive humanitarian catastrophe in Kosovo, but also threatened to destabilize the surrounding region".[11] The granting of the requested provisional measures would enable the FRY to continue these practices.

10 ICJ Public sitting 11 May 1999, verbatim record, CR 99/20, at 15.

11 *Id.*, at 17.

These observations were made at the end of the morning of Tuesday 11 May. During the second round of oral argument, in the morning of Wednesday 12 May, the FRY submitted to the Court a supplement to its original application, in which it invoked a new base of jurisdiction: Article 4 of the 1931 Treaty of Judicial Settlement, Arbitration and Conciliation between the Kingdom of Yugoslavia and the Netherlands, signed at The Hague on 11 March 1931 and in force since 2 April 1932. At the start of the afternoon session of that day the acting President of the Court informed the parties that the Court "will give its consideration to any observations of the Netherlands in regard to the admissibility of the additional ground invoked".[12] That afternoon the Netherlands observed that the invocation of the additional ground for jurisdiction "comes at a very late stage in the proceedings", and should have been invoked in the original application.[13] But the emphasis of the Dutch observations regarding this new ground for jurisdiction was on substance. The Netherlands claimed that the 1931 Treaty was no longer in force. Since the rules of international law relating to state succession in respect of treaties were controversial and unclear, the Netherlands had entered into consultations with the former Socialist Federal Republic of Yugoslavia (SFRY), as it had done with the other former Yugoslav republics. In these consultations, the parties agreed in principle that a number of bilateral treaties in force between the Netherlands and the SFRY could be continued, but the 1931 Treaty was not amongst these treaties. There was therefore no agreement between the parties as to the continued validity of the 1931 Treaty, and the FRY could not unilaterally decide that this treaty had remained in force. Moreover, even if this treaty would be in force, it could not be invoked by the FRY as a ground for jurisdiction because the FRY was not a party to the Statute.

On 2 June 1999 the Court delivered its Order, in which it rejected the request for the indication of provisional measures submitted by the FRY.[14] The Court

12 Order of 2 June 1999, *supra* n. 9, para. 14.

13 *See* ICJ Public sitting 12 May 1999, verbatim record, CR 99/31, at 7.

14 By eleven votes to four. Judges Weeramantry, Shi and Vereshchetin, and Judge ad hoc Kreća voted against. The Court also decided, by fourteen votes to one, to reserve the subsequent procedure for further decision. Judge Oda was the only judge voting against this decision. In his separate opinion, Judge Oda indicated that he was of the view that the Court should remove the case from the General List of the Court – as it had done in the 'Use of Force' cases against Spain and the United States – because it had no prima facie jurisdiction, and because "[i]t would be contrary to judicial propriety to make a distinction between two groups of States, in what is essentially one case dealing with

found that it had no prima facie jurisdiction to entertain the FRY's application – 'prima facie', because at this stage of the proceedings, relating to the request for provisional measures, the Court did not need finally to satisfy itself that it had jurisdiction on the merits of the case, "yet it ought not to indicate such measures unless the provisions invoked by the applicant appear, prima facie, to afford a basis on which the jurisdiction of the Court might be established".[15] The requirement of 'prima facie jurisdiction' is not mentioned in the Court's Statute or Rules, but has been developed in the Court's case law.[16]

The first basis of jurisdiction put forward by the FRY was Article 36, paragraph 2, of the Statute of the Court. The Court concluded that this could not be a basis for jurisdiction in this case, since the acceptance of jurisdiction made by the FRY on 26 April 1999 only related to disputes arising after that date, and the present dispute in essence related to the bombing of the territory of the FRY, which began already on 24 March 1999.[17] In view of this finding the Court did not consider the question whether or not the FRY was a member of the UN and a party to the Statute of the ICJ.[18]

The second basis of jurisdiction put forward by the FRY was Article IX of the Genocide Convention. The Court considered that, in order to determine,

---

the same subject throughout, solely because of the difference in attitudes taken by the States towards the relevant documents which give the Court jurisdiction" (Separate Opinion of Judge Oda, 1999 ICJ Rep. 562, at 577. In the cases against Spain and the United States, the Court concluded that it manifestly lacked jurisdiction to entertain Yugoslavia's application. Spain and the US have not accepted the Court's jurisdiction under the Genocide Convention. Spain has made a declaration recognizing the compulsory jurisdiction of the Court, but in this declaration it has excluded disputes in regard to which the other party or parties have accepted the compulsory jurisdiction of the Court less than 12 months prior to the filing of the application bringing the dispute before the Court. The US has not accepted the compulsory jurisdiction of the Court.

15 1999 ICJ Rep. 542, at 550.

16 This requirement was phrased in this way for the first time in the 1973 Nuclear Tests Case, and is by now firmly established. *See* the analysis by Judge Higgins in her Separate Opinion in this case (relating to the FRY's request for provisional measures), 1999 ICJ Rep. 579, in particular at 580-584.

17 *Id.*, at 551-553.

18 *Id.*, at 553. According to Judge Kooijmans, "the Court's reasoning is flawed from a logical point of view". In his view, the Court should not have avoided the question of Yugoslavia's membership of the UN. "Only after having established that this declaration [of acceptance of the jurisdiction of the Court– NB] is capable of providing the Court with a prima facie basis for its jurisdiction could the Court have considered in a meaningful way whether reservations made in either of the declarations obviously exclude its jurisdiction". *See* Separate Opinion of Judge Kooijmans, ICJ Rep. 591, at 591, 596.

even prima facie, whether a dispute within the meaning of Article IX of the Genocide Convention existed, "the Court cannot limit itself to noting that one of the Parties maintains that the Convention applies, while the other denies it". It therefore found that it had to "ascertain whether the breaches of the Convention alleged by Yugoslavia are capable of falling within the provisions of that instrument".[19] On this point the Court briefly reviewed whether the requirement of 'genocidal intent' was fulfilled and came to the conclusion that it was not.

Thirdly, in relation to the 1931 Treaty, put forward on 12 May 1999 by the FRY as an additional basis for jurisdiction, the Court concluded that that "such action at this late stage, when it is not accepted by the other party, seriously jeopardizes the principle of procedural fairness and the sound administration of justice".[20] This had never occurred before in the Court's practice. The Court therefore decided not to take into consideration this new title of jurisdiction, for the purpose of deciding whether it should indicate provisional measures.[21]

4 The Memorials, the Regime Change and its Implications, and the Judgment

4.1 The Memorials

Following the Order of 2 June, on 28 June 1999, the Court held a meeting with the parties devoted to the subsequent procedure. At that meeting the respondent States requested the Court to deal first with the question of the jurisdiction of the Court, before any proceedings on the merits. Yugoslavia however asked the Court to be permitted to submit a memorial on the merits. In its Order of 30 June 1999 the Court did not limit the next stage of the proceedings to the question of the jurisdiction of the Court and simply fixed the time-limits for the submission of the Memorial of the FRY (5 January 2000), and for the submission of a Counter-Memorial by the Netherlands (5 July 2000).

The FRY submitted its Memorial on 5 January 2000. The first 300 pages of this Memorial discuss facts. Only the final twenty pages concentrate on the jurisdiction of the Court. In this final part, the FRY claims that it is a member

19 1999 ICJ Rep. 542, at 555.

20 *Id.*, at 557.

21 *Id.*

of the UN and a party to the Statute. In relation to the conclusion of the Court in its Order of 2 June that it had no jurisdiction *ratione temporis* (the dispute arose before 26 April 1999), the FRY now claimed that "the dispute aggravated and extended. It got new elements concerning failures of the respondents to fulfil their obligations established by Security Council Resolution 1244 and by the 1948 [Genocide Convention]". According to the FRY, a dispute arises when all its elements have come into existence. In this case, the dispute arose only after 26 April 1999 with all its elements, which would bring it within the scope of the Court's jurisdiction.

As far as the 1931 Treaty is concerned, the FRY stated that the Netherlands had sent a Note (20 May 1997) informing the FRY on bilateral treaties which are in force. The 1931 Treaty was on this list, and should therefore be considered in force.

Finally, in relation to the alleged basis for jurisdiction in the Genocide Convention, the FRY memorial extensively quotes from the Court Order of 2 June, and only adds the following two sentences:

> "By this Memorial, the Applicant has submitted the evidence on the intent to commit genocide referring to acts of the respondents (acts of bombing) and to acts of killing and wounding of Serbs and other non-Albanians in Kosovo and Metohija after the 10th of June 1999. Accordingly, the Applicant claims that the jurisdiction of the Court, based on Article IX of the Genocide Convention is established."

The FRY therefore simply referred to the facts. It did not attempt explicitly to link these facts to the definition of genocide in the Genocide Convention. More specifically, it did not attempt to show that the acts mentioned were committed with the intent to destroy a group. This is in stark contrast with the oral submissions by the FRY during the hearings in April 2004, in particular with the statement by Brownlie, where it became one of the core issues.[22]

On 5 July 2000, the Netherlands submitted its Counter -Memorial, in which it presented a number of preliminary objections. These objections related both to the jurisdiction of the Court and to the admissibility of the claims filed by the FRY.

As for as the jurisdiction of the Court is concerned, the Netherlands first of all submitted that the FRY was not entitled to appear before the Court, since it was not a party to the Statute of the ICJ. Essentially, the Netherlands elabor-

---

22 *See* Paragraph 5, *infra*.

ated the arguments put forward in response to the FRY's request for provisional measures, and reacted to a number of specific arguments in the FRY's Memorial relating to ambiguous elements in UN practice concerning the status of the FRY.[23] Secondly, the Netherlands also elaborated its earlier observations relating to the limitation *ratione temporis* in the unilateral declaration of the FRY, and of course relied also on the Court's Order of 2 June 1999. In its Memorial the FRY submitted that the dispute had aggravated and extended, and new elements were added to the original dispute. The Netherlands submitted that there had only been a continuation and extension of the original dispute, or a reasonably foreseeable follow-up or consequence, but not a new and separate dispute. Thirdly, the Netherlands submitted that the Court did not have jurisdiction on the basis of the Genocide Convention. The FRY simply alleged that a genocidal intent existed, but failed to substantiate these allegations and thereby failed to present an arguable case under this Convention. The jurisdiction claim that was perhaps most difficult to rebut was based on the 1931 bilateral Treaty. In its Counter-Memorial, the Netherlands submitted at some length that the Court did not have jurisdiction on this basis. The essence of its arguments was the same as put forward during the provisional measures proceedings, when there were only a few hours available to prepare the oral submissions. According to the most important argument, the continuation of the 1931 Treaty after the disappearance of the SFRY required the consent of both parties, but such consent did not exist.

In addition to preliminary objections relating to the jurisdiction of the Court, the Netherlands also submitted that the claims presented by the FRY were inadmissible for three reasons. First, the Netherlands put forward that the FRY had not produced even a suggestion of evidence that the alleged breaches had been committed by the Netherlands. The FRY had put forward a large number of facts, but had failed to specify that these were acts undertaken by the Netherlands. Second, according to the Netherlands the FRY claims were inadmissible as a judgment in respect of the Netherlands would necessarily involve a decision in a dispute between the FRY and other entities and States not before the Court. The FRY application was directed against collective measures, taken by NATO or by member states of NATO and by NATO members and other states in the framework of KFOR (the international security presence in Kosovo authorized

23 In particular, a number of letters sent by the UN Secretariat to the authorities of the FRY (that was not recognized as a successor of the SFRY) referring to arrears in the payment of contributions to the UN (due by the SFRY whose membership was not terminated by the General Assembly).

by Security Council Resolution 1244). The Netherlands referred to the *Monetary Gold* and *East Timor* Judgments of the Court, in which the Court emphasized that it could only exercise jurisdiction on the basis of consent and that it could not do so if the legal interests of parties not before the Court would form the very subject matter of its decision.[24] All core decisions of Operation Allied Force were taken by NATO and KFOR. The Netherlands took only a relatively small part in this Operation: approximately five percent of all air sorties were carried out by Dutch aircraft. The largest part was carried out by participants not before the Court. Finally, the Netherlands submitted that some claims by the FRY (based on alleged breaches of obligations established by Security Council Resolution 1244 and by the Genocide Convention related to killings, wounding and expulsion of Serbs and other non-Albanian groups in Kosovo and Metohija after 10 June 1999) were inadmissible since they amounted to a new claim changing the subject of the dispute originally submitted to the Court.

4.2 The Regime Change and its Implications

After the submission of these preliminary objections, a number of developments fundamentally changed the context of the eight *Use of Force* cases before the ICJ. Following elections in the FRY a regime change took place. In October 2000 President Koštunica came to power, and subsequently former President Milošević was transferred to the International Criminal Tribunal for the Former Yugoslavia. In a letter dated 27 October 2000 the FRY applied for UN membership. International organizations generally do not have a reputation of speedy decision-making, but this case was different: within five days the FRY was admitted.[25] This application was processed completely as an application for admission as a new member and did not imply in some way the continuation of membership of the SFRY.

It was not immediately clear what implications these changes would have for the cases pending before the ICJ. Would they be continued by the FRY? Or would they be discontinued, as provided for in Articles 88 and 89 of the

24 Case of the Monetary Gold Removed from Rome in 1943 (Italy *v.* France, United Kingdom and United States), Preliminary Question, Judgment of 15 June 1954, 1954 ICJ Rep. 19; Case Concerning East Timor (Portugal v. Australia), Judgment of 30 June 1995, 1995 ICJ Rep. 15.

25 UN Doc. A/55/528-S/2000/1043; SC Res. 1326; GA Res. 55/12.

Rules of the Court? It was obvious that the eight respondents were in favour of discontinuance, and this was also one of the options considered by the FRY. The case was associated with the *ancien régime* and there was an atmosphere of willingness to start with a clean slate. This also resulted in the replacement of almost all members of the FRY team dealing with this case (Brownlie being the exception). The changes included the Agent for the FRY in this case: Tibor Varady succeeded Rudoljub Etinski as the Agent. The continuation of the case became increasingly surrealistic when the FRY sought a rapprochement with the UN, the Organization for Security and Cooperation in Europe, the Council of Europe, the European Union and even NATO. Several attempts were made at the political and technical level to persuade the FRY to terminate proceedings before the ICJ. However, although the FRY was no longer actively seeking an early judgement on the merits, it did not want to bring these proceedings to an end.

In January 2001 the FRY asked the Court for a stay of proceedings or, alternatively, for the extension of the time limit for the submission of observations of the FRY, for a period of twelve months. The respondents supported this, indicating some preference for a stay of proceedings. The Court however decided to extend the time limits for the submission of observations by the FRY, for the requested period of twelve months.[26] These time limits were again extended subsequently[27] and the case became dormant until December 2002, when the FRY submitted its written observations.[28]

In these very brief observations the FRY referred to "newly discovered facts which have emerged since earlier pleadings were filed". It indicated that these facts had been revealed in the light of the FRY becoming a member of the UN. It observed that it was now clear that the FRY was not a member of the UN before its admission on 1 November 2000.

> "Accordingly, it became an established fact that before 1 November 2000, the Federal Republic of Yugoslavia was not and could not have been a party to the Statute of the Court by way of UN membership".

26 Order of 21 February 2001.

27 Order of 20 March 2002.

28 Available from the Court's website, *see* http://www.icj-cij.org/icjwww/idocket/iyne/iyneframe.htm.

With regard to the Genocide Convention, the FRY observed that it

> "did not continue the personality and treaty membership of the former Yugoslavia, and thus specifically, it was not bound by the Genocide Convention until it acceded to that Convention (with a reservation to Article IX) in March 2001".

In conclusion, the FRY requested the Court "to decide on its jurisdiction considering the pleadings formulated in these Written Observations".[29]

The respondents reacted to these observations, and some of them indicated that these observations by the FRY amounted to a notice of discontinuance of the proceedings. In response the FRY explicitly rejected this interpretation.

For the Netherlands, there was one other development of particular relevance to this case. In 2002 bilateral consultations took place between the Netherlands and the FRY concerning the continuance of treaties concluded between the Netherlands and Yugoslavia. In August 2002 these consultations resulted in an Exchange of Notes with two attachments.[30] Attachment A contains a list of seven treaties that "are in force and represent treaties concluded between the Federal Republic of Yugoslavia and the Kingdom of the Netherlands". Attachment B contains a list of six treaties that "will not be considered in force between the Federal Republic of Yugoslavia and the Kingdom of the Netherlands". The Exchange of Notes states that "the present Exchange of Notes is without prejudice to future discussions regarding the continuance of treaties referred to in Attachment B". The first treaty listed in Attachment B is the 1931 Treaty.[31] This shows that at the time of conclusion of the Exchange of Notes, and therefore also in 1999 when the FRY brought its complaint against the Netherlands before the ICJ, no agreement existed between the Netherlands and the FRY on the continuance of the 1931 Treaty. This development was mentioned in the oral statement by the Netherlands during the hearings in this case.[32]

29 *Id.*

30 This Exchange of Notes was included in a bundle of documents that was submitted to the Court by the eight respondents, pursuant to Article 56 of the Rules of the Court. It has also been published in the relevant issues of the *Tractatenblad* (Netherlands Treaty Series), *see, e.g.* Trb. 2002, 181.

31 *Id.*

32 *See* ICJ Public sitting 19 April 2004, verbatim record, CR 2004/7, at 13 (para. 32).

4.3 Hearings

In November 2003 the Court decided that hearings in these eight cases would be held in April 2004. The Court decided that the judges ad hoc appointed earlier in the proceedings by some of the respondents were not entitled to sit during this new stage of the proceedings, leaving it open that they could sit again should the case enter the merits phase.

None of the parties seemed particularly eager to have hearings in this case. The FRY since it would be forced to defend policies of the *ancien regime*, which must have been somewhat uncomfortable in a period characterized by rapprochement towards its former enemies rather than confrontation. The eight respondents faced the difficulty of determining how they should approach the extremely brief written observations of December 2002 (which came close to a statement that the FRY no longer really disputed their preliminary objections on jurisdiction).

However, to the extent that respondents argued that there was no longer really a dispute on jurisdiction between the parties, the hearings made very clear that the FRY had no intention of discontinuing the cases. Brownlie accused the respondents of having committed genocide, and Varady explicitly stated: "[w]e do have a dispute", and "the applicant State wants the Court to continue the case and to decide upon its jurisdiction – and to decide on the merits as well, if it has jurisdiction".[33]

The Netherlands noted in its oral submissions that it was "difficult, if not impossible" to comply with Article 60, paragraph 1, of the Rules of the Court, according to which the oral statement made on behalf of each party must be directed to the issues that still divide the parties, since there did not seem to be such issues as there was in fact agreement among the parties that there was no jurisdiction. The FRY did not contest the Netherlands' objections to the jurisdiction of the Court, and its written observations of December 2002 were fundamentally different from its original application. According to the Netherlands, the parties now agreed that the Court had no jurisdiction; therefore there was no longer a dispute on the jurisdiction of the Court. In addition, even if the Court would conclude that it was not sufficiently clear whether *according*

33 *See* ICJ Public sitting 21 April 2004, verbatim record, CR 2004/14 (quotations in paras. 3, 37 of the statement by Varady).

to the parties there was no longer a dispute, the Court itself could also, from an *objective* point of view, conclude that this was the case.[34]

4.4 The Judgment

The Court delivered its judgment on 15 December 2004. There was broad agreement within the Court that it had no jurisdiction to entertain the FRY's claims, but there was profound disagreement on the reasons why it had no jurisdiction. On the one hand, the Court *unanimously* concluded that it had no jurisdiction; even Judge ad hoc Kreća supported this conclusion (as he explained in his long separate opinion). On the other hand, behind the veil of unanimity the Court was deeply divided on the grounds for its conclusion, as appears from the joint declaration by seven judges.

In its judgment the Court first dealt with the claim by respondents that, as a result of the changed attitude of the Applicant, the Court would no longer need to adjudge and declare whether it had jurisdiction but could simply dismiss the case. In support of this claim various arguments were used, which were all rejected by the Court. According to one argument, the December 2002 Observations by the FRY amounted to a notice of discontinuance of the proceedings, as provided for in Article 89 of the Rules of the Court. The Court rejected this argument, indicating that the FRY expressly denied that these observations were a notice of discontinuance and wanted the Court to decide on its jurisdiction. Referring to its 1964 Judgment in the *Barcelona Traction* case, it considered that its role in a discontinuance procedure is "simply to record it and to remove the case from its list". However, such a 'simple recording' was not possible in the present case since the FRY did not want to discontinue the case. The Court considered:

> "[i]t may be true that the logical consequence of the contention of Serbia and Montenegro in its Observations could be that the case would go no further; but this would be the result of the Court's own finding and not the placing on record of a withdrawal by Serbia and Montenegro of the dispute from the Court's purview".[35]

---

34 *See* ICJ Public sitting 19 April 2004, verbatim record, CR 2004/7 (statement by Lammers).

35 Judgment, paras. 25-31.

According to another argument by the respondents the Court may of its own motion put an end to a case if necessary for the proper administration of justice. However, the Court found that the present case did not fall into the categories in which it had previously removed cases from its list.[36]

Furthermore, respondents claimed that there was now substantive agreement between the parties on the question of jurisdiction and that as a result the dispute had disappeared. On this point however, the Court concluded that the FRY had not invited the Court to find that it had no jurisdiction;

> "while it is apparently in agreement with the arguments advanced by the respondents in that regard in their preliminary objections, it has specifically asked in its submissions for a decision of the Court on the jurisdictional question".

In addition, more fundamentally, the Court observed that this jurisdictional question is independent of the views or wishes of the parties, since it relates to "the right of a party to appear before the Court under the requirements of the Statute, which is not a matter of consent". The Court therefore has to reach its own conclusions.[37]

In addition, some respondents implied that the position of the FRY might be influenced by the existence of a pending case before the Court, and that the FRY was hoping for a judgment by the Court from which it could benefit in this other case. The Court immediately rejected this argument by finding that "it cannot decline to entertain a case simply because of a suggestion as to the motives of one of the parties or because its judgment may have implications in another case".[38]

The Court therefore concluded that it was unable to find that the FRY "has renounced any of its substantive or procedural rights, or has taken the position that the dispute between the parties has ceased to exist". It could therefore not "remove the cases concerning *Legality of Use of Force* from the list, or take any decision putting an end to those cases *in limine litis*".[39]

The Court therefore examined the question of its jurisdiction in these cases. It noted that it had referred in its earlier case law to "its freedom to select the ground upon which it will base its judgment", and to its freedom to base its decision on one or more grounds of its own choosing, in particular "the ground

---

36 *Id.*, para. 32.
37 *Id.*, paras. 33-35, 42.
38 *Id.*, paras. 38-39.
39 *Id.*, para. 42.

which in its judgment is more direct and conclusive".[40] However, it also observed that in this case law, the parties involved were without doubt parties to the Statute and the Court was open to them under Article 35, paragraph 1, of the Statute. In these eight cases, the fundamental first question to be dealt with was whether indeed the FRY was a party to the Statute. The Court examined this question in detail, as it had done earlier in the Bosnia-Herzegovina *Genocide* case. However, while it had concluded earlier that the legal position of the FRY within the UN during the period 1992-2000 was "highly complex", "ambiguous",[41] "rather confused" and "*sui generis*", it now observed that these earlier qualifications and conclusions were not final and definite, and now came to the conclusion that the FRY had become a member of the UN on 1 November 2000 and that it had not been a member of the UN before that date. Therefore, when the FRY filed its application in 1999 it was not a party to the Statute and it did not have the right to appear before the Court.

In 1999, when the Court delivered its Orders dealing with the request for provisional measures in these cases, the status of the FRY in the UN was obviously less clear and the Court avoided considering this and rejected the request on other grounds. But in 2003, when the Court examined this question in the context of the *Application for Revision* case, the FRY was a member of the UN and a party to the Statute. However, the Court observed that its judgment in that case did not possess "any force of *res iudicata* in the present case".[42] This case related to a request by the FRY under Article 61 of the Court's Statute, to revise the Court's judgment on preliminary objections of 11 July 1996 in the *Genocide* case. Under this procedure the FRY had to show the existence of a fact which was "when the judgment was given, unknown to the Court and also to the party claiming revision".[43] The Court in its *Application for Revision* judgment found the application inadmissible, since the FRY relied on a fact (the admission of the FRY to the UN on 1 November 2000) postdating the 1996 judgment. It did not rule on the question of the status of the FRY in the UN.[44]

Therefore, since the FRY was not a party to the Statute at the time of its application, the Court was not open to it on the basis of Article 35, paragraph 1 of the Statute. Nevertheless, on the basis of Article 35, paragraph 2, of the

40 *Id.*, para. 45.
41 *Id.*, para. 63.
42 *Id.*, para. 79.
43 *Id.*, para. 84.
44 *Id.*, paras. 86-87.

Statute, under certain conditions the Court is also open to non-parties to the Statute. However, the Court concluded that these conditions were not fulfilled in the present case. The Court accordingly found that it had no jurisdiction to entertain the claims by the FRY.

As mentioned above, the Court was unanimous in this conclusion, but was deeply divided on the grounds given in its judgment. As appears from the joint declaration by seven judges, these judges reject the view that the Court first has to establish that parties indeed have the right to appear before it, before considering other objections to its jurisdiction. In their view, if the Court finds that, on two or more grounds, it lacks jurisdiction, the Court may choose the most appropriate ground.[45] In doing so, it should be guided by three criteria: consistency with its own past case law in order to provide predictability; selection of the ground that is most secure in law (principle of certitude); and "as the principal judicial organ of the United Nations, the Court will [...] be mindful of the possible implications and consequences for the other pending cases".[46] The seven judges are of the opinion that these three criteria are not reflected in this judgment. As regards the first criterion, the Court in its 1999 Order concluded that it lacked jurisdiction *ratione temporis* and *ratione materiae*, while it concluded in the present judgment that it lacked jurisdiction *ratione personae*; in addition, this change is at odds with previous decisions of the Court (such as the 2003 *Application for Revision* judgment). With respect to the principle of certitude, the seven judges take the view that no new relevant developments took place since the Court's judgment in the 2003 *Application for Revision* judgment, and that the ground now chosen is less legally compelling and therefore less certain, than the grounds previously relied upon. Finally, the third criterion is not reflected in the judgment because it does not sufficiently look at the implications for other cases.

5 Observations

1.

This is the first case before the Court in which the Netherlands was involved and became the winning party. The case was almost completely intertwined

45 Joint Declaration of Vice-President Ranjeva, Judges Guillaume, Higgins, Kooijmans, Al-Khasawneh, Buergenthal and Elaraby, *see* http://www.icj-cij.org/icjwww/idocket/iyne/iyneframe.htm, at para. 2.

46 *Id.*, para. 3.

with similar cases brought by Serbia and Montenegro against other states that were also members of NATO: nine other states at the stage of the request for provisional measures (1999), of which seven remained after the Court had removed the cases against Spain and the US from the List in view of the Court's manifest lack of jurisdiction.

If the December 2004 judgments in these eight cases are compared, there is very little that distinguishes the judgment in the case against the Netherlands from the other seven judgments. The only difference relates to the considerations of the judgment devoted to the 1931 bilateral treaty; similar considerations can be found only in the judgment in the case against Belgium. However, these considerations show that the Court uses the same argument that it had used to reject the other grounds for jurisdiction of the Court, i.e. the argument that Serbia and Montenegro was not a party to the Statute on 29 April 1999 when it instituted proceedings in these cases.

The Court did not pronounce on the question whether the 1931 Treaty was in force on that date. If the Court would have had to deal with that question, it would have to take into account the fact that the bilateral consultations that took place in The Hague on 24 July 1996 between the Netherlands and the FRY were not completed. Agreement in principle was reached on the continued applicability of most bilateral treaties in force between the Netherlands and the former SFRY, but the 1931 Treaty was not among those treaties. With respect to some treaties, including the 1931 Treaty, it was concluded that the Yugoslav delegation would contact the authorities concerned in Belgrade. It is noteworthy that the Netherlands did not seem to have any objections in principle to the continued application of this treaty. This also appears from the fact that the Netherlands and the other former Yugoslav republics agreed that this was one of the treaties that would continue to be in force between themselves.[47] However, as it happened, the FRY did not give any follow-up to the consultations that took place on 24 July 1996, and therefore agreement was not yet reached on the list of treaties that would continue to be in force, when the FRY invoked the 1931 Treaty as a ground for jurisdiction. It was clear, pending the ICJ proceedings in the *Use of Force* case, that the Netherlands was not in favour of the continued application of the 1931 Treaty. Somewhat unexpectedly, as indicated above, the FRY in the 2002 Exchange of Notes agreed to put the 1931 Treaty on a list of treaties that were not considered in force between the FRY and the Netherlands. Even though the Exchange of Notes

47 Croatia and Slovenia: Trb. 1995, 98; the Former Yugoslav Republic of Macedonia: Trb. 1997, 278; Bosnia-Herzegovina: Trb. 1998, 269.

states that this is without prejudice to future discussions regarding the continuance of treaties referred to in Attachment B, this new development made it less likely that the Court would have accepted this treaty as a basis for jurisdiction in this case, if it would have to deal with this question. However, since the Court in all eight cases used a 'catch all' argument (that Serbia and Montenegro was not a party to the Statute), this issue, which was only relevant in the cases against Belgium and the Netherlands, remained outside the Court's considerations.

2.

Perhaps it is appropriate that the Court used a 'catch all' argument for these eight cases (leaving aside whether the 'non party to the Statute argument' was the best possible 'catch all' argument). After all, these eight cases in fact concerned one single issue. However, while the object of the complaint by the FRY was the use of force *by NATO* against the FRY, the 1999 Applications by the FRY were directed against ten *states* that participated in the NATO operation.

The claims by the FRY in its original application (1999) were formulated along the following lines: the FRY requests the ICJ to adjudge and declare: "by taking part in [...]" the bombing, attacks, destroying, etc. etc., the Netherlands has acted in breach of a number of obligations (such as the obligation not to use force). However, the claims as formulated in the 2000 Memorial were different: the FRY requested the Court to adjudge and declare that "by the bombing [...], by using force [...], by using cluster bombs [...]," etc. etc., the Respondent has acted in breach of a number of obligations. In its Memorial, the FRY simply claimed without much further explanation that acts of NATO (and subsequently of KFOR) were imputable to the respondents. Therefore, while the original claims recognized the fact that the relevant acts were acts in which the Netherlands *took part*, in the final formulation of the claims, the relevant acts were *directly attributed* to the Respondent. However, it is questionable whether the NATO veil could be pierced so easily, and whether the relevant acts that were the subject of the complaints by the FRY were indeed acts for which the respondents could be held responsible.

Nevertheless, this never became a major issue in these ICJ proceedings. It was raised in particular by Canada, France, the Netherlands and Portugal as part of their preliminary objections.[48] For the Netherlands, it was one of the main preliminary objections to the admissibility of the FRY's Application. It claimed in its Memorial that the relevant acts were not imputable to the Netherlands but to NATO. But neither in the written observations by the eight respondents nor during their submissions in the hearings did this become a key issue. This is perhaps surprising. If the relevant acts were indeed acts by NATO and not acts by the respondents, complex questions relating to the responsibility of NATO for these acts, and/or a responsibility of all NATO members or those NATO members that participated in Operation Allied Force would emerge.[49]

The FRY did not have much choice in its application, although it could have decided to bring applications against *all* states that were also members of NATO, including those states that did not participate in Operation Allied Force, as was done by the applicants in the *Banković* case before the European Court of Human Rights. But it could not successfully bring an application against NATO, as international organizations do not have *locus standi* before the ICJ. As Judge Kooijmans has noted in his separate opinion in another case:

> "[t]he system of international judicial dispute settlement is premised on the existence of a series of bilateral inter-State disputes, artificial as this sometimes may be, as became clear, for example in the *Legality of the Use of Force* cases".[50]

Nevertheless, the respondents did not really choose to hide behind the NATO veil (and follow a '*Flucht in der Organisation* strategy') in this case. Perhaps this is because it could have been perceived as too facile an escape of responsibility for the 1999 NATO operation in the current climate of accountability.

48 France also raised this issue before the European Court of Human Rights in the Banković case (Appl. No. 52207/99), Banković, and others *v.* Belgium, and others, Decision on Admissibility, 12 December 2001, para. 32. The European Court did not pronounce on this issue.

49 In the Banković case, the applicants lodged their application not only against those NATO members that participated in Operation Allied Force, but against all 17 NATO members that were also party to the European Human Rights Convention. On the question whether NATO and/or its members would be responsible for these acts, *see* T. Stein, *Kosovo and the International Community. The attribution of Possible Internationally Wrongful Acts: Responsibility of NATO or of its Member States?, in* C. Tomuschat (ed.), Kosovo and the International Community – A Legal Assessment, 181 (2002); A. Pellet, L'imputabilité d'éventuels actes illicites – Responsabilité de l'OTAN ou des États members, in Tomuschat (ed.), *id.*, 193.

50 Case Concerning Armed Activities on the Territory of the Congo (Democratic Republic of the Congo *v.* Uganda), Judgment of 19 December 2005, 2002 ICJ Rep., para. 11.

Perhaps it was expected that there was no chance at all that the Court would accept this argument. Nevertheless, as could be seen during all the stages of the proceedings, the collective nature of the 1999 NATO Operation pervaded each of the individual cases. While each respondent had its own team and prepared its own submissions, regular consultations took place amongst the respondents during all stages of the proceedings.[51]

Operation Allied Force was a NATO operation, and in practice it was considered as such. The operation took place on the basis of NATO decisions (in particular: the relevant Activation Orders). All decisions to move to another phase of the air campaign were taken by the NATO Council. The military implementation (covering the decisions where, when and how targets were attacked) was left to NATO military authorities. The Netherlands transferred command and control over the participating Dutch units to NATO commanders.[52]

It was important for the respondents to prevent the collective nature of the operation from being crumbled in the legal aftermath. They succeeded in this, even though the collective nature of Allied Force was not given the same prominence by each of the eight respondents. At the same time it appears that NATO solidarity in the legal aftermath has not *really* been put to the test since the case did not reach the stage of the merits. If the cases would have arrived at that stage, the fundamentally different views amongst the respondents on the legal basis for the operation (in short: implied authorization by the Security Council or humanitarian intervention) would come fully into the spotlight.

The collective nature of the operations also appears from the way in which the FRY and the Court have handled these cases. It is reflected in the fact that, "due to substantive and technical reasons, the Applicant has prepared an identical text of the Memorial in all eight pending cases. The substance of the dispute in all eight cases is identical".[53] The Court has attempted to streamline the proceedings in these cases. For example, the FRY could present one set of oral submissions for all eight cases, and the President of the Court did not read out eight separate judgments in these cases, but made one single 'merged' presentation.

---

51 In the Banković case before the European Court of Human Rights, cooperation between NATO members was more intense. For example, in that case the submissions were made on behalf of all respondents, by the United Kingdom; *supra* n. 48, para. 3.

52 *See, for more details,* Preliminary Objections by the Netherlands (5 July 2000), para. 7.2.

53 FRY Memorial, Introduction, para. 11.

However, it seems that in one respect ICJ has gone too far in streamlining these proceedings. In its Order of 23 December 2003, the Court decided, pursuant to Article 31, paragraph 5 of the Statute, that

> "taking into account the presence upon the Bench of judges of British, Dutch and French nationality, the judges *ad hoc* chosen by the respondent States should not sit during the current phase of the procedure in these cases; it was made clear to the Agents that this decision by the Court did not in any way prejudice the question whether, if the Court should reject the preliminary objections of the respondents, judges *ad hoc* might sit in subsequent stages of the cases".[54]

However, it was precisely during this stage of the proceedings, when the Court had to deal with the preliminary objections by the respondents, that there were important differences between the positions of the parties. In the cases against France, Germany and Italy, jurisdiction could exclusively be claimed on the basis of the Genocide Convention. In the cases against Canada, Portugal and the United Kingdom, jurisdiction could potentially also be based on the unilateral declarations of these states. Finally, in the cases against Belgium and the Netherlands, there was a third potential basis for jurisdiction: the bilateral treaties concluded with Yugoslavia by these two countries in the 1930s. As a result of the Order of the Court, five respondents did not have a judge *ad hoc* when the Court decided on the preliminary objections by these countries. In the view of the Court, all eight respondents were "in the same interest", as mentioned in Article 31, paragraph 5 of the Statute. However, there were substantial differences between the parties as far as the basis for jurisdiction in these cases was concerned. In particular, it was widely recognized that Belgium and the Netherlands were in a special position in view of their bilateral treaties with Yugoslavia. But while there was a judge of Dutch nationality on the Bench, this was not the case for Belgium. While one may criticize the phenomenon of the judge *ad hoc*, as long as it is part of the structure of the Court and accepted in the Court's Statute it should allow a party before the Court to have a judge of its nationality on the Bench in case it has an interest that is not the same as that of other parties before the Court. It is submitted that this was not the case for five of the respondents in these eight cases, in particular for Belgium.

54 *See* Judgment of 15 December 2004, para. 17.

3.

Another characteristic of the eight cases is the question whether there was a real dispute between the parties on jurisdiction of the Court. It is certain that there was such a dispute in 1999, when the FRY brought its application, and in 2000 until the regime change. But it was not so certain after the regime change. Following a period of internal changes and policy reorientation, the brief written observations of the FRY of December 2002 explicitly state that it considered itself not a member of the UN before its admission on 1 November 2000, and therefore not a party to the Statute by way of UN membership. However, the FRY did not draw any conclusions from these written observations. The Court was in fact asked to do so. In these cases, the Court was faced with an applicant with two faces during the successive stages of the proceedings.

Nevertheless, even if it is assumed that there was hardly any dispute left after the regime change, there was a dispute when the FRY brought its application. At that moment, the FRY formulated its claims, and the Court has no alternative but to decide on that basis unless the FRY would change these claims or would inform the Court that it would not go on with the proceedings, in accordance with Article 89 of the Rules of the Court, or if the Court would itself decide to remove the case from the List. The FRY did not fundamentally change its claims, nor did it want to discontinue proceedings. Moreover, it explicitly requested the Court to decide on the issue of jurisdiction. And, when respondents claimed in response to the FRY's written observations of December 2002 that the dispute had disappeared, the FRY was apparently triggered to emphasize that it wanted the Court to continue the proceedings. Moreover, the FRY's conduct during the hearings was far from conciliatory. Rather, it stressed that a conflict continued to exist between the parties. Inter alia, it claimed in a submission by Brownlie that NATO had committed genocide against the population of Serbia and Montenegro.[55] In these circumstances, the requirements of procedure make it difficult for the Court to remove *of its own motion* these cases from its List. There was some support for such a 'catch all' approach. In particular, judges Higgins and Kooijmans favoured this approach in their separate opinions. But it would require the Court to take a more active and autonomous stance – in particular *vis-à-vis* Serbia and Montenegro – than it had now decided to take.

One of the options for the FRY following the regime change was to terminate these cases. One can only speculate why this was not done. First, and

55 *See* ICJ Public sitting 21 April 2004, verbatim record, CR 2004/14.

perhaps most important for the FRY, it considered that an ICJ judgment in these cases could be instrumental for the FRY defence in the two pending 'genocide cases' against the FRY. In these 'genocide cases' the FRY was relying on similar arguments as the eight respondents in the 'use of force cases'. A finding by the Court that the FRY had committed genocide could entail severe political and financial consequences. The interrelatedness of these cases will briefly be discussed below.

Secondly, although a regime change had taken place, there was still substantial support for the *ancien régime*. A simple termination of these cases would perhaps favour the still considerable anti-Western, nationalist political sentiments in the country. In the parliamentary elections in Serbia of 28 December 2003 Milošević's Socialist Party of Serbia and the Serbian Radical Party of Vojislav Šešelj obtained 104 of the 250 seats in Parliament; the Serbian Radical Party becoming the largest party.[56] Moreover, even though a regime change had taken place, there was widespread criticism at the NATO bombardments, and this was precisely the subject matter of these ICJ cases.

A third reason is perhaps the degree of political pressure from the eight respondents. Although, following the regime change, some political pressure was exerted on the FRY to terminate these cases, this may not have been strong enough. If in response to the FRY's rapprochement to its former enemies, and to the UN, the OSCE, the Council of Europe, the EU, and even NATO, the condition would have been posed to terminate these cases, the cases would perhaps be discontinued. This condition does not seem to have been posed in strong terms. Perhaps this is because of the awareness that it would be difficult for such a course to obtain sufficiently broad support internally within the FRY, perhaps also because after 2000 these cases before the ICJ were not as high on political agendas as in 1999 during the provisional measures stage of the proceedings.

4.

An important issue in this case was the possibility that the Court's judgment would not only bring these cases to an end but would also have major implications for two other cases still pending before the Court: the *Case concerning Application of the Convention on the Prevention and Punishment of the Crime*

56 *See* OSCE/ODIHR Election Observation Mission Report (Doc. ODIHR.GAL/13/04, 27 February 2004): www.osce.org/documents/odihr/2004/02/2177_en. At the time of these elections, both Milošević and Šešelj were detained by the International Criminal Tribunal for the Former Yugoslavia.

of Genocide (Bosnia and Herzegovina v. Yugoslavia) and the *Case concerning the Application of the Convention on the Prevention and Punishment of the Crime of Genocide* (Croatia v. Yugoslavia). Since the Court had found in the 'use of force cases' that the Court was not open to the FRY because it was not a party to the Statute at the time of its application in 1999, the question is whether the Court was nevertheless open to the FRY a few years before, in 1993, when Bosnia and Herzegovina filed its application, and on 2 July 1999, when Croatia filed its application. It does not seem easy for the Court to give an affirmative answer to this question, certainly not in relation to the 1999 Croatia case, but also in relation to the 1993 Bosnia-Herzegovina case.

While previously the Court has carefully avoided making final determinations on the status of the FRY in the UN, in the December 2004 judgment the Court concluded that the FRY was not a member of the UN in 1999, after it had analyzed "the rather confused and complex state of affairs that obtained within the United Nations surrounding the issue of the legal status of the Federal Republic of Yugoslavia in the Organization" during the period between 1992 to 2000.[57] It is true that the December 2004 judgments in the eight 'use of force' cases are applicable between the parties only, but it is unlikely that the Court in other cases would come to different conclusions on issues as complex and sensitive as the status of the FRY in the UN.

Nevertheless it may be relevant that, although the December 2004 judgment was made unanimously, there was profound disagreement amongst the judges as to the reasoning of the Court. A joint declaration of seven judges of the Court was appended to the judgment, in which these judges in strong terms disagreed with the ground upon which the Court had found that it had no jurisdiction. In particular, these seven judges disagreed with the Court's findings concerning the status of the FRY in the UN in the period 1992-2000. It is not certain whether this largest possible minority will also represent the minority view in possible future judgments in the two pending 'genocide cases', also in view of the changes in membership of the Court.[58] Nevertheless, as the seven judges mention in their joint declaration, if the Court has the possibility of determining its jurisdiction on more than one ground, in making a choice the Court

57 Judgment, para. 72.

58 As of 6 February 2006, three of the seven judges who signed the joint declaration are no longer members of the Court. Of the judges who did not sign the joint declaration (excluding the judge *ad hoc*), two are no longer members of the Court.

> "must ensure consistency with its own past case law in order to provide predictability. Consistency is the essence of judicial reasoning. This is especially true in different phases of the same case or with regard to closely related cases".[59]

It would seem difficult for possible future judgments in the two pending 'genocide cases' to follow a fundamentally different course than it has done in December 2004 on the issue of the status in the UN of the FRY in the period 1992-2000.

5.

The Court's finding that it had no jurisdiction was not surprising in view of the difficult jurisdictional hurdles the FRY had to take. The seven judges of the joint declaration also found that "this case cannot, as a matter of law, proceed to the merits".[60] But the main ground on which the Court based its finding was surprising. Not many observers would have expected that the Court, in these eight cases, would draw such firm conclusions on the status of the FRY in the UN in the period 1992-2000, in particular in view of the possible implications for the pending genocide cases (as discussed above) and in view of the Court's 2003 judgment in the *Application for Revision* case. In the 2003 judgment, the Court carefully avoided drawing such firm conclusions. In the eight *Use of Force* cases, the Court does not fail to explain what appears to be a change of approach. In its explanation, it emphasizes that, in its view, the 2003 judgment does not predetermine the Court's findings in the eight *Use of Force* cases and has to be interpreted in the specific context of the revision procedure of Article 61 of the Statute.

However, in the 2003 judgment the Court states that General Assembly Resolution 47/1 (1992) "did not *inter alia* affect the FRY's right to appear before the Court or to be a party to a dispute before the Court under the conditions laid down by the Statute", and that

> "General Assembly Resolution 55/12 of 1 November 2000 cannot have changed retroactively the *sui generis* position which the FRY found itself in vis-à-vis the United Nations over the period 1992-2000, or its position in relation to the Statute of the Court and the Genocide Convention".[61]

59 Joint Declaration of Vice-President Ranjeva, Judges Guillaume, Higgins, Kooijmans, Al-Khasawneh, Buergenthal and Elaraby, para. 3.

60 *Id.*, para. 1.

61 2003 Judgment, paras. 70-71.

In the eight *Use of Force* judgments, the Court refers to these statements in the 2003 judgment and finds that "[t]hese statements cannot however be read as findings on the status of Serbia and Montenegro in relation to the United Nations and the Genocide Convention".[62] It is not clear how the Court can deny that the quoted sentences of the 2003 judgment "cannot [...] be read" in this way, as there does not seem to be any other way in which they can be read. The precise purpose of these sentences was to carefully avoid pronouncing upon or determining definitely the ambiguous legal status of the FRY within the UN in the period 1992-2002. The precise result of the eight 2004 judgments was the opposite: to bring this ambiguity to an end by determining "that the FRY was not a member of the United Nations, and in that capacity a State party to the Statute of the International Court of Justice".[63]

6.

This case, and the other *Use of Force* cases, involved sensitive political issues, as always in disputes relating to the use of force in international relations. The case attracted considerable attention in Dutch media and politics at the stage of the request for provisional measures. In consultations with Parliament Minister of Foreign Affairs Van Aartsen agreed to send to Parliament the text of the observations by the Netherlands presented during the hearings,[64] and declared that the Netherlands would abide by ICJ orders and judgments in this case.[65] The reports of these consultations show that members of Parliament had read the text of the Dutch observations for the hearings.[66] Van Bommel of the Socialist Party introduced a motion asking the Government to respect the decision the ICJ would take on the request for provisional measures by the FRY. Only subsequently, in its 2001 judgment in the *LaGrand* Case, was the Court to state that such orders have binding effect.[67] Therefore, at the time of these debates in Parliament the legal status of an order of the Court made in the context of a request for provisional measures was not yet clear. Minister Van Aartsen stated that the Netherlands had never before been confronted with an ICJ Order in a request for provisional measures, but that it was standing practice

62 Judgment, para. 87.

63 *Id.*, para. 78.

64 *See* TK 1998-1999, 22181, Nos. 272 and 280 (p. 12).

65 *See* Handelingen 1998-1999, No. 81, pp. 4698-4703.

66 TK 27 May 1999, 81-4698 – 81-4703.

67 ICJ, LaGrand Case (Germany v. United States of America), Judgment of 27 June 2001, 2001 ICJ Rep., paras. 92-109.

for the Netherlands to respect and observe similar Orders made by the European Court of Human Rights. Minister Van Aartsen referred in this context to the Dutch Constitution, in which an important role was given to international law. He mentioned as an additional reason to follow decisions of the Court the fact that the Netherlands is the host state of the ICJ. Minister Van Aartsen therefore concluded that the motion introduced by Van Bommel was superfluous. The subsequent vote on this motion showed that only the Socialist Party supported it; it was therefore rejected.[68]

Since the two sets of decisions in the *Use of Force* cases (the ten Orders of 1999 and the eight judgments of 2004) did not pass the jurisdiction hurdle, the Court did not discuss the relevant substantive questions, in particular the legality of humanitarian intervention. Nevertheless, the importance of these substantive questions was mentioned in these decisions and in some of the separate or dissenting opinions. Judge Shi, in his dissenting opinion to the 1999 Orders, was of the opinion that, "confronted with that urgent situation, the Court ought to have contributed to the maintenance of international peace and security in so far as its judicial functions permit"; he found it "deplorable" that the Court did not issue a "general statement appealing to the parties to act in compliance with their obligations under the Charter of the United Nations and all other rules of international law relevant to the situation, including international humanitarian law, and at least not to aggravate or extend their dispute".[69] According to Judge Vereshchetin,

> "[t]he Court should have promptly expressed its profound concern over the unfolding human misery, loss of life and serious violations of international law which by the time of the request were already a matter of public knowledge. It is unbecoming for the principal judicial organ of the United Nations, whose very raison d'être is the peaceful resolution of international disputes, to maintain silence in such a situation".[70]

At the end of its Order of 2 June 1999, the Court only made a general reference to, *inter alia*, the obligation of the parties to resolve their disputes by peaceful means, and the "special responsibilities under Chapter VII of the Charter" of

68 *Id.*

69 1999 ICJ Rep. 542, at 602.

70 *Id.*, at 604.

the Security Council; in addition, it stated that the parties "should take care not to aggravate or extend the dispute".[71]

No matter how urgent the situation, the Court cannot change the fact that its jurisdiction is based on consent, "even if one might regret this state of affairs as we approach the twenty-first century", as Judge Higgins sighed in her separate opinion to the 1999 Orders.[72] If there is no jurisdiction – and the Court was in full agreement on this in its 2004 judgments in the eight *Use of Force* cases – the Court cannot fulfil its judicial function. The case *Legality of the Use of Force (Yugoslavia v. Netherlands)*, and the other *Use of Force* cases, started as highly political disputes about the use of armed force. They ended following the regime change in Yugoslavia when the FRY almost agreed with the respondents that the Court did not have jurisdiction but requested and obtained a judgment by the Court to that effect.

71 *Id.*, at 557.
72 *Id.*, at 586.

3

THE NETHERLANDS AND THE INTERNATIONAL TRIBUNAL FOR THE LAW OF THE SEA

How a state may find itself before the tribunal "against its will"

Robert van Dijk[*]

1 INTRODUCTION

The Netherlands and the sea are intrinsically linked. Grotius – through his *Mare Liberum* – has become the personification of this intimate connection between the Netherlands, the sea and international law. Less well known is that Grotius spent a good part of his life in government service.[1] For purposes of this article, however, there is no need to dig back that far in history. Two predecessors of Johan Lammers, Willem Riphagen and Adriaan Bos, were active participants in the United Nations Conference on the Law of the Sea (1973-1982). The Conference led to the adoption of the 1982 United Nations Convention on the Law of the Sea ("Convention"), often referred to as the "Constitution for the Oceans" because it provides the regulatory framework for the numerous uses of ocean space.

* Legal counsel at the International Law Division of the Ministry of Foreign Affairs of the Kingdom of the Netherlands, and former official of the International Tribunal for the Law of the Sea. The opinions expressed are solely the author's and do not necessarily represent those of the Kingdom of the Netherlands.

1 Grotius was in the service of the States of Holland *inter alia* involved in discussing access to the East Indian Regions at the Court of James I of England. *See* L.E. van Holte & C.G. Roelofsen (eds.), Grotius Reader – A Reader for Students of International Law and Legal History (1983) at 29.

N. Blokker, R. Lefeber, L. Lijnzaad & I. van Bladel (eds.), *The Netherlands in Court. Essays in Honour of Johan G. Lammers*, © 2006 Koninklijke Brill NV. Printed in the Netherlands, pp. 51-70.

An integral part of the Convention is its comprehensive system of dispute settlement.[2] Disputes arising under the Convention are subject to binding third-party settlement with the exception of certain optional exclusions.[3] It is relatively well known that the system provides for States to make a choice between four fora for dispute settlement: the International Tribunal for the Law of the Sea ("Tribunal"), the International Court of Justice, an arbitral tribunal or a special arbitral tribunal.[4]

Although the Netherlands has not made a declaration accepting the jurisdiction of the Tribunal, there is still a reasonable chance that the Netherlands and other States that have not accepted the jurisdiction of the Tribunal under Article 287 of the Convention may find themselves sooner or later involuntarily ("against their will") before the 21-member bench of the Tribunal.[5] It is surprising that little attention has been paid to the number of ways in which the Tribunal may be seized unilaterally, and thus by action of one State may pronounce on matters of extreme importance to another State. Telling in this respect is that this unilateral jurisdiction of the Tribunal is not mentioned in the Dutch Explanatory Memorandum (*Memorie van Toelichting*), accompanying the Convention when submitted to Parliament.[6]

Although the Netherlands has not appeared before the Tribunal, it would seem appropriate briefly to explore the different ways in which a State that has not accepted the jurisdiction of the Tribunal under Article 287 may nonetheless find itself before ITLOS. This contribution will examine the relevant provisions of the Convention in light of the practice of the ten-year-old independent judicial body.

---

2 Part XV UNCLOS, its Annexes V, VI, VII and VIII, and Section 5 of Part XI UNCLOS.

3 Art. 286 UNCLOS.

4 Art. 287 UNCLOS.

5 The term "against their will" may be perceived as misleading, as in all cases the jurisdiction of an international court or tribunal depends on the consent of the parties involved which may be expressed in different ways either before or after a dispute has arisen. The element of involuntariness referred to here is contained in the lack of an express choice of the Tribunal by the parties involved either under Art. 287 UNCLOS (forum choice) or by special agreement (*ad hoc* agreement to submit a dispute to the Tribunal).

6 See *Memorie van Toelichting*, TK 1995-1996, 24 433 (R 1549), No. 3. *Goedkeuring van het op 10 december 1982 te Montego Bay tot stand gekomen Verdrag van de Verenigde Naties inzake het recht van de zee, met bijlagen; en van de op 29 juli 1994 te New York tot stand gekomen Overeenkomst betreffende de uitvoering van Deel XI van genoemd Verdrag, met bijlage.*

2 Some General Remarks Concerning Dispute Settlement under the Convention

Before embarking on an in-depth discussion of the specific provisions conferring jurisdiction on the Tribunal, a few general observations on the dispute settlement provisions of the Convention must be made.

The comprehensive nature of the compulsory procedures leading to binding decisions makes the dispute settlement mechanism under the Convention unique.[7] The Convention echoes the basic principle of the Charter of the United Nations that disputes must be resolved by peaceful means.[8] However, where no settlement has been reached by enquiry, mediation, conciliation, arbitration, judicial settlement, resort to regional agencies or arrangements, Article 286 of the Convention provides that a dispute may in general be submitted – by a single State – to a court or tribunal. It stipulates that:

> "Subject to section 3 any dispute concerning the interpretation or application of this Convention shall, where no settlement has been reached by recourse to section 1, be submitted at the request of any party to the dispute to the court or tribunal having jurisdiction under this section."[9]

Any decision rendered by such a court or tribunal shall be final and must be complied with by all the parties to the dispute.[10]

As mentioned above, under Article 287 of the Convention, States may choose between four judicial institutions to submit their disputes. This choice of procedure resulted from the failure of States to agree on one single forum for dispute settlement under the Convention. Certain, mainly western, States preferred the International Court of Justice, others, mainly developing States, the Tribunal and again others, mostly the then communist block, arbitration. The compromise between these different views resulted in Article 287, which reads as follows:

7 Section 2 of Part XV UNCLOS.

8 *See* Art. 279 UNCLOS which refers to Arts. 2(3) and 33(1) of the UN Charter.

9 Art. 286 UNCLOS. The (optional) exclusions of Section 3 include certain disputes over fisheries, marine scientific research, maritime delimitation, military and law enforcement activities and Security Council measures.

10 Art. 296(1) UNCLOS.

Choice of procedure

1. When signing, ratifying or acceding to this Convention or at any time thereafter, a State shall be free to choose, by means of a written declaration, one or more of the following means for the settlement of disputes concerning the interpretation or application of this Convention:
(a) the International Tribunal for the Law of the Sea established in accordance with Annex VI;
(b) the International Court of Justice;
(c) an arbitral tribunal constituted in accordance with Annex VII;
(d) a special arbitral tribunal constituted in accordance with Annex VIII for one or more of the categories of disputes specified therein.
2. A declaration made under paragraph 1 shall not affect or be affected by the obligation of a State Party to accept the jurisdiction of the Seabed Disputes Chamber of the International Tribunal for the Law of the Sea to the extent and in the manner provided for in Part XI, section 5.
3. A State Party, which is a party to a dispute not covered by a declaration in force, shall be deemed to have accepted arbitration in accordance with Annex VII.
4. If the parties to a dispute have accepted the same procedure for the settlement of the dispute, it may be submitted only to that procedure, unless the parties otherwise agree.
5. If the parties to a dispute have not accepted the same procedure for the settlement of the dispute, it may be submitted only to arbitration in accordance with Annex VII, unless the parties otherwise agree.
6. A declaration made under paragraph 1 shall remain in force until three months after notice of revocation has been deposited with the Secretary-General of the United Nations.
7. A new declaration, a notice of revocation or the expiry of a declaration does not in any way affect proceedings pending before a court or tribunal having jurisdiction under this article, unless the parties otherwise agree.
8. Declarations and notices referred to in this article shall be deposited with the Secretary-General of the United Nations, who shall transmit copies thereof to the States Parties.

The dispute resolution system of Article 287 is as simple as it is ingenious; if both States have accepted the same forum, any dispute may be submitted to that forum. If they have not, their dispute may be submitted only to arbitration, unless the parties otherwise agree.

Shabtai Rosenne has commented that the former Netherlands Legal Adviser Willem Riphagen was instrumental in developing the forum choice procedure contained in Article 287 that allowed some of the major powers to agree to the far reaching system of dispute settlement procedures under the Convention.[11] Today, this dispute settlement mechanism is binding on all 149 States that have ratified the Convention, including the Netherlands.[12]

States are supposed to file a declaration designating one or more institution(s) when signing, ratifying or acceding to the Convention, or at any time thereafter. Not surprising for the country which is host to the International Court of Justice, the Netherlands, upon ratification of the Convention, made a declaration under Article 287 of the Convention choosing the International Court of Justice as its preferred means for dispute resolution for conflicts arising under the Convention.[13] When both parties to a dispute concerning the interpretation or application of the Convention have made a declaration designating the same institution, the dispute may be submitted to that institution. If States have designated different institutions, or at least one has failed to designate an institution, the case may be submitted to arbitration only. At present, only thirty-seven States have filed such declarations. Also, the declarations filed have very different contents. Therefore, most disputes would most likely result in arbitration.[14] The practice since the entry into force of the Convention confirms this. All disputes that have arisen under Article 287 to date have, at least initially, been submitted to arbitration under Annex VII of the Convention.

Arbitration is, however, a costly procedure. A recent media report reveals that Trinidad and Tobago spent US $ 13 million on the arbitration with Barbados relating to the delimitation of the Exclusive Economic Zone and

---

11 S. Rosenne, *UNCLOS III – The Montreux (Riphagen) Compromise*, *in* A. Bos and H. Siblesz (eds.), Realism in Law-making, Essays on International Law in Honour of Willem Riphagen 169 (1986).

12 Status on 10 August 2006. The Convention entered into force on 16 November 1994. The Netherlands ratified the Convention on 28 June 1996. For a complete overview of the states which have ratified the Convention see: http://www.un.org/Depts/los/reference_files/chronological_lists_of_ratifications.htm.

13 The Kingdom of the Netherlands made the following declaration: "The Kingdom of the Netherlands hereby declares that, having regard to Art. 287 UNCLOS, it accepts the jurisdiction of the International Court of Justice in the settlement of disputes concerning the interpretation and application of the Convention with State Parties to the Convention which have likewise accepted the said jurisdiction".

14 Status on 1 May 2006. On this date, of the thirty-eight states, twenty-three had designated ITLOS and twenty-three had designated the International Court of Justice as a forum for dispute settlement under Art. 287 UNCLOS (sixteen of these have designated both the International Court of Justice and ITLOS). See for an overview of declarations made under Art. 287: http://www.un.org/Depts/los/settlement_of_disputes/choice_procedure.htm.

Continental Shelf between them.[15] Although the government of Trinidad and Tobago claims it was money well spent, it could have seriously cut back expenses by agreeing with Barbados to transfer the arbitral proceedings to a standing court such as the International Court of Justice or the Tribunal.

If a case goes to arbitration, the parties must pay the salaries of the arbitrators and their staff and for the infrastructure at the seat of the tribunal. Since the International Court of Justice is paid from the regular budget of the United Nations and the Tribunal is paid for by means of annual contributions from the States Parties, no such costs have to be borne by parties to a case before these standing courts. This could make it attractive for States to transfer arbitral proceedings to the International Court of Justice or the Tribunal or to commence proceedings in these fora in the first place. Another key reason for transferring proceedings to the International Court of Justice or the Tribunal is efficiency. The judges, the court building, the procedural rules, the staff to service the meetings, are all in place.

In two instances where proceedings were initially submitted to arbitration, the proceedings were transferred to the Tribunal by agreement between the parties. Both the arbitral proceedings in the *M/V "SAIGA" (No. 2)* case *(Saint Vincent and the Grenadines* v. *Guinea)* and in the *Case concerning the Conservation and Sustainable Exploitation of Swordfish Stocks in the South-Eastern Pacific Ocean (Chile/European Community)* were transferred to the Tribunal. In *M/V "SAIGA" (No. 2)* the proceedings were transferred to the whole Tribunal.[16] The *Case concerning the Conservation and Sustainable Exploitation of Swordfish Stocks in the South-Eastern Pacific Ocean* was transferred to a chamber of the Tribunal.[17] In those instances where a dispute arises between two States and the application of Article 287 would lead to the submission of the dispute to an arbitral tribunal, States would be well advised to consider submitting the proceedings to a standing court or tribunal.

15 Arbitration between Barbados and the Republic of Trinidad and Tobago, relating to the delimitation of the Exclusive Economic Zone and Continental Shelf between them, submitted under Part XV of the United Nations Convention on the Law of the Sea (UNCLOS) to an arbitral tribunal constituted in accordance with UNCLOS Annex VII. *See* local news item of the Caribbean Broadcasting Corporation: $12 million case, Tuesday, 25 April 2006 at http://www.cbc.bb/content/view/5205/10/.

16 ITLOS Press Release No. 13, available at http://www.itlos.org.

17 Order 2003/3 of 20 December 2000 in the Case concerning the Conservation and Sustainable Exploitation of Swordfish Stocks in the South-Eastern Pacific Ocean (Chile *v.* European Community) available at http://www.itlos.org. This case is still pending at the time of writing.

3 PROVISIONS PROVIDING SPECIFICALLY FOR COMPULSORY JURISDICTION OF THE TRIBUNAL

Apart from the dispute settlement procedure under Article 287 of the Convention, which, would normally lead to jurisdiction of an arbitral tribunal, the Convention provides for three categories of disputes that may by unilateral action of one State be submitted to the Tribunal and may lead to decisions that will bind parties that did not want to submit to the jurisdiction of the Tribunal.[18]

3.1 Prompt Release Proceedings

The compulsory jurisdiction of the Tribunal with respect to the prompt release of vessels and crews is provided for in Article 292 of the Convention. Three categories of prompt release cases have been identified that may be submitted to the Tribunal: apprehension of a vessel for violation of fisheries regulations in the exclusive economic zone, pollution in the EEZ, and lack of seaworthiness.[19] To date only apprehension for violations of fisheries regulations in the EEZ has been invoked. Article 292 reads as follows:

Prompt release of vessels and crews

1. Where the authorities of a State Party have detained a vessel flying the flag of another State Party and it is alleged that the detaining State has not complied with the provisions of this Convention for the prompt release of the vessel or its crew upon the posting of a reasonable bond or other financial security, the question of release from detention may be submitted to any court or tribunal agreed upon by the parties or, failing such agreement within 10 days from the time of detention, to a court or tribunal accepted by the detaining State under Article 287 or to the International Tribunal for the Law of the Sea, unless the parties otherwise agree.
2. The application for release may be made only by or on behalf of the flag State of the vessel.

---

18 *See supra* n. 5.

19 The M/V "SAIGA" Case (Saint Vincent and the Grenadines *v.* Guinea), Prompt Release (1997) para. 52. The provisions referred to are Arts. 73(2), 220(6) and (7), and 226(1)(c) UNCLOS.

3. The court or tribunal shall deal without delay with the application for release and shall deal only with the question of release, without prejudice to the merits of any case before the appropriate domestic forum against the vessel, its owner or its crew. The authorities of the detaining State remain competent to release the vessel or its crew at any time.
4. Upon the posting of the bond or other financial security determined by the court or tribunal, the authorities of the detaining State shall comply promptly with the decision of the court or tribunal concerning the release of the vessel or its crew.

The Tribunal has, from its inception, had seven prompt release cases on its docket, comprising slightly more than half of the total of cases until now.[20] In all cases, the vessels were allegedly arrested for violating fisheries regulations. The Tribunal set high bonds for the release of vessels and crews allegedly involved in illegal, unregulated and unreported ("IUU") fishing. It pointed out that it understood the international concerns about IUU fishing, but stressed that it could only take this into account by reference to the penalties that may be imposed for the alleged offences under the laws of the arresting State.[21] Greenpeace, which has kept a close watch at the Tribunal, has welcomed the outcome of proceedings before the Tribunal, while at the same time expressing concern that vessels and crews, once released, would take up IUU fishing again.[22]

In the *Camouco*, *Monte Confurco* and *Grand Prince* cases, in a period of a little less than fifteen months, three separate applications were filed for the release of three vessels arrested by France for illegal fishing in Antarctic

20 Status on 20 August 2006. Seven out of thirteen cases related to an application for the release of a vessel.

21 The "Volga" Case (Russian Federation *v.* Australia), Prompt Release, Judgment, paras. 66-67.

22 Greenpeace Press Release of 7 February 2000: Greenpeace welcomes today's decision of the International Tribunal on Law of the Seas to take action against pirate fishing, at: http://archive.greenpeace.org/pressreleases/oceans/2000feb7.html and http://www.greenpeace.org/australia/news-and-events/media/releases/overfishing/russians-free-toothfish-pirate.

waters.[23] France made no secret of its annoyance at being required to appear before the Tribunal for trying to maintain law and order in the Antarctic.[24]

For the proceedings to be effective, they must be expeditious. As stated in the commentary to the transmittal of the Convention to the US Senate:

> "Article 292 provides specifically for expedited dispute settlement to address allegations that a State Party has not complied with the Convention's provisions for the prompt release of a vessel flying the flag of another State Party and its crew".[25]

Therefore, both the Convention and the Rules of the Tribunal provide for quick action. Article 112 of the Rules of the Tribunal provides for hearings to commence within fifteen days commencing with the first working day following the date on which the application is received and the judgment to be read not later than fourteen days after the closure of the hearing. The *Volga* case, for example, took only three weeks from its filing with the Registry of the Tribunal to the delivery of the judgement.[26] Hearings were held for two days. Article 292, paragraph 4, of the Convention requires further that the detaining State complies expeditiously with the terms of a prompt release judgment. Article 292 ensures that a vessel can continue with her commercial operations and the crew can continue with their lives upon the posting of a reasonable bond or other financial security.

In prompt release cases, the Tribunal may only deal with the question of the release and the determination of the bond or other security. The procedure does not include a determination of the merits of the underlying dispute nor does it prejudice such a determination by a court or tribunal. The Tribunal stated this clearly in its decision in the first prompt release case submitted to it:

> "[W]hile the States which are parties to the proceedings before the Tribunal are bound by the judgment adopted by it as far as the release of the vessel and the bond

23 The "Camouco" Case (Panama *v.* France), Prompt Release; The "Monte Confurco" Case (Seychelles *v.* France), Prompt Release; and The "Grand Prince" Case (Belize *v.* France), Prompt Release.

24 Verbatim records in the "Grand Prince" Case, ITLOS/PV.01/2 of 5 April 2001 p.m., at 10, where Counsel for France stated that the pleasure to appear before the Tribunal would probably become less if it were to happen too frequently.

25 Commentary to the transmittal of the Convention to the US Senate of 7 October 1994, at 85.

26 The "Volga" case was filed on 2 December 2002 and the Judgment delivered on 23 December 2002.

> or other security are concerned, their domestic courts, in considering the merits of the case, are not bound by any findings of fact or law that the Tribunal may have made in order to reach its conclusions."[27]

The Convention provides for the proceedings to be brought either by or on behalf of the flag State. Although the flag State is normally represented by a State agent, private lawyers retained by the vessel's owners shoulder most of the workload.[28]

It is quite possible that the Netherlands may find itself involved in prompt release proceedings before the Tribunal. Vessels flying the flag of a State Party to the Convention may be detained by Dutch authorities, and vessels flying the flag of the Netherlands may be detained abroad for reasons falling within the ambit of the Convention. In this respect the constitutional structure of the Netherlands adds an interesting dimension to the prompt release procedure.

The Kingdom of the Netherlands is at present composed of three countries: the Netherlands, the Netherlands Antilles and Aruba. Each of the three countries of the Kingdom has its own ship registry, but all vessels fly the flag of the Netherlands.[29] Only the Kingdom of the Netherlands has international legal personality. It is the Kingdom of the Netherlands that takes on the obligations under the Convention and that is responsible for their fulfilment.

The Kingdom of the Netherlands has, however, at present only ratified the Convention with respect to the part of the Kingdom that is situated in Europe. It may be expected that the Kingdom of the Netherlands will only seek the

---

27 The M/V "SAIGA" Case (Saint Vincent and the Grenadines *v.* Guinea), Prompt Release (1997) para. 49.

28 The "Volga" Case (Russian Federation *v.* Australia), Prompt Release (2002), Dissenting Opinion of Judge *ad hoc* Shearer, para. 19: "It is notable that in recent cases before the Tribunal, including the present case, although the flag state has been represented by a state agent, the main burden of presentation of the case has been borne by private lawyers retained by the vessel's owners. A new 'balance' has to be struck between vessel owners, operators and fishing companies on the one hand, and coastal Sates on the other".

29 *See* the advice of the Netherlands Council of State (*Raad van State*) and the reaction thereupon of the Minister of Transport, *Advies Raad van State en Nader Rapport, Voorziening om ter uitvoering van besluiten van instellingen van de Europese Unie regels te kunnen stellen ten aanzien van buitenlandse schepen (Wet buitenlandse schepen*", TK, 2003-2004, 29 394, No. 4. *Wijziging van de Wet voorkoming verontreiniging door schepen, de Wet verontreiniging zeewater en de Scheepvaartverkeerwet in verband met de instelling van de Nederlandse exclusieve economische zone en enkele ander onderwerpen*, TK, 2002-2003, 28 984, A, and *Regels omtrent de bemanning van zeeschepen (Zeevaartbemanningswet)*, TK, 1996-1997, 25 233, B.

release of vessels registered in the Netherlands, since it would be doubtful whether an application made with respect to a ship registered in a territory for which the application of the Convention is explicitly excluded at present could be entertained by the Tribunal.

3.2 Provisional Measures Proceedings

The jurisdiction of the Tribunal to prescribe binding provisional measures is contained in Article 290 of the Convention. Particularly relevant is paragraph 5 of Article 290, paragraph 5, that provides for the compulsory jurisdiction of the Tribunal to prescribe binding provisional measures pending the constitution of an arbitral tribunal; the constitution of which is the result of the application of Article 287 of the Convention. Article 290 reads as follows:

Provisional measures

1. If a dispute has been duly submitted to a court or tribunal which considers that prima facie it has jurisdiction under this Part or Part XI, section 5, the court or tribunal may prescribe any provisional measures which it considers appropriate under the circumstances to preserve the respective rights of the parties to the dispute or to prevent serious harm to the marine environment, pending the final decision.
2. Provisional measures may be modified or revoked as soon as the circumstances justifying them have changed or ceased to exist.
3. Provisional measures may be prescribed, modified or revoked under this article only at the request of a party to the dispute and after the parties have been given an opportunity to be heard.
4. The court or tribunal shall forthwith give notice to the parties to the dispute, and to such other States Parties as it considers appropriate, of the prescription, modification or revocation of provisional measures.
5. Pending the constitution of an arbitral tribunal to which a dispute is being submitted under this section, any court or tribunal agreed upon by the parties or, failing such agreement within two weeks from the date of the request for provisional measures, the International Tribunal for the Law of the Sea or, with respect to activities in the Area, the Seabed Disputes Chamber, may prescribe, modify or revoke provisional measures in accordance with this article if it considers that prima facie the tribunal which is to be constituted would have jurisdiction and that the urgency of the situation so requires. Once constituted, the tribunal to which the dispute has been submitted may modify, revoke or affirm those provisional measures, acting in conformity with paragraphs 1 to 4.

6. The parties to the dispute shall comply promptly with any provisional measures prescribed under this article.

On 30 July 1999, New Zealand and Australia filed separate requests for the prescription of provisional measures against Japan to conserve the southern bluefin tuna stock. The stock gave cause for serious biological concern since it was severely depleted and at its historically lowest levels.[30] Australia and New Zealand claimed that Japanese fisheries threatened serious or irreversible damage to the stock, which would result in a loss of revenue and unemployment in the fishing industry. The media dubbed the conflict the "sushi war". The bluefin tuna is a highly valuable stock, used for sushi and sashimi, with a single fish fetching up to US$ 50,000. A single fish can live as long as 40 years, weigh up to 200 kilograms and grow to be over two metres long. The Tribunal considered that the parties should in the circumstances act with prudence and caution and ordered parties to stick to previously agreed quota and not increase their catches.

The dispute over bluefin tuna catches is one example out of five cases that have been submitted to the Tribunal for the prescription of provisional measures. Others included a dispute between the UK and Ireland about the environmental impact of the opening of a new nuclear mixed oxide fuel (MOX) processing plant at Sellafield and a dispute between Malaysia and Singapore concerning land reclamation by Singapore in and around the Straits of Johor.

All these cases resulted from requests made for provisional measures pending the constitution of an arbitral tribunal under Annex VII of the Convention. The request for provisional measures may be brought to the Tribunal, because Article 290, paragraph 5, provides that pending the constitution of an arbitral tribunal – which may take a while – a request for provisional measures may be submitted to the Tribunal.[31]

Provisional measures are a kind of interim injunction: an order prohibiting certain behaviour pending final decision on the merits or substance of a case. As stated by the present President of the Tribunal, Judge Rüdiger Wolfrum: "Generally speaking, in international adjudication provisional measures are meant to safeguard the rights of parties to a conflict or to prevent irreparable

30 Southern Bluefin Tuna Cases (New Zealand *v.* Japan; Australia *v.* Japan), Order of 27 August 1999, para. 71.

31 Art. 290(5) UNCLOS.

damage until the final decision."[32] Wolfrum continues to point out that, as is the case with the International Court of Justice, provisional measures are only justified "if there is urgency in the sense that action prejudicial to the rights of either party to the dispute is likely to be taken before the final decision is given".[33]

The Tribunal may prescribe provisional measures that it "considers appropriate under the circumstances to preserve the respective rights of the parties to the dispute or to prevent serious harm to the marine environment".[34] The addition of the prevention of "serious harm to the marine environment" as a basis to prescribe provisional measures is new when compared with the jurisdiction of the International Court of Justice. It will be interesting to see how the Tribunal will apply this provision. Moreover, the Tribunal may only prescribe provisional measures if it considers that, prima facie, the arbitral tribunal that is to be constituted would have jurisdiction.[35]

Even though these strict criteria apply, precedent shows that provisional measures have been requested in many cases submitted to international adjudication. In five out of eight cases submitted to arbitration under Annex VII of the Convention since its entry into force, provisional measures were requested from the Tribunal, and in a further case provisional measures were requested directly from the arbitral tribunal.[36] A commentator of the work of the International Court of Justice has written that:

> "[T]he inherent nature of provisional measures proceedings and the factor of urgency supply an element of drama which fits in well with modern practices of diplomacy by television and the Internet."[37]

---

32 R. Wolfrum, *Provisional Measures of the International Tribunal for the Law of the Sea*, 37 Indian Journal of International Law (1997) at 422.

33 *Id.*, at 430.

34 Art. 290(1) UNCLOS.

35 Art. 290(5) UNCLOS.

36 As at 24 August 2006. In the arbitral proceedings commenced by Guyana against Suriname, provisional measures were directly requested from the arbitral tribunal. *See* T.W. Donovan, *Guyana Invokes Annex VII of United Nations Convention on Law of the Sea Against Suriname for Disputed Maritime Boundary*, ASIL Insight, April 2004, at http://www.asil.org/insights/insigh131.htm.

37 S. Rosenne, The Law and Practice of the International Court, Vol. III (2006) at 1416.

He continues quoting a Judge of the Tribunal:

> "Sometimes one has the impression that the real objective of the applicant is to bring to the Court a request for provisional measures, rather than institute proceedings in the Court. The previous institution of proceedings is often seen only as a legally necessary prerequisite for requesting provisional measures."[38]

These comments, although made with reference to the International Court of Justice, hold equally true for the Tribunal and underline the importance attached to these proceedings. Significantly, any State Party to the Convention may, by instigating arbitral proceedings, request provisional measures from the Tribunal and thus force another State Party into court. States – such as the Netherlands – that have not accepted the jurisdiction of the Tribunal under Article 287 may consequently be taken by surprise when confronted with the compulsory jurisdiction of the Tribunal.

Although it has been argued that provisional measures should avoid prejudging the merits of the case,[39] this is not always possible. Often a decision on provisional measures is read as giving a strong indication of a court's inclination on the merits. Provisional measures are binding on the parties to the dispute.[40] Provisional measures that have been prescribed may be modified or revoked as soon as the circumstances justifying them have changed or ceased to exist.[41] The Convention also specifically stipulates that once the arbitral tribunal is established, it can modify or revoke the provisional measures prescribed by the Tribunal.[42]

In certain circumstances, it will not be the full Tribunal that decides upon provisional measures. The Statute of the Tribunal provides that the Chamber of Summary Procedure consisting of at least three judges, could, if the Tribunal is not in session or a sufficient number of members is not available to constitute a quorum, make a binding decision. Provisional measures prescribed by the

38 T. Trevis, *The* Political *Use of Unilateral Applications and Provisional Measures Proceedings*, *in* J.A. Frowein *et al.* (eds.), Verhandeln für den Frieden/Negotiating for Peace: Liber Amicorum Tono Eitel, 463 (2002) at 466, as quoted by Rosenne, *supra* n. 37, at 1416.

39 Separate Opinion Judge B. Ajibola, Case Concerning the Land and Maritime Boundary between (Cameroon *v.* Nigeria), Request for Provisional Measures, Order of 15 March 1996, 1996 ICJ Rep. 35, at 48.

40 Art. 290(6) UNCLOS.

41 Art. 290(2) UNCLOS.

42 Art. 290(5) UNCLOS.

Chamber would be subject to review and revision by the Tribunal.[43] Interestingly, also the President of the Tribunal may call upon parties to act in such a way as will enable any order the Tribunal may make to have its appropriate effects.[44]

3.3 Seabed Dispute Chamber of the Tribunal

The third and last category of provisions providing for compulsory jurisdiction of the Tribunal, or rather its Seabed Disputes Chamber, concerns disputes arising from the exploration and exploitation of the deep seabed (Area).[45] Provisions concerning the jurisdiction of the Tribunal may be found throughout the Convention, but centre around Article 187 of the Convention.[46] Article 187 reads as follows:

Jurisdiction of the Seabed Disputes Chamber

> The Seabed Disputes Chamber shall have jurisdiction under this Part and the Annexes relating thereto in disputes with respect to activities in the Area falling within the following categories:
> (a) disputes between States Parties concerning the interpretation or application of this Part and the Annexes relating thereto;
> (b) disputes between a State Party and the Authority concerning:
> (i) acts or omissions of the Authority or of a State Party alleged to be in violation of this Part or the Annexes relating thereto or of rules, regulations and procedures of the Authority adopted in accordance therewith; or
> (ii) acts of the Authority alleged to be in excess of jurisdiction or a misuse of power;
> (c) disputes between parties to a contract, being States Parties, the Authority or the Enterprise, state enterprises and natural or juridical persons referred to in Article 153, paragraph 2(b), concerning:

43 Art. 25(2) of the Statute of the Tribunal and Art. 28(6) of the Rules of the Tribunal.
44 Art. 90(4) of the Rules of the Tribunal.
45 Art. 1(1) UNCLOS, which defines the Area as the seabed and ocean floor, and subsoil thereof, beyond the limits of national jurisdiction.
46 Parts XI (in particular Section V) and XV UNCLOS and its Annex VI.

(i) the interpretation or application of a relevant contract or a plan of work; or

(ii) acts or omissions of a party to the contract relating to activities in the Area and directed to the other party or directly affecting its legitimate interests;

(d) disputes between the Authority and a prospective contractor who has been sponsored by a State as provided in article 153, paragraph 2(b), and has duly fulfilled the conditions referred to in Annex III, article 4, paragraph 6, and article 13, paragraph 2, concerning the refusal of a contract or a legal issue arising in the negotiation of the contract;

(e) disputes between the Authority and a State Party, a State enterprise or a natural or juridical person sponsored by a State Party as provided for in article 153, paragraph 2(b), where it is alleged that the Authority has incurred liability as provided in Annex III, article 22;

(f) any other disputes for which the jurisdiction of the Chamber is specifically provided in this Convention.

The Convention provides that the Area and its resources are the common heritage of mankind[47] and establishes the International Seabed Authority (Authority) in Jamaica to administer the resources of the Area.[48] The exploration of the deep seabed appeals to the imagination with the potato-shaped polymetallic or manganese nodules that are believed to cover the deep seabed in sheer inexhaustible numbers ready to be harvested. The potentially valuable polymetallic nodules have been known for over a century, but exploration has not been forthcoming because the nodules were located in very deep water, in excess of 5,000 metres, where commercial mining was not considered viable. Recent scientific studies have aroused interest in other resources of the deep seabed such as polymetallic sulphides and cobalt-rich crusts.[49] Other resources, such as gas hydrates, oil and gas, phosporites and precious metals have also stirred up the interests of research institutions and mining companies.[50]

47 Art. 136 UNCLOS.

48 Art. 157 UNCLOS.

49 *See,* most recently, UN Doc. ISBA/10/C/WP.1/Rev.1.

50 *See* website of the International Seabed Authority at: http://www.isa.org.jm.

The Seabed Disputes Chamber of the Tribunal has near-exclusive jurisdiction with respect to disputes relating to the activities in the Area.[51] The Chamber is composed of eleven Judges selected from the twenty-one Judges of the Tribunal. The Judges are selected from among the elected members of the Tribunal. As is the case with the composition of the Tribunal, as a whole, representation of the principal legal systems of the world and equitable geographical distribution must be assured. The Assembly of the Seabed Authority may adopt recommendations of a general nature relating to the representation and distribution.[52] The Chamber functions as a court within a court with its own jurisdiction *ratione materiae* and *ratione personae*. Importantly, the jurisdiction of the Seabed Disputes Chamber covers not only disputes between States, as is the case with the International Court of Justice, but also between a State and the Authority, between the Authority and a (prospective) contractor, and between the parties to a contract, including State enterprises and natural or juridical persons.[53] A further unusual feature of this Chamber is that its decisions against natural and juridical persons are enforceable in the territory of States Parties in the same manner as judgements or orders of the highest court of the State Party in whose territory the enforcement is sought.[54] Other remarkable features are the advisory jurisdiction of the Chamber, and the duty of a commercial arbitral tribunal to refer to the Chamber any question involving the interpretation of Part XI of the Convention.

The exploration and exploitation of the deep seabed has, so far, been relatively uninteresting because of the high costs of extracting minerals from the Area. It may therefore come as no surprise that to date no disputes have been referred to the Chamber. This may, however, change in the future with land reserves of minerals nearing depletion and rising prices of minerals rendering exploitation of the resources of the deep sea profitable. Calculations were made in the 1960s with regard to the depletion of land and sea mineral resources indicating that sufficient supplies of certain minerals exist in the deep sea to

51 For a detailed description of the jurisdiction of the Chamber to decide contentious cases and to give advisory opinions (and the limits to its jurisdiction), *see* J. Akl, *The Sea-bed Disputes Chamber of the International Tribunal for the Law of the Sea,* 37 Indian Journal of International Law 435 (1997).

52 Art. 35(2) of the Statute of the Tribunal.

53 J.G. Merrills, International Dispute Settlement (1998) at 188.

54 Art. 39 of the Statute of the Tribunal; Art. 188 UNCLOS.

satisfy consumption for thousands of years at least at the 1960 world rate of consumption.[55]

4 Concluding Remarks

Even though the Netherlands may not, at the time of the negotiations of the Convention, have liked the idea of the establishment of a new tribunal with a jurisdiction partly overlapping with the International Court of Justice,[56] as a State Party to the Convention the Netherlands is bound by its provisions. As a consequence it has accepted the compulsory jurisdiction of the Tribunal with respect to provisional measures, prompt release of vessels and the exploration and exploitation of the Area.

Interestingly, where States failed to agree on a single forum for compulsory dispute settlement for disputes, resulting in the four options contained in Article 287 of the Convention, they were able to agree on a single forum, *i.e.* the Tribunal, for dispute settlement with respect to the three categories of disputes discussed above. The reason for this seems to be that the expedited nature of the proceedings with respect to prompt release and provisional measures has persuaded the drafters of the Convention to derogate from the general rule codified in Article 287 that disputes be submitted to arbitration. A standing court had to be found to adjudicate these matters; it would simply not be feasible to wait for the creation of an arbitral tribunal.

The importance of ensuring uniform interpretation of the new regime concerning the exploration and exploitation of the resources of the ocean floor is the salutary rationale behind the creation and the compulsory jurisdiction of the Seabed Disputes Chamber. It also explains the wide range of parties that may appear before it, apart from States, including those involved in the exploration and exploitation of the Area. The compulsory jurisdiction of the Seabed Disputes Chamber was an important step to protect the integrity of the regime applicable to the common heritage of mankind.

Prompt release proceedings and provisional measures may only be submitted to the Tribunal, failing agreement between the parties to the dispute to submit

55 *See* Address of Ambassador Pardo (Malta) to the UN General Assembly on 1 November 1967, Official Records of the Twenty-Second Session, First Committee, 1515th Meeting, para. 26.

56 R. van Dijk *et al.*, *Een geslaagde tewaterlating? De inwerkingtreding van het VN Zeerechtverdrag*, 70 NJB 551 (1995).

the request to another court or tribunal. States may thus avoid proceedings before the Tribunal by agreeing to submit disputes to another court or tribunal. However, it may be doubtful that the States involved will be able to agree to this.

Distinct from the three ways in which a State may find itself before the Tribunal by unilateral action of another State described above, there is a fourth way in which a State may be bound by a decision of the Tribunal "against its will", namely through legal precedent. Although the Statute of the Tribunal (Annex VI of the Convention) stipulates clearly that "[t]he decision [of the Tribunal] shall have no binding force except between the parties in respect of that particular dispute",[57] it has been pointed out that the protection of this statutory provision is largely illusory partly due to "the force of persuasive precedent".[58] This is particularly true when the interpretation and application of a multilateral instrument such as the Convention is at stake. Interestingly, the International Court of Justice itself observed in the Aegean Sea Continental Shelf case that it is evident that any pronouncement as to the status of a multilateral instrument may have implications going beyond the parties to the dispute.[59]

However, it is particularly the interpretation given by the Tribunal to a provision of the Convention that it is going to influence the way the law is perceived by States, including States that have not been a party to the dispute in which the interpretation was at issue. This may explain why the founding fathers of the Convention decided to allow third party intervention whenever the interpretation or application of the Convention or any other international agreement is in question.[60] Whether States are going to make use of this right and how much the Tribunal will allow for this kind of third party intervention remains to be seen. If a State uses this right, the interpretation given by the judgment will be equally binding upon it.[61]

57 Art. 33(2) of the Statute of ITLOS; Art. 296(2) UNCLOS.

58 Rosenne, *supra* n. 37, at 1590-1598. The remarks were made by former International Court of Justice President Sir Robert Jennings with respect to Art. 59 of the Statute of the International Court of Justice, but hold equally true for ITLOS.

59 Aegean Sea Continental Shelf Case (Greece *v.* Turkey), Judgment of 19 December 1978 (Jurisdiction), 1978 ICJ Rep. 3, at 17-18. The Court discussed the implications of its finding the General Act for the Pacific Settlement of Dispute of 1928 in force or to be no longer in force.

60 Art. 32(1) and (2) of the Statute of the Tribunal.

61 Art. 32(3) of the Statute of the Tribunal.

In sum, the Tribunal has a remarkable jurisdiction to deal with disputes, even those involving States that have not accepted the jurisdiction of the Tribunal under Article 287 of the Convention. It would seem important for States to realize that the Tribunal may be called upon to decide issues of profound State interest without the need of establishing the State's agreement to its jurisdiction, provided the State is a State Party to the Convention.

4

THE INTERNATIONAL CRIMINAL COURT AT WORK IN ITS EARLY YEARS: SOME REFLECTIONS

*Adriaan Bos**

1 INTRODUCTION

I have been asked to offer some reflections on the International Criminal Court ('ICC' or 'the Court'). According to its President, speaking at the fourth meeting of the Assembly of States Parties, the Court stands at the threshold of the most crucial period of its brief history.[1] While institutional developments are still under way, the first investigations have actually begun. It is therefore tempting to ask what the Court's place will be in the international criminal law community. Since the establishment of the International Criminal Tribunal for the former Yugoslavia (ICTY) in 1993, it has become apparent to the international community that international tribunals offer a way of trying grave breaches of international humanitarian law. Although the Nuremberg and Tokyo Tribunals were obvious precedents, it proved impossible to build on them for over half a century. This failure was due in part to criticisms that they dispensed victor's justice and partly contravened the law that applied at the time. But above all it was due to the onset of the Cold War after the Nuremberg and Tokyo trials.

---

* Former Legal Adviser at the Ministry of Foreign Affairs of the Kingdom of the Netherlands, Chairman of the Ad Hoc Committee and the Preparatory Committee on the Establishment of an International Criminal Court. Thanks are due to Herman A.M. von Hebel, who was so kind to read my draft and made useful comments.

1 Speech given on 28 November 2004. The text can be found at http://www.icc-cpi.int/presidency/presspeeches.html.

N. Blokker, R. Lefeber, L. Lijnzaad & I. van Bladel (eds.), *The Netherlands in Court. Essays in Honour of Johan G. Lammers*, © 2006 Koninklijke Brill NV. Printed in the Netherlands, pp. 71-87.

For half a century, the political circumstances ruled out any possibility of setting up successors to these tribunals.

Over the last couple of decades, the situation has changed. Serious crimes threatening the peace, security and well-being of the world have no longer gone unpunished. The fact that some of these crimes were committed in Europe and practically on our doorstep will have had something to do with this.[2] The international community judged that the perpetrators of such crimes should be held individually liable and should be tried either by national courts or by mixed or international courts. After the Nuremberg and Tokyo trials, a second generation of international criminal justice developed in an extremely diverse manner, with the Tribunals for Rwanda and the former Yugoslavia, followed by the International Criminal Court and a series of hybrid institutions.
A third generation can also be identified. These are the national courts that, based on their universal jurisdiction, are becoming increasingly active in the endeavour to ensure that the most serious international crimes are not committed with impunity. A good example of this is what is now happening in Croatia and Bosnia-Herzegovina, with referrals by the ICTY of cases to national courts in these countries. The third generation is being enabled to carry out these tasks with the aid of the second generation. This illustrates the speed of the developments in international criminal justice. In this multifaceted judicial system, determining the place of the ICC is no easy task.

Below I will set out some reflections on the establishment of the Court, its unique character as an international organization, its place in the international criminal law community, and comparisons of the statutes of the two *ad hoc* Tribunals with that of the ICC. In so doing I refer to its historical background and elements from the Rome Statute of the International Criminal Court ('the Statute'). These reflections attempt in particular to shed light on the problems the Court may encounter in the near future in its operational phase. Exhaustive treatment of the subject is naturally not possible within the scope of this contribution.

2 C. Del Ponte, *Der Internationale Strafgerichtshof*: Vortrag, gehalten vor der Juristischen Gesellschaft Mittelfranken zu Nürnberg e.V. am 9. November 2000 im historischen Gerichtssaal 600 des Justizgebäudes in Nürnberg (2001).

2 The Establishment of the ICC

The Statutes of the ICTY and the International Criminal Tribunal for Rwanda ('ICTR') were established by the United Nations Security Council on the basis of Chapter VII of the Charter of the United Nations. The ICTY and the ICTR are subsidiary organs of the Security Council and are embedded in the organization of the United Nations. As they are backed up by the authority of the Security Council, all States are obliged to implement the resolutions by which they were instituted. The time required for the drafting, acceptance and entry into force of a treaty, combined with the uncertainty as to whether the States in question would become parties to such a treaty, were important reasons for opting for this approach at the time. The fact that the tribunals were limited in their jurisdiction to a certain time and place also played a role. The ICC was set up in the traditional manner by international treaty requiring the approval of States. Looking back at the establishment and entry into force of the Statute and the early years of functioning of the ICC, we can say without any exaggeration that something that was considered a utopia over two decades ago had become a reality in – by international standards – record time.[3]

Since the Statute took the form of a treaty, no questions will be raised as to the legitimacy of the ICC of the kind that were raised in the first proceedings before both *ad hoc* Tribunals and indeed are still raised today. This being said, the position of States that are not parties to the Statute can be expected to give rise to problems. Will they be willing to cooperate with the Court and under what conditions might their citizens come under its jurisdiction?

It must be said that the Court cannot yet be viewed as a universal representative organ of the international community and cannot therefore yet pretend to be in a position comparable with, for example, the International Court of Justice. There are still too many States – and too many important States – that have yet to accede to the Statute. In the outcome document of the UN world summit of heads of State and government in September 2005, for example, it proved impossible to include any reference to the ICC.[4] This is by no means insignificant. The Court will have to prove its expertise and independence, primarily through its actions, in order to persuade those States that are not yet parties to accede to the Statute and to afford the Court universal status.

---

3 The Statute was adopted on 17 July 1998 and entered into force on 1 July 2002. The number of States to have ratified the Statute by 1 January 2006 was 100.

4 UN Doc. A/Res/60/1.

3 THE ICC AS AN INTERNATIONAL ORGANIZATION

The ICC is a novelty in that it is the first worldwide permanent international organization that exercises criminal jurisdiction and supervision over individuals rather than States.[5] Its task is to adjudicate on crimes committed after the entry into force of the Statute. It is designed to render superfluous the establishment of *ad hoc* Tribunals. The Statute is a multifaceted instrument that bears the mark of difficult negotiations. It also embraces a wide range of issues. It is the constitution of a new international organization with its own international legal personality, with rules governing the structure and powers of its organs and the dealings of the organization with the outside world. It is also a set of procedural rules, addressing matters of jurisdiction, investigation, prosecution and judicial procedures, as well as penalties and their execution. It also includes a number of substantive criminal law provisions, including definitions of three categories of crimes, a number of general principles of international criminal law and a summary of various forms of criminal responsibility. With regard to the substantive and procedural provisions, the authors of the Statute often had to find compromises between the civil law and common law systems and also to take account of the major legal systems of the world.[6] Finally, it includes provisions on the role of the States Parties and final clauses. In the process leading up to the negotiations, little if any attention was paid to the consequences of setting up the Court by means of a multilateral treaty and the consequences of this curious blend of constitutional and criminal law provisions. Efforts were made, however, to find a structure that guaranteed the independence of the judges and the Prosecutor and distinguished between the Court proper with the organs listed in Article 34 of the Statute and the Court in a broad sense including the Assembly of States Parties.

3.1 The Court Proper

When the ICTY and the ICTR got under way, each encountered considerable practical difficulties regarding the working relationships between its judges, prosecutor and registrar and their respective responsibilities. These difficulties stemmed from the fact that the judges invoked their judicial independence, the

5 *See* K. Gallant, *The International Criminal Court in the System of States and International Organizations*, 16 LJIL, 553 (2003).

6 *Cf.* Art. 38(1)(c) of the Statute of the International Court of Justice.

prosecutors asserted their independence as enshrined in the respective statutes, while the registrars – by virtue of the status of the *ad hoc* Tribunals as subsidiary organs of the Security Council – were also accountable to the UN Secretary-General. Both Tribunals are moreover facing growing pressure from the Security Council to complete their work. This is exerting an ever greater influence on the way this work is organised and on the referral of cases back to the countries concerned. Similar problems are to be expected with regard to the cooperation between and respective responsibilities of the various organs of the ICC. It is doubtful whether, at an institution such as an international criminal court, tensions of this kind between judges, prosecutor and registrar can ever be entirely avoided. In fact, the problem is inherent in the organizational structure of an international criminal court, with its various functions. The extent to which serious problems arise in practice will undoubtedly depend in part on the personalities of those involved.

3.2 The Court in a Broader Sense

Political and management tasks fall under the remit of the Assembly of States Parties to the Rome Statute. In the case of the *ad hoc* Tribunals, these tasks are the responsibility of UN organs. But among the decisions requiring the approval of the Assembly are those that directly affect the judicial process, such as the approval of the Rules of Procedure and Evidence and the Elements of Crimes and the appointment of the judges and the Prosecutor. The Assembly is thus very closely involved in the work of the Prosecutor and the judges. Only time will tell how internal coordination within the ICC between the organs of the Court proper and the organs of the Court in a broader sense will develop in practice. The ICC would, however, do well to draw on the wealth of experience garnered at both the *ad hoc* Tribunals and other international tribunals instituted in the recent past.

3.3 Cooperation with the UN

The conclusion of a Relationship Agreement on 13 September 2004[7] between the UN and the ICC[8] represented an important step towards the establishment of an independent permanent ICC in relationship with the UN system.[9] A great deal will depend, however, on its practical implementation.

On 2 December 2004, the General Assembly of the UN adopted a resolution that ties in with Article 4 (2) of the Relationship Agreement. The Court was granted observer status in the General Assembly.[10] Article 6 of the Relationship Agreement provides that the Court may report to the UN on its activities. The Court presented the first report of this kind at the recent session of the General Assembly in 2005.[11] The importance of the Relationship Agreement was underlined by the General Assembly in a resolution adopted by consensus at its session in the autumn of 2005.[12] However, the US did not join this consensus. At its fourth session, the Assembly of States Parties decided to set up a Liaison Office in New York to further the implementation of the Relationship Agreement.[13]

The Security Council and the ICC are both instruments for the maintenance of peace and security. In view of their shared task, it is vitally important that these two organs work together. A close and above all constructive relationship is desirable to underline the universality, authority and permanence of the Court. In the past, however, there have been repeated conflicts in the Security Council and the General Assembly. The fiercest debate took place in 2002 in response to Resolution 1422, in which the Security Council called on the Court, in accordance with article 16 of the Statute, not to institute any investigation or prosecution of conduct by UN peacekeeping troops from States that were not parties to the Statute. This Resolution was extended in 2003 for another 12 months by Resolution 1487. In 2004, however, the US gave up attempts to again renew this Resolution when it transpired that seven members of the Security Council were threatening to abstain when the question came to a vote. This was the time when the publicity surrounding the treatment by the US of

7 UN Doc. A/Res/58/318.

8 Relationship Agreement between the United Nations and the International Criminal Court, UN Doc. A/58/874.

9 *See* para. 9 of the Preamble to the Rome Statute.

10 UN Doc. A/Res/59/512 and A/59/PV 65 (2004); GA/10309.

11 UN Doc. A/60/177.

12 UN Doc. A/Res/60/29.

13 Res. ICC-ASP/4/Res.4, para. 25.

prisoners in Afghanistan and Iraq was at its height. In August 2003, however, Resolution 1497 established a multinational force for Liberia and provided that current or former officials or personnel from a contributing State which was not a party to the Statute should, without any time limit, be subject to the exclusive jurisdiction of that contributing State for all alleged acts or omissions arising out of or related to the multinational force. This amounted to permanent immunity.

In all the above cases, the Security Council was criticised because these decisions were at odds with the Statute and with the obligations that the parties to the Statute had assumed. Resolution 1593 (2005), in which the situation in Darfur was referred by the Security Council to the Court, provided that the expenses relating to this referral would not be borne by the UN.[14] Article 115 (b) of the Statute, under which in these very cases of referral by the Security Council the UN can in fact contribute to the costs, was thereby completely disregarded. In addition, this Resolution again excludes nationals of States that are not party to the Statute from the jurisdiction of the ICC. These examples offer little encouragement as regards the working relationship with the UN. It will be an important but also difficult task for the Court to interpret the Statute in such a way that constructive cooperation with the UN remains possible without infringing on the Statute. The referral to the ICC by the Security Council of the situation in Darfur is significant. It offers hope that the US may be taking a more constructive approach and it might herald the end of the antagonism between supporters and opponents of the ICC at the UN.

Darfur

It remains to be seen how the Court and the organs of the UN will work together in the context of Resolution 1593 and what assistance the Court will receive from the UN in performing its tasks. The Resolution in operational paragraph 2 urges the government of Sudan and all other parties to the conflict in Darfur to cooperate with and provide any necessary assistance to the Court. This wording is somewhat confusing since all States have an obligation to cooperate under resolutions based on Chapter VII.[15] Nor is it clear who is meant by 'all other parties to the conflict' and what form the cooperation should take. Does it imply that not all non-parties to the Statute are included? And is cooperation to be understood as defined in the Statute for the States Parties

14 Para. 7 of S/Res/1593 (2005).

15 Art. 29 of the ICTY Statute and Art. 28 of the ICTR Statute clearly state that 'States shall cooperate'.

or is it to be interpreted more broadly? In the Resolution, the Prosecutor is invited to address the Security Council every six months on actions taken pursuant to the Resolution. Three meetings have accordingly taken place to date. In his first report, the Prosecutor states that the process of information gathering is under way in order to determine whether there is a reasonable basis to initiate proceedings, that is to say whether there is a reasonable basis to believe that a crime within the jurisdiction of the Court has been committed, whether the case is admissible under Article 17 of the Statute and whether prosecution would serve the interests of justice.[16]

To date, the Sudanese authorities have in practice given no indication whatsoever of willingness to cooperate actively with the ICC, and they contend that they themselves are able to try any crimes. The Prosecutor responds in his report by saying that he has absolutely no wish to discourage national proceedings in any way. Nevertheless, on the basis of information he has gathered, he does see grounds for pursuing his investigations on certain issues. In the third of his reports, the Prosecutor again sets forth the cooperation he has received from the Sudanese authorities but also states that, in particular, interviews in Sudan itself are needed to complement the investigation.[17]

3.4 Budget

The ICC's success will depend in no small part on whether it is able to secure the funding it needs to carry out its tasks. In the process leading up to the negotiations, the best option was considered to be funding via the regular budget of the UN, without ruling out voluntary contributions from States and other sources. This was not followed up at the time. As we now know, the expenditure of the two *ad hoc* Tribunals has risen to very high, unforeseen levels. The ICTY's budget for the period 2006 to 2007 is currently over USD 305 million, while that of the ICTR for the same period is almost USD 270 million.[18] This has given rise to serious concerns in the Security Council about

16 Report of the Prosecutor of the International Criminal Court, Mr Luis Moreno Ocampo, to the Security Council pursuant to UNSCR 1593 (2005), *see* UN Doc. S/PV.5216.

17 Third Report of the Prosecutor of the International Criminal Court, Mr Luis Moreno Ocampo, to the UN Security Council Pursuant to UNSCR 1593 (2005) of 14 June 2006, *see* S/PV.5459 or: http://www.icc-cpi.int/library/cases/OTP_ReportUNSC_3-Darfur_English.pdf#search=%22Third%20Report%20on%20Sudan%22.

18 *See*, respectively, UN General Assembly, A/Res/60/243 and A/Res/60/241.

the funding needed to set up international criminal tribunals. These expenditure levels have also played a major role in the Security Council in the fashioning and tightening up of the completion strategy for the two ad hoc Tribunals. Moreover, the Special Court for Sierra Leone could only become operational once it had been firmly established in the Security Council that States' financial contributions were sufficient to fund its work for three years. In addition, experience at the two ad hoc Tribunals has shown that there are virtually no limits to the criminal investigation designed to establish the responsibility of suspects – especially high-ranking suspects – for crimes committed. Investigation and prosecution are also very expensive and time-consuming where the crimes in question relate to armed conflicts that are still ongoing. In fact all three situations currently being actively addressed by the Court fall into this category. A shortage of funds can soon become an issue, not just because of the number of situations to be dealt with, but also because of their nature.

The need for good coordination between the Assembly and the Court has already been demonstrated by the discussions on the 2004 budget concerning the funding required for the Prosecutor's activities. The Prosecutor invoked Article 42 of the Statute, under which he has full authority over the management and administration of his Office, and warned of the danger that he would not be able to fulfil his duties because of budgetary restrictions, while the Assembly, in this instance the budget committee, is responsible for sound and efficient financial management. The budget committee has since established that it is not clear from the current provisions of the Statute or the Financial Regulations and Rules[19] who is accountable on behalf of the Court in this matter.[20] When preparing the budget for 2005, the Assembly set up a contingency fund totalling € 10 million for a period of four years in order to be a position to cope with unexpected expenditure and situations. The budget for 2005 highlighted the need to adjust expectations. It transpired that no account had been taken of the cost of offices abroad to provide information about the Court in the countries where the crimes had been committed, or of the costs of protecting victims and witnesses. The budget for 2006 is based on the expectation that the Prosecutor will monitor eight situations and will start a fourth investigation in the second half of the year. The first hearing was due to start in May 2006, followed by

19 Arts 38, 42 and 43 of the Statute; Reg. 10 of the Financial Regulations and Rules.

20 Official Records of the Fourth Session of the Assembly of States Parties to the Rome Statute of the International Criminal Court, at 245.

a hearing on another situation in July 2006.[21] The budget also provided for additional staff. The total budget for 2006 is € 82,464.4 million.

It is crucial that the contributions from the parties to the Statute and also the other sources referred to in Article 116 of the Statute remain sufficient to enable the Court to perform its duties.

4 The Position of the ICC in the International Criminal Law Community

The successful establishment of the Court also explains the strong opposition, or in some cases the guarded attitude, on the part of States which are still reluctant to transfer powers relating to the administration of criminal justice. There are doubts as to the legitimacy of the justice administered by a Court of this nature; doubts as to whether the Court will be able to perform its tasks properly; doubts about the substance of certain provisions in the Statute; and doubts as to the value of the Court, in that this attempt to end the impunity of the perpetrators of such serious crimes might turn out to be a vain hope. Within the international legal system, based as it is on equality and reciprocity, criminal justice is regarded as an exclusively national matter. A supranational Court that is an instrument of the international public interest – in other words a product of the globalization of international responsibility – cannot be introduced into such a system without a struggle. The international community apparently believes that traditional sanctions, such as reprisals, civil and economic sanctions and the doctrine of State responsibility, are no longer adequate forms of action against wrongful acts on the part of States. There is now a clear tendency to hold individuals liable when grave breaches of international law are committed.

However, the ICC cannot yet rely on a solid foundation of norms that are generally accepted by the international community, comparable to national criminal law systems. The international system of criminal law is still in its

21 As regards the situation in Uganda, five international arrest warrants have since been issued for members of the Lord's Resistance Army (LRA) – 14 October 2005, *see* ICC Press Releases No. ICC-20051014-110 or http://www.icc-cpi.int/pressrelease_details&id=114&l=en.html. As regards the situation in the Democratic Republic of the Congo, an international arrest warrant for Thomas Lubanga Dyilo has recently been executed in that country. Lubanga is now being held at the detention unit in Scheveningen pending his trial – 17 March 2006, *see* ICC Press Releases No. ICC-CPI-20060302-125 or http://www.icc-cpi.int/press/pressreleases/132.html.

infancy and unanimous answers at global level to general questions, such as the significance of international criminal justice, whether or not there is an obligation to prosecute, alternatives to sentences and the aim of sentences, are still a long way off. National criminal law developed in response to the violation of norms laid down by the State. But the State often has a hand in the crimes over which the ICC has jurisdiction. Those who commit international crimes are therefore tried in a context of conduct by the State that is – normatively speaking – unacceptable. Trying an individual does not release the State from its international responsibility. This creates tension between the responsibility of the State and that of the individual and hence makes certain States reluctant to accede to the Statute.

Understandably, the two *ad hoc* Tribunals only gradually came to terms with the fact that international justice is essentially different from national justice, in both organization and substance. The ICC, on the other hand, can build on their experience. This gives it a major advantage.

It is worth pointing out that when the two Tribunals were developing their completion strategy and their rules of the road, they realised that it would be very useful to take note of the practice of the Nuremberg Tribunal.[22] It was even acknowledged that the ICTY might have avoided certain mistakes had it done so at an earlier stage. This is a good illustration of the gradually increasing awareness, in practice, of the existence of a body of international criminal law.[23]

Apart from the fact that international criminal law is still developing, and that international courts have no clear framework within which to operate, the ICC is also subject to limitations arising from the Statute itself. The Court is dependent on the cooperation of States to do its work. It has no powers to arrest suspects, to collect evidence or question witnesses at the scene and so on. For these purposes it must rely on the cooperation of the State in question. Under the terms of the Statute, it is the responsibility of the Assembly of States Parties to enforce compliance with the ICC's decisions, except in situations that are referred to the ICC by the Security Council. As the experience of the Tribunals shows, cooperation of this kind is extremely difficult, even though States are obliged by the UN Charter to take all measures necessary to implement a Security Council decision. Effective international political pressure is essential

---

22 D.A. Mundis, *Completing the Mandates of the Ad Hoc International Criminal Tribunals: Lessons From the Nuremberg Process?* 28 Fordham International Law Journal 591.

23 *See also* J.M. Sjöcrona & A.M.M. Orie, Internationaal Strafrecht vanuit Nederlands perspectief (2002) at 10.

to compel States to comply, but the position taken by a number of States, particularly the US, means that it is not always possible to exercise effective political pressure.

4.1 The ICC's Statute Compared with Those of the Two Tribunals

The resolutions establishing the two *ad hoc* Tribunals assumed, as the UN Secretary-General pointed out in his report on the *nullum crimen sine lege* principle, that the Tribunals may only apply such provisions of international humanitarian law as indubitably form part of customary international law, regardless of whether that law has been codified in conventions or whether the States in question are party to the said conventions.[24] One reason for adopting this approach was undoubtedly to forestall criticisms of the legality of the judgments handed down, like those voiced at the time of the Nuremberg and Tokyo Tribunals. The Statutes of the *ad hoc* Tribunals make no mention of the *nullum crimen sine lege* principle. Clearly, no sufficiently codified rules on individual criminal responsibility existed then, any more than a code of international criminal law. Moreover, it was specifically decided not to develop such rules in the resolution. This had consequences for the judicial practice of the Tribunals. Particularly in the early days of the ICTY, its judges felt it appropriate to include *obiter dicta* in their judgments, so as to contribute to the future development of international criminal law.[25] The idea was to compensate for the non-existence of an international legislative body and an international court with compulsory universal jurisdiction; they also did so because, as stated above, international criminal law was still underdeveloped. The ICTY set itself the task of clarifying customary international law and the applicable treaty rules and principles, without infringing on the rights of suspects or the *nullum crimen* principle.[26] As a result, the conclusions of law in these judgments went somewhat further than contemporary customary law required. The distinction between *lex lata* and *lex ferenda* was quite frequently tenuous. In turn, these *obiter dicta* accelerated the development of customary law. The "customary" law formulated by the ICTY and the ICTR had a significant, direct

24 Report of the Secretary-General Pursuant to Paragraph 2 of Security Council Resolution 808 (1993), UN Doc. S/25704 (1993), para. 34.

25 *See* A. Cassese *The ICTY: A Living and Vital Reality*, 2 Journal of International Criminal Law 585 (2004) at 589.

26 *Id.*, at 590.

influence on the wording of certain provisions in the ICC Statute and so further contributed to the rapid development of certain legal rules. The ICC Statute is in many respects the antithesis of the Statutes of the *ad hoc* Tribunals. One of the features of the ICC Statute, which is an international treaty, is that the States Parties intended to regulate everything in detail. Like the Statutes of the Tribunals, the UN International Law Commission's draft Statute for the ICC assumed that the definitions of the crimes referred to must be found in pre-existing international criminal law.[27] The aim of the Code of Crimes against the Peace and Security of Mankind, which the International Law Commission began to draft after the Second World War, was to codify international criminal law. The drafting process took a very long time, and was not completed until 1996, when negotiations on the ICC were already under way. The General Assembly confined itself to drawing the attention of the States that were negotiating on the ICC to the relevance of the Code to their work. This meant that the connection which had previously always been made between the Code and the establishment of the ICC was in fact abandoned, and from then on attention was focused entirely on the Statute. While the Code of Crimes as such declined in importance as the negotiations proceeded and received no further follow-up after the negotiations were completed, its relevance was demonstrated by the provisions of the new ICC Statute. However, what is still lacking is coherent, consistent transposition of the Statute's provisions into the national legislation of the States Parties. The freedom that the statutes of the ICTY and the ICTR still allowed the judges – a freedom of which they took advantage – was used in the negotiations as an argument for including more clearly defined rules in the ICC Statute. Throughout the negotiations, it was clear that States were disinclined to surrender any sovereignty and highly suspicious of international courts, and were not prepared to allow the judges much latitude in interpreting and applying the Statute. In addition, the national criminal law experts who played an important part in the negotiations constantly referred to the legal principles of *nullum crimen* and *nulla poena sine lege.* This stress on legality was a major factor in the negotiations,[28] and was reinforced by the fact that

27 J. Crawford, *The ILC adopts a Statute for an International Criminal Court*, 89 AJIL 405 (1995).

28 M. Boot, Nullum Crimen Sine Lege and the Subject Matter Jurisdiction of the International Criminal Court (2002) at 363. Boot observes that the *nulla poena* principle received little attention. She regards this as an indication that the negotiators were more concerned about maintaining their own sovereignty than about safeguards for individuals.

the content of international criminal law was still far from clear.[29] This uncertainty formed an argument for defining the crimes in the Statute, formulating elements of crimes and drafting rules of procedure and evidence.[30] However, the Statute did not go so far as to produce an entirely new codification and to refer for example to serious human rights violations instead of war crimes and crimes against humanity.[31] Nevertheless, the negotiations overlooked the fact that the *nullum crimen* principle does not require international norms to be elaborated in detail.[32] This can be attributed to the fact that the principle was being included in an international criminal law system for the first time. But an international legal system cannot be equated with a national legal system. The two types of system differ fundamentally in the nature and extent of the authority at their disposal and their ability to use coercive measures.[33] In international law, generally recognised sources of international law may be regarded as *lex* within the meaning of the *nullum crimen sine lege* principle.[34] For it to be possible to hold an individual responsible, it is enough that clear, accessible rules applied to the offender's actions at the time the crime was committed and that agreement exists on the crime and the attribution of individual criminal responsibility for it, and on the right of the international community as a whole or of its individual members to prosecute international crimes of this nature.

Whether all the norms laid down in the Statute can already be regarded in their entirety as customary law cannot yet be said with certainty. Too many

29 Sjöcrona, *supra* n. 23, at 3.

30 The inclusion of these elements was a concession to the United States. They are obviously inspired by the US legal system, especially the uniform code of justice applied by the US courts martial. Elements of this kind are not defined in the legislation of the civil law countries, which means that every element of a crime must be proved beyond reasonable doubt.

31 W.A. Schabas, An Introduction to the International Criminal Court (2004) at 28.

32 *See* A. Pellet, *Applicable Law, in* A. Cassese, P. Gaeta and J.R.W. Jones (eds.), The Rome Statute of the International Criminal Court: A Commentary, Vol. II, at 1057.

33 *See* Prosecutor *v.* Dusko Tadić, Decision on the Defence Motion for Interlocutory Appeal on Jurisdiction, Case No. IT-94-1, Appeals Chamber, 2 October 1995, paras. 42-43.The Appeals Chamber endorsed the view that requirement that a tribunal must be established by law is a general principle of law, but considered that it could not purely and simply be transposed to the international sphere due to the absence of any separation of powers in international society.

34 *See* W. Heintschel von Heinegg, *Criminal International Law and Customary International Law, in* A. Zimmerman (ed.), International Criminal Law and the Current Development of Public International Law 27 (2003).

compromises were reached for this to be possible, and parts of the Statute clearly reveal progressive development. Nor is everything which can be counted as customary law codified in the Statute. That was never the aim of the negotiations leading to the establishment of the ICC. This also explains the inclusion of Article 10. Its original aim was to ensure that the definitions of crimes in the Statute, which some negotiators regarded as too restrictive in comparison with prevailing law, should not be interpreted as limiting or prejudicing existing or developing rules. However, the end product of the negotiations on this point was more progressive in parts than originally assumed, especially with regard to war crimes and crimes against humanity. Other parts are regarded as less far-reaching than the provisions of customary international law. This gave another meaning to Article 10: it protected the Statute from future as well as current developments.[35] In fact, Article 10 may be invoked in support of either a broader or a stricter interpretation. What effects will these developments have on the work of the judges? Can judicial practice take sufficient account of the – still ongoing – development of customary international law or will the extensive codification contained in the Statute, the Rules of Procedure and Evidence, and the Elements of Crimes allow the judges too little scope to take account of new developments? Is there a real risk that further progressive development of international criminal law will take place outside the Statute, and what will that mean for the position of the Court?

4.2 Outreach

If the ICC is to be a success, it is essential for the victims of crimes and the people in the countries or regions concerned to believe in the Court's legitimacy and to believe that it will give them justice. In the case of the ICTY, the importance of this factor was not recognised until late in the day, and, in the view of many, without success, when an outreach programme was set up in 1999. The Security Council then encouraged this initiative for both *ad hoc* Tribunals. Certain "mixed" tribunals also aim to keep their judicial practice as close as possible to the practice of the country in question, so as to make it clear to the victims that justice is being done to them. The Special Court for Sierra Leone, for example, does a great deal of outreach work. However, there will always be the question of whether justice can be dispensed independently, efficiently

35 M.H. Arsanjani, *The Rome Statute of the International Criminal Court*, 93 AJIL 22 (1999) at 36.

and safely in countries where armed conflicts are still raging or where the courts can barely function. The Security Council took the view that this was not the case in Rwanda, which is one reason why that country was opposed to the setting up of the Rwanda Tribunal. And since the trial of Saddam Hussein began in Iraq on 19 October 2005, for example, the President of the Iraqi Special Tribunal has resigned and been replaced; two members of the defence team have been assassinated, one has left the country after being injured; and the court proceedings have been, in a word, chaotic.

The impression given by what the ICC has done in the three situations now pending is that it understands how important it is for the local population to learn to know and respect the Court. The ICC has set up offices in the Democratic Republic of the Congo (DRC), Uganda and, for Darfur, Chad. The aim is to make it possible for the Court to discharge its obligations to keep the local population informed, to offer support and protection to victims and witnesses and to inform victims of the possibility of participating in the proceedings in order to obtain compensation. The Court makes its existence and its procedures known through training courses and in other ways. This creates an important task for NGOs. In the investigation into the situation in the DRC a dispute evolved already about the rights of the victims. In this case especially about the extent to which they can be involved in the investigation phase.[36] This case may assist the development of the position of victims under the Statute in proceedings before the ICC, a section that has received much praise.

5 Conclusion

I have endeavoured in the foregoing to illustrate the challenges facing the International Criminal Court in terms of organization and comparative law. The Preamble to the Statute states that the international community is determined to put an end to impunity for the perpetrators of serious crimes of concern to the international community and thus to contribute to the prevention of such crimes.[37] To this end, the universal support of the international community is of paramount importance. Furthermore, the establishment of the Court is putting a strain on international criminal law. Despite being still in its infancy, international criminal law will have to be accepted, interpreted and applied by an array of courts, both national and international. The situations that the ICC

36 *See* ICC-01/04 concerning the situation in the DRC, www.icc-cpi.int.

37 Preamble to the Statute, para. 5.

is investigating and that have led to summonses being issued demonstrate once again that peace and justice are often, if indeed not always, at odds with each other. Faced with these challenges, the Court must show that it can make a meaningful contribution, as a judicial body, to the peace, security and well-being of the international community.

5

HELPING TO CHART UNCHARTED WATERS: THE NETHERLANDS BEFORE THE INTERNATIONAL CRIMINAL TRIBUNAL FOR THE FORMER YUGOSLAVIA

Olivia Swaak-Goldman[*]

1 INTRODUCTION: THE NETHERLANDS AS BOTH GOOSE AND GANDER TO THE ICTY

As is well known, in response to the wide scale violence committed in the Balkans in the early 1990s, the international community – in the form of the UN Security Council – established the International Criminal Tribunal for the former Yugoslavia (ICTY) to hold individuals accountable for serious violations of international humanitarian law committed in the territory of the former Yugoslavia since 1991.[1] The ICTY, with its seat in The Hague, was based on the precedents of the Nuremberg and Tokyo tribunals established in the aftermath of the Second World War. These precedents were, however, of limited value. In addition to developments in international law – notably international human rights and humanitarian law – since the Second World War, the ICTY was in a markedly different position vis-à-vis the international community than its predecessors. This difference has various facets: the character of the tribunals; the context in which they are required to accomplish their tasks; and their

* Legal counsel at the International Law Division of the Ministry of Foreign Affairs of the Kingdom of the Netherlands. The opinions in this essay are solely the author's and do not necessarily represent those of the Kingdom of the Netherlands.

1 SC Res. 808, UN Doc. S/RES/808 (1993) and 827, UN Doc. S/RES/827 (1993).

N. Blokker, R. Lefeber, L. Lijnzaad & I. van Bladel (eds.), *The Netherlands in Court. Essays in Honour of Johan G. Lammers*, © 2006 Koninklijke Brill NV. Printed in the Netherlands, pp. 89-104.

competences. As noted by ICTY President Antonio Cassese in the ICTY's first Annual Report to the Security Council:[2]

> "[U]nlike the Nürnberg and Tokyo Tribunals, the Tribunal is truly international. It has rightly been stated that the Nürnberg and Tokyo Tribunals were 'multi-national tribunals, but not international tribunals in the strict sense', in that they represented only one segment of the world community: the victors. This was recognised by the Nürnberg Tribunal itself when it pointed out that, in creating the Nürnberg Tribunal and defining the law it was to administer, the four signatory Powers to its Charter 'have done together what any one of them might have done singly'. In other words, at Nürnberg each of the four victorious Powers could have tried the defendants itself; they preferred instead to set up a joint tribunal, acting simultaneously on behalf of all of them. [...] By contrast, the Tribunal is not the organ of a group of States; it is an organ of the whole international community."

With regard to their context and competences, it should be noted that while the Nuremberg and Tokyo trials took place in occupied territory after the conclusion of hostilities, the ICTY was, at least in its early years, attempting to adjudicate crimes in the midst of an ongoing conflict occurring thousands of miles away, without the benefit of an enforcement arm. Again, President Cassese made this point eloquently in the first Annual Report:

> "It is well known that the Allied Powers that set up the international tribunals at Nürnberg and Tokyo wielded full authority and control over the territory of Germany and Japan respectively and, in addition, had already apprehended the defendants when trials commenced. Consequently, those tribunals did not need the cooperation of the defendants' national authorities or those of other countries for the prosecutors' investigations and collection of evidence. The situation is totally different for the Tribunal. The Security Council, when it established the Tribunal, was aware that it lacked any direct authority over the territories of States Members of the United Nations and, in particular, of the successor republics of the former Yugoslavia. Thus, the Tribunal was not endowed with direct enforcement powers: it has no law enforcement agents at its disposal entitled to carry out investigations, subpoena witnesses, or serve arrest warrants in the territories of States Members of the United Nations. To fulfil all these tasks, the Tribunal must rely upon the domestic legal system and the enforcement machinery of each State. [...] In this respect it must,

2 First Annual Report of the International Tribunal for the Prosecution of Persons Responsible for Serious Violations of International Humanitarian Law Committed in the Territory of the Former Yugoslavia since 1991, UN Doc. A/49/342, S/1994/1007 (1994), para. 10, citations omitted.

however, be emphasized that all States are under a strict obligation to cooperate with the Tribunal and to comply with its requests and orders."[3]

As a result of these differences with its predecessors, the ICTY was to a certain extent sailing in uncharted waters with regard to its relationship with States. As both host State to the ICTY and Member State of the United Nations the Netherlands has been at the forefront of helping to map this difficult terrain. On the one hand the Netherlands is in the same position as all Member States of the UN and is obliged to comply with requests for assistance by the ICTY. On the other hand the Netherlands, by virtue of its status as host State, has a special relationship with the ICTY. Both of these relationships, and the parameters of the corresponding obligations, have been the subject of litigation at the ICTY. Two examples of this litigation will be discussed below.

2 The Netherlands' Obligations as a Member State of the UN

As mentioned above, the Netherlands is a Member State of the UN and as such it is obliged to cooperate with the ICTY. This obligation is far reaching in that the ICTY was established under Chapter VII of the UN Charter[4] as a measure to restore international peace and security. This obligation is not only binding on all States as a result of Article 25 of the UN Charter, but must also be given priority over other international obligations, in accordance with Article 103 of the UN Charter.[5]

Article 29 of the ICTY's Statute is quite explicit with regard to the obligation of States to cooperate: States are obliged to cooperate with the ICTY in the investigation and prosecution of persons accused of committing serious international crimes. Specifically, States are required to comply "without undue delay with any request for assistance or an order issued by a Trial Chamber" concerning a variety of requests, a few examples of which are given, including the production of evidence.[6]

---

3 *Id.*, para. 84, citations omitted.

4 1945 Charter of the United Nations, 1983 Yearbook of the United Nations 1325.

5 *Id.* Article 103 states: "In the event of a conflict between the obligations of the Members of the United Nations under the present Charter and their obligations under any other international agreement, their obligations under the present Charter shall prevail".

6 SC Res. 827, UN Doc. S/RES/827 (1993); reprinted *in* 32 ILM. 1192 (1993). Article 29 states:

Although broadly formulated, the exact parameters of this obligation were unclear. For example, does this obligation extend to providing sensitive intelligence information to defence counsel? The Netherlands, as well as NATO and its other Member States, was asked to do exactly that by General Dragoljub Ojdanić, former Chief of Staff of the armed forces of the Federal Republic of Yugoslavia, who stands accused of crimes against humanity and violations of the laws and customs of war committed in Kosovo in 1999. In response, the Netherlands, along with several other of the requested States, argued that the cooperation obligation in Article 29 did not extend this far. While, as discussed below, the obligation to provide information has previously been the subject of litigation, this was the first time that States were asked to provide sensitive intelligence data in response to a general request. Nevertheless, it is not unique in that it is an example of how States, including the Netherlands, use litigation to determine the boundaries of their obligations.

In the case of *Prosecutor* v. *Ojdanić*, the accused requested the Trial Chamber to order NATO and certain States,[7] including the Netherlands, to produce three categories of information:

(a) All recordings, summaries, notes or text of any intercepted communications (electronic, oral or written) during the period 1 January through 20 June 1999, to which General Dragoljub Ojdanić was a party;

(b) All recordings, summaries, notes or text of any intercepted communications (electronic, oral or written) during the period 1 January through 20 June 1999, originating in the Federal Republic of Yugoslavia, and relating to Kosovo, in which General Dragoljub Ojdanić was mentioned or referred to in the communication; and

---

1. States shall cooperate with the International Tribunal in the investigation and prosecution of persons accused of committing serious violations of international humanitarian law.

2. States shall comply without undue delay with any request for assistance or an order issued by a Trial Chamber, including but not limited to:

(a) the identification and location of persons;

(b) the taking of testimony and the production of evidence;

(c) the service of documents;

(d) the arrest of detention of persons;

(e) the surrender or the transfer of the accused to the International Tribunal.

7 Albania, Belgium, Bosnia and Herzegovina, Bulgaria, Canada, Croatia, Czech Republic, Denmark, Former Yugoslav Republic of Macedonia, France, Germany, Greece, Hungary, Iceland, Italy, Luxembourg, Netherlands, Norway, Poland, Portugal, Romania, Spain, Turkey, United Kingdom and United States of America.

(c) All correspondence, memoranda, reports, recordings or summaries of any statements made by General Dragoljub Ojdanić during the period 1 January through 20 June 1999 to any representative of your organization, including sources of information working on your behalf.[8]

The accused argued, *inter alia*, that the absence of incriminating evidence in these recordings or statements would establish his innocence.

The Netherlands, despite its desire to assist the ICTY, argued that its obligation to cooperate with the ICTY as laid down in Article 29 of the Statute could not be interpreted in a manner which would require compliance with this request. In its written pleadings filed 28 February 2003[9] as well as during the oral hearings held from 1-2 December 2004,[10] the Netherlands objected to this request on several grounds. First, it noted that in accordance with Rule 54 *bis* (B)(i) of the ICTY's Rules and Procedures of Evidence, the Trial Chamber can reject the Application if it determines that

> "the documents or information sought are not relevant to any matter at issue in the proceedings before [it] or are not necessary for a fair determination of any such matter."[11]

The Netherlands argued that the request should be rejected on both of these grounds. Further, it noted that even if the request were deemed to be sufficiently relevant and necessary to warrant the production of information in general, it did not warrant overriding the legitimate national security concerns of the Netherlands.

---

8 Prosecutor *v.* Milan Milutinović, Nikola Šainović and Dragoljub Ojdanić, "General Ojdanić's Application for Orders to NATO and States for Production of Information", Case No. IT-99-37-PT, 15 November 2002; (hereinafter "Application").

9 *Id.*, Written Response of the Government of the Netherlands to the Application of General Ojdanić for Orders to NATO and States for Production of Information, 28 February 2003.

10 On 7 March 2003 the accused submitted his reply memorandum: "General Ojdanić's further Submission in Support of Application for Orders to NATO for Production of Information". By Order of 13 May 2003 the Trial Chamber directed the accused to provide a further submission addressing the relevance of the material sought in more detail. The accused filed this submission on 20 June 2003 ("General Ojdanić's Further Submission in Support of Application for Orders to NATO and States for Production of Information"). As a result of negotiations between the accused and several of the requested States, a stay was ordered on 14 November 2003, which remained in place until the oral hearing was scheduled from 1-2 December 2004.

11 *See also* Rule 54 *bis* (A).

Specifically, with regard to necessity, the Netherlands argued that the request failed to establish that the information requested was necessary for a fair determination of any matter at issue in this case. It noted that although ICTY jurisprudence exists to support the granting of a request for categories of documents, unduly *broad* categories, such as those at issue in this case, are explicitly prohibited.[12]

The Netherlands argued that categories of information requested by the accused were impermissibly broad in terms of source material, subject matter, time frame and place. In fact, the Netherlands argued, the extreme breadth of the request, together with the failure of the request to refer to any specific information, indicated that the accused sought to engage in a 'fishing expedition'; he was not even certain that such information exists, rather he sought to use the power of the ICTY to ascertain whether this was in fact the case. Relying on a Separate Opinion by Judge David Hunt in *Prosecutor* v. *Delalić*,[13] the Netherlands argued that such mere speculation is insufficient to justify an order for the production of information.

The Netherlands further argued that the request also failed to satisfy the necessity requirement because of the considerable burden that such an order would place on the requested States. The Netherlands noted that the Appeals Chamber stated that deciding whether to grant a request:

> "entails the striking of a balance between the need, on the one hand, for the Tribunal to have the assistance of States in the collection of evidence for the purpose of prosecuting persons responsible for serious violations of international humanitarian law and the need, on the other hand, to ensure that the obligation upon States to assist the Tribunal in the evidence collecting process is not unfairly burdensome".[14]

Further, the Netherlands relied on the statement of the Appeals Chamber in the *Prosecutor* v. *Blaskić*, that

> "a party cannot request hundreds of documents, *particularly when it is evident that the identification, location and scrutiny of such documents by the relevant national*

---

12 *See* Prosecutor *v.* Dario Kordić and Mario Čerkez, Decision on the Request of the Republic of Croatia for Review of a Binding Order, Case No. IT-95-14/2, Appeals Chamber, 9 September 1999, para. 38.

13 *See* Prosecutor *v.* Zejnil Delalić, Zdravko Mucić, Hazim Delić and Esad Landžo, Separate Opinion of Judge David Hunt on Motion by Esad Landžo to Preserve and Provide Evidence, Case No. IT-96-21, Appeals Chamber, 22 April 1999, paras. 4, 7.

14 Prosecutor *v.* Kordić, *supra* n. 12, para. 41.

authorities would be overly taxing and not strictly justified by the exigencies of the trial".[15]

According to the Netherlands, this was precisely the situation in this case.

In this case, given the unparalled breadth of the request and the large number of States to which it was directed, the burden imposed on the requested States is considerable. This burden is additionally compounded due to the sensitive nature of certain of the information sought; access to intelligence information is by necessity extremely limited and thus there are few individuals that can be entrusted with responding to these requests. The Netherlands argued that this imposition manifestly outweighs the limited necessity, if any, established by the request. Moreover, should the requested order be granted, one could expect other defendants to follow suit in the hope that national governments would be ordered to sift through their sensitive intelligence information for any indication of information that might be of use for their case. Such a precedent would thus magnify the already undue burden placed on the requested States. This, in turn, would limit their ability to cooperate with ICTY requests.

Finally, the Netherlands argued that the accused had not established that the requested order was necessary in that the requested information could not be obtained elsewhere. Particularly concerning communications to which the accused was a party or statements made by him, resort to an order to a State seems unnecessary. The accused was well suited to know which statements or communication he had made. Relying on the Separate Opinion of Judge Hunt in *Prosecutor* v. *Delalić* and the Appeals Chamber decision in *Prosecutor* v. *Blaskić*, the Netherlands noted that various less onerous means exist for bringing this information to the attention of the Trial Chamber,[16] and that the ICTY should reserve its mandatory compliance powers "for cases in which they are really necessary",[17] and that this was not such a case.

With regard to its second basis for challenging the request, relevance, the Netherlands argued that the information sought was of questionable relevance to the accused's case. The accused argued that the information requested is "directly relevant" to show whether he

15 Prosecutor *v.* Tihomir Blaskić, Judgment of the Appeals Chamber on the Request of the Republic of Croatia for Review of the Decision of Trial Chamber II of 18 July 1997, Case No. IT-95-14, Appeals Chamber, 29 October 1997, para. 32, emphasis added.

16 *See* Prosecutor *v.* Delalić, *supra* n. 13, Separate Opinion of Judge Hunt, paras. 4, 7.

17 Prosecutor *v.* Blaskić, *supra* n. 15, para. 31.

> "participated in any of the crimes [...] alleged [...], whether war crimes were reported to him or brought to his attention [...], and to show his state of mind concerning the events occurring in Kosovo and the prevention and punishment of war crimes".[18]

However, in formulating his specific request he did not limit it to these issues. Rather, he requested copies of all communications during a six-month period to which he was a "party" or in which he was "mentioned or referred to", as well as correspondence concerning "statements" made by him during this period. There was thus no requirement that any such communications or statements have any bearing on the accused's participation in, knowledge of, or state of mind concerning the crimes alleged. As a result, the Netherlands argued that the accused had failed to establish that the requested information was relevant to any matter at issue in the case.

As a final objection, the Netherlands noted that its national security was called into question as a result of this request. In this regard it noted that ICTY jurisprudence[19] and Rule 54 *bis* (F) of the Rules of Procedure and Evidence establish that States are permitted to object to requests for production of information based on national security concerns.

Rule 54 *bis* (F)(i) requires States to "identify, to the extent possible, the basis upon which its national security interests will be prejudiced". In this regard the Netherlands pointed out, in particular with respect to the first two categories of information sought, the sensitive nature of information relating to the existence of intercepted communications. It noted that the very disclosure of such information would cause serious prejudice to national security interests by jeopardising not only the methods and sources utilised to generate that specific information, but also the requested State's ability to gather such information in the future. It argued that these concerns also applied to the third category of requested information – statements made by the accused – to the extent that it includes human intelligence. Although noting that provisions can be made to protect the information,[20] the Netherlands pointed out that some risks inevitably remain inherent. It argued that the ICTY should only ask States to undergo such inherent risks if it is convinced that the accused has met the heightened burden accompanying these risks.

18 Application, para. 15.

19 Prosecutor *v.* Blaskić, *supra* n. 15, paras. 61, 65 and 67.

20 Rule 54 *bis* (F) (ii), (G) and (I).

On 23 March 2005 the Trial Chamber issued its Decision.[21] In it, the Trial Chamber ordered the accused to reformulate his request for documents with respect to certain States and to give those States a further opportunity to respond voluntarily. As examples, the Trial Chamber recommended that, with regard to paragraphs (A) and (B), the accused identify the particular matters in issue in the case to which the documents sought are said to be relevant, and indicate how they are relevant to these matters, "stipulating as far as possible the place and dates of intercepted communications that relate to matters which are the subject of the Indictment".[22] With regard to paragraph (C) the Trial Chamber recommended identifying specifically the documents sought and how such documents relate to the matters in issue in the case.

The accused subsequently reformulated his request.[23] For example, with regard to paragraph (A), the reformulated request sought:

> "[c]opies of all recordings, summaries, notes or text of any intercepted communications ... during the period 1 January 1999 and 20 June 1999 in which [the Accused] was a party and which (1) [the accused] participated in the communication from Belgrade [FRY]; (2) the communication was with one of the persons listed in Attachment 'A'; and (3) may be relevant to one of the following issues in the case,"

following which comes a list of issues.[24] The reformulation of paragraph (B), although not exactly the same, is similarly formulated. With regard to paragraph (C), the reformulated request continues to seek "any reports, evaluations or comments" concerning various contacts with the accused. The reformulated request was sent to the twelve remaining States.[25] While arguing that the reformulated request remained insufficiently specific, and with regard to paragraph (C) without an adequate explanation of the relevance or necessity of the requested documents, the Netherlands nevertheless chose a pragmatic approach: in an attempt to assist the ICTY it had made a good faith examination of its

---

21 Prosecutor *v.* Milan Mulutinovic, Nikola Sainovic and Dragoljub Ojdanić, *supra* n. 8, Decision on Motion of Dragoljub Ojdanić for Modification of Decisions on Application for binding Orders Pursuant to Rule *54bis*, Trial Chamber, 23 March 2005, amended on 19 April 2005.

22 *Id.*

23 Prosecutor *v.* Milan Mulutinović, Nikola Šainović and Dragoljub Ojdanić, *supra* n. 8, General Ojdanić's *Ex Parte* Request to NATO and States Pursuant to Trial Chamber's Decision of 23 March 2005, 19 April 2005.

24 *Id.*, paras. 3-4.

25 Belgium, Canada, Czech Republic, France, Germany, Hungary, Iceland, Luxembourg, Netherlands, Poland, United Kingdom and United States of America.

records and not found any documents responsive to the request.[26] As a result, the request for an order with respect to the Netherlands was denied. The accused, however, continued his request with regard to other States.[27] A second oral hearing was held to consider this request in October 2004, and the Trial Chamber ordered those States which had not already done so, and NATO, to comply with paragraphs (A) and (B) of the request.[28]

This case indicates the important boundaries within which the ICTY has to work. As has been noted, the ICTY, unlike its predecessors, lacks an enforcement arm and is thus dependant on States to fulfil a variety of functions, from the apprehension of suspects to the production of evidence. While the ICTY has wide-ranging powers based on its Statute and its origins as a subsidiary organ of the UN Security Council based on Chapter VII of the UN Charter, it must take the legitimate concerns of States into consideration. States, for their

---

26 Prosecutor *v.* Milan Mulutinović, Nikola Šainović and Dragoljub Ojdanić, *supra* n. 8, Response of the Government of the Netherlands to "General Ojdanić's *Ex Parte* Request to NATO and States Pursuant to Trial Chamber's Decision of 23 March 2005", Case No. IT-99-37-PT, 17 June 2005.

27 On 27 June 2005 the accused submitted a second application for binding orders against NATO and eleven States, (Belgium, Canada, Czech Republic, France, Germany, Hungary, Iceland, Luxembourg, Poland, United Kingdom and United States of America). Prosecutor *v.* Milan Mulutinović, Nikola Šainović and Dragoljub Ojdanić, *supra* n. 8, General Ojdanić's Second Application for Orders to NATO and States for Production of Information, 27 June 2005. Paragraph (C) (1) was reformulated to request "any reports, evaluations or comments concerning the speech given by General Ojdanić to the military attaches of foreign governments in Belgrade during July-August 1998".

28 After continuing negotiations with the relevant States, the accused filed "General Ojdanić's Report on Status of Second Application to NATO and States for the Production of Information (Rule 54*bis*)", notifying the Trial Chamber of the responses received from the States concerned and requesting that an oral hearing be held on the Second Application. The oral hearing was held on 4 October 2005. By then the Second Application had been restricted to five States (Canada, Iceland, Luxembourg, the United Kingdom and the United States of America) and NATO, although with regard to the United Kingdom the accused had limited his application to paras. (C)(2) and (C)(3). *See* Hearing Transcript, 4 Oct. 2005, T. 119, in Prosecutor *v.* Milan Milutinović, Nikola Šainović, Dragoljub Ojdanić, Nebojša Pavković, Vladimir Lazarević, Vlastimir Dordević and Sreten Lukić, Decision on Second Application of Dragoljub Ojdanić for Binding Orders Pursuant to Rule 54 *bis,* Case No. IT-05-87-PT, 17 November 2005, para. 7. The Trial Chamber ordered that Canada, Iceland, Luxembourg, the United States and NATO comply with the request in paragraphs (A) and (B) of the Second Application, while giving them 21 days to request protective measures; with respect to the United Kingdom, the Trial Chamber noted that it had complied with the requests in (A) and (B). Paragraph (C) was denied in its entirety. At the time of writing the appeal on this decision was pending.

part, must comply with their obligation to cooperate with the ICTY and seek in good faith to ascertain the limits of this obligation. This case, as have others before and after it, helped to further define where those boundaries lie.

3 THE NETHERLANDS AS HOST STATE

In addition to helping to define the confines of States' obligations to assist the ICTY, the Netherlands has also had the opportunity to help explore the boundaries of the rights of accused before the ICTY. This opportunity arose as a result of the Netherland's role as host State to the ICTY. Specifically, the ICTY asked the Netherlands to give its opinion on the limitations that can be placed on an accused who is granted provisional release. This was not an issue that its predecessors, the Nürnberg and Tokyo tribunals, had to address. These tribunals conducted relatively short trials and kept the accused in custody pending their outcome. In contrast, the ICTY's trials are quite long and human rights norms concerning the right to provisional release have developed, thus creating the necessity in certain cases to provisionally release accused. An additional complicating factor is that, unlike its predecessors, the institution trying the accused (the ICTY), is not an organ of the State on whose territory the institution is located (the Netherlands).

These issues arose in the case *Prosecutor* v. *Dragan Jokić*,[29] in which the accused was granted provisional release in accordance with Rule 65 of the ICTY's Rules of Procedure and Evidence. Rule 65 provides that once detained, an accused may not be released except: upon an order of a Trial Chamber (A); and that release may be ordered only after giving the host State and the State to which the accused seeks to be released an opportunity to be heard and only if it is satisfied that he or she will appear for trial and, if released, will not pose a danger to any victim, witness or other person (B). The Trial Chamber may impose conditions upon the release of the accused (C), and, provisions are in place to appeal a decision on provisional release (D), (E), (F) and (G).

The accused in this case, Dragan Jokić, had applied for provisional release on 21 January 2002. In accordance with Rule 65(B), the Netherlands was given an opportunity to comment on this request. It did so by replying that it did not object to his release, and that it was its understanding that upon his release the accused would leave the territory of the Netherlands. The accused's request

29 Prosecutor *v.* Vidoje Blagojević, Dragan Obrenović, Dragan Jokić and Momir Nikolić, Case No. IT-02-60-PT.

for provisional release was rejected by the Trial Chamber on 28 March 2002, but was subsequently granted on appeal two months later.[30] He was released to the Republika Srpska, Bosnia and Herzegovina, subject to certain conditions, including that he would report to the police every week and not leave the area without notifying them, not have any contact with co-accused in the case or with victims or potential witnesses, and not discuss the case with anyone other than his counsel and immediate family.[31] The government of Republika Srpska gave a guarantee providing, *inter alia*, that it would provide security for the accused and would immediately arrest him should he try to escape or violate any of the provisions of the Provisional Release Decision.

On 11 November 2002 the Trial Chamber issued a scheduling order setting a Status Conference for 27 November 2002. It ordered the accused to return to the UN Detention Unit ("detention unit") during his return to the ICTY for the Status Conference and held that following the Status Conference his provisional release would continue under the same conditions as set out in the Provisional Release Decision. The accused, however, objected to the idea of returning to the detention unit and filed a confidential motion on 15 November 2002 requesting that he be allowed to stay in a hotel in The Hague while in the Netherlands for the Status Conference.[32] The Trial Chamber issued its decision on 21 November 2002, in which it granted the accused's request, pursuant to certain conditions including, *inter alia*, that he remain in the hotel or the premises of the ICTY, that he obey the instructions of the Dutch police, that he not have any direct contacts or in any way interfere with victims or potential witnesses, and that he not discuss the case with anyone other than his counsel and members of his immediate family. It also requested the Registrar to consult with the authorities of the Netherlands to ensure that the practical arrangements for the accused were taken care of.[33]

---

30 Prosecutor *v.* Vidoje Blagojević, Dragan Obrenović, Dragan Jokić, Decision on Application by Dragan Jokic for Provisional Release, Case No. IT-02-53-AR65, Trial Chamber, 28 May 2002 ("Provisional Release Decision").

31 *Id.*, para 4.

32 Expedited Motion to Modify Conditions of Appearance for Status Conference, 27 November 2002, filed confidentially 15 November 2002, cited in Prosecutor *v.* Vidoje Blagojević, Dragan Obrenović, Dragan Jokić, Momir Nikolić, *supra* n. 29, Request to the Netherlands to Attend a Status Conference on 27 November 2002, 25 November 2002, para. 2.

33 Prosecutor *v.* Vidoje Blagojević, Dragan Obrenović, Dragan Jokić, Momir Nikolić, *supra* n. 29, Request to the Netherlands to Attend a Status Conference on 27 November 2002, 25 November 2002, at 4.

This ruling came as quite a surprise to the Netherlands, and the government quickly filed its objections. It noted that allowing the accused to stay outside of the detention unit would violate its condition to his provisional release, namely that he leaves the territory of the Netherlands, and that it therefore could not agree to the accused staying in a hotel while in The Hague.[34] A temporary solution was found by the accused agreeing to return to the detention unit, but the Trial Chamber struggled to achieve a longer term solution. As such, it requested the Netherlands to attend a Status Conference to be held on 27 November 2002 and to present its opinion in the capacity of an *amicus curiae* brief on the question of whether it is necessary or even mandatory for the accused, and for accused in general, to be detained in the detention unit during the pre-trial phase and/or during the trial phase.[35]

In providing its reply to this question, the Netherlands noted that it was its understanding that the requirement in Rule 65(B) to consult the host State applied not only to whether provisional release should be granted, but also to the conditions under which this release should take place. Thus, before the Trial Chamber modified the conditions of the accused's provisional release, by allowing him to stay in a hotel in the Netherlands, it should have been consulted. The objections of the government spring from its responsibility for the accused's security while in the Netherlands outside of the detention unit. This responsibility arises not only from the ICTY Headquarters Agreement,[36] but also as an independent responsibility for the Dutch police and security authorities. As such, the Netherlands seeks to restrict this responsibility to a minimum given the risks and the considerable financial costs involved. The ICTY's decision to allow the accused to stay in a hotel presumes the additional involvement of the Dutch police and security authorities during his stay. The accused is required to obey any instructions of the Dutch police and the Dutch authorities are apparently expected to monitor the accused's compliance with the conditions of his provisional release, including the possibility of arresting him should he fail to comply with these conditions. The Netherlands thus objected

34 Letter of the Netherlands Ministry of Foreign Affairs, 22 November 2002.

35 Prosecutor *v.* Vidoje Blagojević, Dragan Obrenović, Dragan Jokić, Momir Nikolić, *supra* n. 29, Request to the Netherlands to Attend a Status Conference on 27 November 2002, 25 November 2002, at 5-6.

36 Agreement between the Kingdom of the Netherlands and the United Nations concerning the Headquarters of the International Tribunal for the Prosecution of Persons Responsible for Serious Violations of International Humanitarian law Committed in the Territory of the former Yugoslavia since 1991, Trb. 1994, 35.

to the ICTY's imposing on it the burden of monitoring the compliance of accused with the conditions of his or her provisional release.

The Netherlands attempted to put this scenario in a broader perspective. First, it noted that, with the exception of transfer to and from the detention unit, it is not under any obligation to agree to the presence on its territory outside of the detention unit of an accused who has been provisionally released by the ICTY. While the Headquarters Agreement has a provision governing the entry into, exit from and movement within the territory of the Netherlands for explicitly named categories of persons, accused persons are not included.[37] The Netherlands argued that the Headquarters Agreement assumes in principle that accused persons will remain in the detention unit while on Dutch territory[38] and that it is its standard understanding, when commenting on the appropriateness of provisional release, that an accused will leave Dutch territory upon his or her provisional release.

Having made the argument that it is not under any obligation to accept provisionally released accused on its territory, the Netherlands turned to the question whether it is disproportionate and in contradiction of the status of a provisionally released person to require him or her to stay in the detention unit upon his or her return to the ICTY. In addressing this issue the Netherlands accepted, for the sake of argument, that in most jurisdictions provisionally released individuals are not usually required temporarily to return to pre-trial detention. However it noted, firstly, that in a national legal system a person who does not have legal title to stay in that jurisdiction will usually not be granted provisional release at all, and thus the issue of having to return to pre-trial detention would not arise. Secondly it questioned the transposition of a principle from national legal systems, according to which provisionally released individuals may not be required to be returned to pre-trial detention, to accused provisionally released by the ICTY. It noted that for a variety of reasons the situation in a national jurisdiction differs from the situation of the ICTY

37 *Id.* Article XXIII of the Headquarters Agreement provides that "All persons referred to in Article XIV [Judges, the Prosecutor and the Registrar], XV [officials of the Tribunal], XVII [persons performing missions for the Tribunal], XVIII [witnesses and experts appearing before the Tribunal] and XIX [counsel] of this Agreement as notified as such by the Registrar to the Government shall have the right of unimpeded entry into, exit from and movement within, the host country, as appropriate and for the purposes of the Tribunal. [...]"

38 In exceptional circumstances accused have been allowed to remain in a safe house. For example, in the case Prosecutor *v.* Tihomir Blaskić, General Blaskić was allowed to remain in a safe house while awaiting trial.

provisionally releasing an accused in the territory of the Netherlands. The ICTY, as an international tribunal, is not an organ of a State that has its own territory. It has jurisdiction over crimes committed in the territory of the former Yugoslavia and all of the accused have a nationality other than that of the Netherlands, which is the territory in which the ICTY is located;

> "[i]ndeed, in a national legal system the court granting the release will be part of the legal order in which the released person is to stay during his release, and the court will take the specific legal, social and political circumstances of that legal order into account, and any burden connected with the safeguarding or the security naturally rests on the state of the Court".[39]

In addition to these arguments, the Netherlands submitted that there was no indication that obliging an accused who has been provisionally released to temporarily return to detention, under circumstances similar to those in the present case, could be considered a violation of international norms, as codified in the European Convention on Human Rights. Further, argued the Netherlands, because what is granted is *provisional* release, this could be interpreted – in the specific context of the ICTY – to be limited to the State to which the accused is released. This will usually be that State which provides a guarantee to the ICTY; "in such an interpretation, the provisional release would, as it were, be geographically restricted and would not extend to the territory of the host State".[40]

Finally, the Netherlands noted that if a provisionally-released accused were allowed to stay on Dutch territory outside of the detention unit, legal difficulties would arise with regard to the power of the Dutch authorities to monitor the compliance of that accused with the conditions of his or her release and to arrest the individual if necessary. These measures impose a restriction of liberty – one which was not foreseen in the legislation implementing the Netherlands' obligations with regard to the ICTY. This legislation[41] only provides for such restrictions of liberty in the case of transferring an individual to and from the ICTY, and in the case of a request by the ICTY to the Netherlands for the arrest and surrender of an accused. Therefore, if it proved necessary to arrest a

---

39 Letter of the Netherlands Ministry of Foreign Affairs, 22 November 2002, para. 19.

40 *Id.*, para. 22

41 Wet van 21 april 1994, houdende bepalingen verband houdende met de instelling van het Internationaal Tribunaal voor de vervolging van personen aansprakelijk voor ernstige schendingen van het internationale humanitaire recht, begaan op het grondgebied van het voormalige Joegoslavië sedert 1991, Stb. 1994, 308.

provisionally-released accused, it might be necessary to utilize formal arrest and surrender proceedings.

As such, based on the specifics of the *Jokić* case[42] as well as the situation for accused in general, the Netherlands found that their right to provisional release granted by the ICTY could not be extended to provisional release on the territory of the Netherlands.

Despite these principal objections the Netherlands, in traditional Dutch fashion, tried to find a pragmatic solution to this problem. In January 2004 the Netherlands reached an agreement with the ICTY whereby provisionally-released accused, who return to the ICTY for a Status Conference or other hearing and therefore return to the Netherlands for a maximum of two nights, can stay in a hotel. The Netherlands and the ICTY agreed to a notification procedure for these individuals in which, *inter alia*, the ICTY would take responsibility for meeting the individuals upon their arrival and during their stay in the Netherlands. The accused, however, remain responsible for paying the costs of their stay, and as result this procedure has not been utilized as often as was originally envisaged.

4 Conclusion

Through both its roles as a Member State of the UN and as the host State to the ICTY, the Netherlands has helped to define the obligations States have toward the ICTY and the extent of accused's right to provisional release. As such, it has helped to chart the unknown terrain which the ICTY has to traverse. It has tried to do so in a way that is both principled yet practical, and operating from the premise that cooperation with the ICTY should be given where possible without jeopardizing its legitimate national interests.

42 *Supra* n. 29.

6

IUDEX NON CALCULAT

Experiences in Management of International Criminal Tribunals – Sierra Leone on a Shoestring?

Carl Peersman[*]

1 INTRODUCTION AND SUMMARY

This contribution attempts at indicating that in practice too little attention has been paid to the fact that international criminal tribunals, while some checks and balances may be present, do not operate in the same *trias politica* as domestic courts can.[1] For this reason, there is no executive organ, which, in the same way as a ministry of justice (or as in the Netherlands, an autonomous institution such as the Council for the Judiciary) takes care of all managerial issues necessary for the independent functioning of a court of law. In the two cases – the former Yugoslavia and Rwanda- in which the Security Council of the United Nations decided to establish an international criminal tribunal, based on Chapter VII of the UN Charter, it is at least formally possible to enforce policy. The arrears in contributions that existed and still exist in the financing of international criminal tribunals are just one example of how difficult the practice is. Against this background, it is understandable that the management

* Legal counsel at the International Law Division of the Ministry of Foreign Affairs of the Kingdom of Netherlands and representative of the Netherlands in the Management Committee for the Special Court for Sierra Leone from 2001-2005. The opinions in this essay are solely the author's and do not necessarily represent those of the Kingdom of the Netherlands.

1 On *trias politica* and international criminal courts, *see* D. Raab & H. Bevers, *The International Criminal Court and the Separation of Powers,* 3 International Organizations Law Review 93 (2006) at 132.

N. Blokker, R. Lefeber, L. Lijnzaad & I. van Bladel (eds.), *The Netherlands in Court. Essays in Honour of Johan G. Lammers*, © 2006 Koninklijke Brill NV. Printed in the Netherlands, pp. 105-124.

and budget of the tribunals in Sierra Leone and Cambodia, paid for out of voluntary contributions, is yet more complicated. To support both institutions there is oversight by and dialogue with a group of States, for example in a management committee or a group of interested States. Experience proves how difficult it is to distinguish between purely logistic and managerial issues and the administration of justice itself. To put it differently: many actors in the international field often do not make that principal difference.

This situation makes a prosecutor – and judges – less independent than he or she should be: it may well be so that a prosecutor has the pure and simple policy "to go where the evidence leads him"[2] ; in practice, he can only go as far in that direction as the voluntary contributions by the donor community to the criminal tribunal allow.

In addition, an even more fundamental problem may arise: the international community, often represented by the United Nations, wants assurances that international standards, such as human rights, due process, and independence of the judiciary, will be respected before any voluntary contribution is made. In some cases, the highly politicised situation in which a temporary tribunal has to be founded, often tailor-made to a specific situation in a specific State, can make this difficult: many of those involved have interests at stake which may stand in the way of their cooperation with independent adjudication. Due to this fact, international standards may be insufficiently met in the eyes of the international community, which then remains reluctant to contribute.

For these problems there is no panacea, but the new permanent International Criminal Court certainly can be part of the solution.

2 The Origin of International Criminal Tribunals

2.1 The Desirability of an "International Judicial Authority"

During the second half of the last century, there have been approximately 250 armed conflicts, both international and non-international. These conflicts have cost more than 86 million non-combatant civilians their lives, most of them women and children, and have caused an accumulated total of refugees and displaced persons of about 170 million people. After World War II, in reaction to this human suffering, international humanitarian law developed rapidly and

2 Maxim of David Crane, first Prosecutor of the Special Court for Sierra Leone.

substantially. Without credible international administration of justice to combat impunity for grave violations of international humanitarian law, however, this law often remains in the eyes of the victims to a high extent theoretical, even though it is true that it has been generally recognized that criminal tribunals are not the only means necessary to accomplish lasting and durable peace.[3] A difference with alternative mechanisms, such as for instance "truth commissions" is, however, that independent administration of justice does not lend itself for changing policy very easily. Once the law and procedures have been established, the tribunal has been installed and the defendant has been led to the dock, justice most literally must have its course, even if the most obvious political expedience of the day would command differently. It is cumbersome on the one side to negotiate with politicians like Milošević for peace in the former Yugoslavia and on the other to demand that he be prosecuted by a criminal tribunal for his role in the war preceding that peace. However, once the rules have been established, it is too late for a "peace versus justice" debate.[4] In the Rome Statute of the International Criminal Court, this has been implicitly recognised in Article 16, which gives the possibility for the deferral – not cancellation – of an investigation and/or prosecution.

In the General Assembly of the United Nations already in 1948, after the Nuremberg and Tokyo trials, the desirability of the existence of an international judicial authority to exercise jurisdiction over crimes such as genocide was introduced.[5] In 1951, there already was a draft statute, but not enough political momentum could be gained for its completion. The road to the entry into force of the Statute of the International Criminal Court began with initiatives to establish *ad hoc* and hybrid tribunals. Directly after the Cold War it was not possible to come to a permanent institution. The United States in particular, but also Russia, China and India refused and still refuse to allow for administration of justice that, as they see it, could surpass their own jurisdiction, effective-

3 *See also* S. Linton, *Cambodia, East Timor and Sierra Leone: Experiments in International Justice*, 12 Criminal Law Forum (2001) at 185: "For international tribunals to be correctly understood, they must first be recognised as being one of a range of transitional justice options, from those of a judicial nature to non-judicial truth seeking mechanisms [...] a single initiative on its own is unlikely to bring about a peaceful, stable and restored nation".

4 *Cf.* L. van den Herik, *Het Rwanda Tribunaal: Een waardevolle exercitie of weggegooid geld?*, 4 Justitiële Verkenningen 27 (2006) at 30.

5 *See* H. von Hebel, *An International Criminal Court – a Historical Perspective*, *in* H. von Hebel, J.G. Lammers & J. Schukking (eds.), Reflections on the International Criminal Court – Essays in Honour of Adriaan Bos 13 (1999) at 23.

ly opposing universality to date. At the same time, however, these four States did support the creation of some ad hoc tribunals. In 1993, the Security Council decided, two years after the outbreak of the civil war in Yugoslavia, to establish the International Criminal Tribunal for the former Yugoslavia (ICTY).[6] While establishing the ICTY, the Security Council clearly indicated which objectives it had in mind:

(1) to take effective measures to bring to justice the persons who are responsible for "flagrant violations of international humanitarian law";
(2) to provide redress to the victims;
(3) to halt further violations;
(4) to contribute to the restoration of peace by prosecuting the responsible persons.[7]

In 1994, the establishment of the International Criminal Tribunal for Rwanda (ICTR) followed,[8] and in the 2002, the Special Court for Sierra Leone.[9]

Also in 2002, the Rome Statute of the International Criminal Court came into force. On 11 April, the necessary number of 60 ratifications was met.[10] As indicated before, universality is yet to be achieved. In addition, the Statute of the International Criminal Court does not allow for retroactive exercise of

6 The ICTY was established by SC Res. 827 of 25 May 1993 in reaction to serious violations of international humanitarian law committed on the territory of the former Yugoslavia since 1991, and as an answer to the threat to international peace and security which followed from those violations.

7 Fifth, sixth and seventh preambular paragraphs of SC Res. 827 of 23 May 1993.

8 The International Criminal Tribunal for Rwanda was established by SC Res. 955 of 8 November 1994. The ICTR has jurisdiction to prosecute persons responsible for genocide and other grave violations of international humanitarian law, committed on the territory of Rwanda between 1 January 1994 and 31 December 1994. In addition, Rwandan nationals who committed such crimes on the territory of neighbouring states can be prosecuted.

9 The Special Court for Sierra Leone was established by treaty between the United Nations and Sierra Leone and is a separate international organisation, not an UN-institution. The mandate to negotiate such an agreement on behalf of the UN has been given to the Secretary-General in SC Res. 1315 of 14 August 2000.

10 As of 22 August 2006, there are 102 States parties to the Rome Statute, a majority of the 192 member states of the United Nations.

jurisdiction.[11] Therefore, it is clear that there is still place for other international, mixed or hybrid criminal tribunals.

The best-known examples of these tribunals are, in descending measure of international involvement, the mentioned Special Court for Sierra Leone, the Extraordinary Chambers in the Courts of Cambodia for the Prosecution of Crimes committed during the period of Democratic Kampuchea,[12] the Mixed Panels in Kosovo and the Special Panels for Serious Crimes in East Timor. Those last two examples are less relevant for the purpose of this contribution, since as part of UN missions, the United Nations Mission in Kosovo (UNMIK) and the United Nations Temporary Administration of East Timor (UNTAET), their management and budget are part of the responsibility of the United Nations itself.

The War Crimes Chamber in Bosnia is actually part of the Bosnian judiciary. Only the Registry is established by agreement between Bosnia and the High Representative.[13]

Mixed and hybrid forms of tribunals raise the issue who is responsible for the administration of those tribunals. In most cases, responsibility for the good functioning of the courts of law in a national jurisdiction is given to a ministry of justice, which is of all the government institutions best placed and closest to the functions of the court system. Therefore, the *trias politica* not only gives legitimacy, but in practical terms also a logistic and management framework.

11 Article 11 reads:
1. The Court has jurisdiction only with respect to crimes committed after the entry into force;
2. If a State becomes a Party to this Statute after its entry into force, the Court may exercise jurisdiction only with respect to crimes committed after the entry into force of this Statute for that State, unless that State made a declaration under article 12, paragraph 3.

12 The United Nations and Cambodia concluded an agreement on 6 June 2003, which regulates the establishment and functioning of the Extraordinary Chambers. The Chambers are part of the Cambodian judiciary, not a separate international organisation. The mandate for the United Nations to negotiate the agreement is given in GA Res 57/228 of 13 May 2003. The personal jurisdiction of the Chambers is limited to the top level leadership of the Khmer Rouge and those most responsible for crimes and serious violations of the Cambodian penal law, international humanitarian law, customs and international conventions, recognised by Cambodia, committed in the period April 1975 until January 1979, *see* Art. 5(3) of the Agreement.

13 A. Nollkaemper & S. Nouwen, *Gemengde tribunalen en hooggespannen verwachtingen*, 4 Justitiële Verkenningen 37 (2006) at 41, n. 14.

In the community of nations, there is no such thing as *trias politica*. All States are equal and sovereign. There is no government of the world, nor is there a world parliament. In spite of diplomacy and international negotiations, at the end of the day on a global level and in the absence of any law to the contrary, the maxim *par in parem imperium non habet* prevails. The General Assembly of the United Nations generally does not have the power to adopt binding resolutions. One of the exceptions of great practical importance here is Article 17 (1): "The General Assembly shall consider and approve the budget of the organisation".[14]

In addition, the Security Council, which for some instances has been given the powers normally reserved to the executive in a State, cannot be compared to a government.

2.2 Budgeting and Financing for the ICTY and the ICTR

In the case of the ICTY and ICTR however, both in respect of legitimacy and management and budgetary matters, there is still a reasonable degree of clarity. To begin with, all States are under the obligation to comply with resolutions adopted by the Security Council under Chapter VII of the Charter and furthermore, the budget is secured in a better way: it is the General Assembly, which adopts the budget and the scale of assessment for contributions.

The costs of the UN tribunals for Rwanda and Yugoslavia are both in relative and absolute sense very high. The budget for ICTY for the period 2006-2007 exceeds USD 305 millionD, while the budget for the ICTR for the same period is nearly USD 270 million.[15]

The total costs are borne by the membership contributions of 192 member States, which are mainly assessed according to their Gross National Product. This entails amongst others that half of the budget of the UN tribunals is assessed in the ordinary manner of the UN budget and the other half according to the assessment used for peacekeeping operations.[16] The budget of the tribu-

14 *See* M. Shaw, International Law (1997) at 3.

15 GA Res. 60/243 and GA Res. 60/241.

16 T. Ingadottir, *The Financing of Internationalized Courts and Tribunals*, *in* C. Romano, A. Nollkaemper & J. Kleffner (eds.), Internationalized Criminal Courts 271 (2004). The precise scale for peacekeeping operations is based on a case-by-case basis and approved by the General Assembly. The methodology used was approved by the GA in its Resolution of 11 December 1973. Under the method, the assessment of the poorer countries is reduced in accordance with the regular budget scale, and the reduction is

nals has to be approved, as is the case for the rest of the UN budget, by the General Assembly after it has passed the Fifth Committee of the United Nations. Preceding the Fifth Committee, the Advisory Committee on Administrative and Budgetary Questions has to give its advice first. By putting the budget in the framework of the Charter, a sanction has been created against non- or late payment of contributions. If a member State owes the Organization a total of contribution of last two years, Article 19 of the Charter is applied. This means that in principle such member State will lose its vote in the General Assembly. Doubts are expressed in the literature whether this sanction is severe enough to force States to pay in time, looking at the gross total of arrears. It has been suggested that the United Nations resort to measures that are more stringent such as interest on late payment or limitations on the hiring of nationals of States that are in arrears.[17]

3 The Special Court for Sierra Leone

From 1991 to 2000, a particularly vicious civil war raged in Sierra Leone between its government and the rebel Revolutionary Front, which abducted and recruited by force thousands of child soldiers. In this civil war, tens of thousands non-combatants perished. The winds of peace seemed to have prevailed when the warring parties signed the Lomé Peace Agreement on 22 May 1999.[18] In addition to the general ceasefire, this Agreement granted amnesty to the Revolutionary Front leader Foday Sankoh and his followers, appointed him Vice-President and made provision for the establishment of a truth and reconciliation process. When signing the Lomé Agreement, the Special Representative of the Secretary-General of the UN appended a statement that the United Nations understood that the amnesty provisions would not apply to international crimes of genocide, crimes against humanity, war crimes and other serious violations of international humanitarian law. Shortly thereafter, the United Nations Mission in Sierra Leone (UNAMSIL) was established to help

added to the assessment of the permanent members of the Security Council. When the ICTY and the ICTR were established, some states argued that contributions for the Tribunals should be assessed solely based on the peacekeeping budget scale, as the Tribunals were sub-organs of the Security Council.

17 Ingadottir, *supra* n. 16, at 273.

18 Peace Agreement between the Government of Sierra Leone and the Revolutionary United Front of Sierra Leone, Lomé (Togo, 18 May 1999), UN Doc. S/1999/777.

implement the Lomé Agreement and assist the disarmament, demobilisation and reintegration process.[19]

However fighting between government and rebel forces resumed in violation of the agreement. Revolutionary Front attacks on United Nations peacekeepers, in particular the abduction of 500 of them, hardened the position of the international community, and peace was only finally restored in spring 2000, also by intervention of the Economic Community of West African States (ECOWAS). These events all renewed the impetus to restore the rule of law in Sierra Leone through the means of criminal justice.

3.1 The Creation of the Special Court for Sierra Leone

In the summer of 2000, after the civil war in Sierra Leone had finally ended, President Kabbah of that country wrote a letter to the United Nations, dated on 12 June, in which he made a plea to the international community to prosecute those most responsible for the serious violations of international humanitarian law that had occurred.[20] When the letter was discussed in the Security Council, several members showed hesitance to establish a third UN tribunal, as the preceding two were widely perceived as slow and expensive. The Security Council eventually reached unanimity on 14 August 2000 when it adopted Resolution 1315, which included a mandate for the Secretary-General to conclude an agreement with the government of Sierra Leone on the establishment of an independent special tribunal based on voluntary contributions. The political will to come to a full-fledged third UN tribunal simply was not there. The US Ambassador literally said on this issue: "We wanted an international umbrella over the court but we didn't want to create a third tribunal, because they are very expensive and very slow."[21]

The Secretary-General had strongly opposed the creation of a court on the basis of voluntary contributions. He clearly writes in his Report on the Establishment of a Special Court for Sierra Leone: "[t]he risks associated with the establishment of an operation of this kind with insufficient funds, or without long-term assurances of continuous availability of funds, are very high, in terms

19 SC Res 1270 (1999).

20 Annex to the Report by the Secretary-General on Sierra Leone, UN Doc. S/2000/751, 31 July 2000.

21 *UN to Establish a War Crimes Panel to Hear Sierra Leone*, New York Times, 15 August 2000.

of both moral responsibility and loss of credibility of the Organization, and its exposure to legal liability", and concluded therefore that "... the only realistic solution is financing through assessed contributions".[22] The Netherlands, then a member of the Security Council supported this view. Financing and managing international criminal tribunals in practice are difficult tasks, as goes to show from the mushrooming budget and persistent arrears at ICTY and ICTR. Financing and managing an international criminal tribunal based on voluntary contributions is no less difficult and even more uncertain. The decision in favour of voluntary contributions was justified by some Security Council members by the fact that it was not the Security Council itself, which took the initiative to prosecute those most responsible for serious crimes of international humanitarian law during the Sierra Leonean civil war, but the President of Sierra Leone, Kabbah. Many in the Security Council did not feel it was justified to use its powers to bind the rest of the United Nations because of a request of one of its members and were afraid this might lead to a proliferation of requests for more expensive international tribunals.

The UN Secretariat was ordered to develop "a model similar in form, substance, and international legitimacy to the ad hoc tribunals, but one which respects a nation's vision of justice, its choice of means of bringing it about, and its ownership, at least in part, of the judicial process".[23] This process eventually led to the "Agreement between the United Nations and the Government of Sierra Leone and the Establishment of a Special court for Sierra Leone", which was concluded in Freetown on 12 January 2002.[24] The Agreement is the legal basis for both jurisdiction and legal personality of the Court. It should thus be borne in mind that by the Agreement a new international organisation was created. In this, the Special Court is different from the ICTY and ICTR, which are UN institutions. Privileges and immunities for the international prosecutor, judges and international staff are regulated by Articles 11 and 12 of the Agreement.

22 UN Doc. S/2000/915 (2000) at 13.

23 D. Shraga, *The Second Generation UN-Based Tribunals: A Diversity of Mixed Jurisdictions*, *in* Internationalized Criminal Courts, *supra* n. 16, at 15 *et seq.*

24 *See* http:/www.sierra-leone.org/specialcourtagreement.html.

3.2 The Creation of the Management Committee of the Special Court for Sierra Leone

In the case of the Special Court (as was also the case for the Extraordinary Chambers in Cambodia – see below) in the beginning there was nothing more or less than the free will of the parties concluding the agreement, the UN and the State in question, which was the basis for both substantive and procedural law. In addition, the limitations of any agreement show immediately: it cannot bind third parties. The agreement cannot force by itself Nigeria or Liberia to assistance and cooperation, as was necessary for the extradition of Charles Taylor, the former president of Liberia and one of the most important indicted persons by the Court.

One of the solutions found in practice to prevent a temporary criminal tribunal from functioning in a total vacuum is to install a management committee. The Security Council in the case of the Special Court for Sierra Leone has chosen this possibility.[25]

In a management committee, States that are willing and able to contribute can participate and in such manner keep an eye on both costing and financing of the court. In the case of Sierra Leone, this led to the situation that those countries most involved in the Security Council joined forces and formed a Management Committee with Sierra Leone and the Secretary-General, namely Canada, the Netherlands, United Kingdom and the United States. Nigeria and Lesotho also joined later.

In the Agreement between the United Nations and the Government of Sierra Leone on the establishment of a Special Court for Sierra Leone the parties agree in Article 7 that:[26]

(a) a Management Committee will be established;
(b) it will established by interested States, which are important contributors;

25 Letter by the President of the Security Council, UN Doc. S/2000/1234 (2000), para. 2.

26 Agreement between the United Nations and the Government of Sierra Leone on the establishment of a Special Court for Sierra Leone, Article 7, Management Committee: "It is the understanding of the Parties that interested States will establish a Management Committee to assist the Secretary General in obtaining adequate funding, and provide advice and policy direction on all non-judicial aspects of the operation of the Court, including questions of efficiency, and to perform other functions as agreed by interested States. The Management Committee shall consist of important contributors to the Special Court. The government of Sierra Leone and the Secretary-General will also participate in the Management Committee." *See* website of the Sierra Leone Special Court: http://www.sc-sl.org/documents.html.

(c) this Management Committee will assist in obtaining adequate funding;
(d) it will advise on all non-judicial matters of the Court, including efficiency;
(e) it will also perform other functions, as it agrees.

In 2002, the Management Committee elaborated its tasks more precisely in the following terms of reference:

(a) assisting in establishing the Special Court, including identifying possible candidates as registrar, prosecutor and judges for appointment by the UN Secretary-General;
(b) assess reports by the Special Court, and advising on all institutional aspects of its operations;
(c) monitoring the annual budget and other financial reporting and advising the UN Secretary-General on these issues;
(d) assisting the UN Secretary-General in obtaining adequate funds;
(e) encourage all States to co-operate with the Special Court;
(f) to report to a group of interested States (GIS).

The identification of judges and other officials in practice turned out to be a matter which the UN Secretariat was able to solve itself. The assessment and monitoring of progress in the establishment of the Court and later the "exit strategy" proved to be tasks that were labour intensive. The Management Committee consulted with the Court on the Financial Regulations, which it also adopted, and decided on a procedure for independent auditing of the budget. The Management Committee also played a role in assigning the contract for the construction of the building of the Special Court. The most important and most labour intensive however, turned out to be the never-ending quest for voluntary contributions.

The Management Committee is the point of contact between the Special Court and the whole of the UN community and therefore, the most important donors. The Management Committee institutionalised and thus enhanced this contact by establishing a group of interested States. This has proven to be very useful as an instrument to raise awareness in the UN community and to increase willingness to contribute.

In addition, this interaction made clear to the Court and the Management Committee that willingness to contribute also depended on the political opinion of States on the Special Court. They wanted to be sure that it made things better, rather than more complicated. In addition, they wanted to be sure that its goals were achievable.

One of the most debated issues here was the indictment of Charles Taylor, the former president of Liberia. The complication here was that Taylor, to facilitate the launching of peace negotiations between the Liberian government and the Rebels on 17 June 2003, was granted asylum from 4 June 2003 in Nigeria, a member of the Management Committee. Nigeria was only willing to extradite Taylor to Liberia. After the civil war and the election of the new President Ellen Johnson Sirleaf in 2005, Liberia requested the extradition of Taylor. After Taylor himself chose to flee from his place of exile in Calaba, Nigeria's president Obasanjo consented to this request. Liberia handed over Charles Taylor to the Special Court in Freetown. The Special Court, concerned with security risks requested the cooperation of the Netherlands, the seat of the International Criminal Court, to have Charles Taylor's case transferred to the Netherlands. To give legal basis for Taylor's transfer, custody and trial in the Netherlands, the Security Council adopted Resolution 1688 on 16 June 2006. The Netherlands subsequently agreed a headquarters agreement with the Special Court.[27] Although Resolution 1688 is sufficient as a legal basis for Taylor's trial in the Netherlands, to guarantee clear and adequate implementation, the Netherlands also adopted complementary legislation on transfer, security, immunities of witnesses, detention and legal cooperation.[28] Charles Taylor has been in custody at the detention centre of the International Criminal Court since 20 June 2006.[29]

The Management Committee after some debate, also enquired into the possibility of private funding, for instance by the Ford Foundation. However, after some enquiry on this issue, it was not possible to find private sources for the items that were suitable for private financing. Not all budget items lend themselves easily for private funding because of the need to maintain the independence of the Court.

Finally yet importantly, the Management Committee has supported calls from the Special Court directed at the Security Council and the General Assembly drawing attention to the often critical financial situation of the Court. All these actions were necessary to prove the limitations of voluntary financing. In this way, the Court was in a stronger position to ask for a subvention out of the UN budget, after the voluntary contributions had run out.

27 Trb. 2006, 131.

28 Stb. 2006, 315, 6 July 2006, *Wet Speciaal Hof voor Sierra Leone.*

29 ICC Press Release, *The Special Court for Sierra Leone to use ICC Facilities for Trial of Charles Taylor,* 21 June 2006.

3.3 Comparison with the Involvement of the UN Community with the Khmer Rouge Trials

Whereas cooperation between the United Nations and Sierra Leone on the Special Court most of the time seems to be good, cooperation between Cambodia and the United Nations on the Khmer Rouge trials proved to be difficult from nearly the beginning. With these cumbersome working relations, contact between Cambodia and the donor community was also difficult.

Some background information on the genesis of the Extraordinary Chambers therefore is indispensable. The first letter by Cambodia on the issue, in which both acting Prime Ministers, Prince Ranaridhh and Hun Sen, turned to the UN with a request for assistance in establishing the Khmer Rouge trials, already dates from 21 June 1997.[30] On 15 March 1999, an expert group, appointed by the UN Secretary-General, advised that an international tribunal should be installed. To this advice Cambodia reacted in June 1999. The then sole Prime Minister, Hun Sen, amended the request: the assistance should be directed at national administration of justice with participation of international judges and prosecutors. The UN in its place, tried to obtain enough guarantees that the trials would comply with international standards of justice. A critical point for the UN was to obtain enough certainty that a treaty to be concluded with the UN on assistance would prevail over national law. After minister Sok An, on 21 November 2001 communicated to the UN Legal Counsel, Under Secretary-General Hans Corell in a letter,[31] that this guarantee could not be given, the United Nations, after ascertaining that this was Cambodia's final position, broke off the negotiations on 8 February 2002. These were not reopened until after the General Assembly on 18 December 2002 adopted Resolution 57/228, in which the Secretary-General was requested to renew these negotiations. France and Japan took the initiative for this Resolution. Negotiations were restarted on 13 March 2003 in Pnom Penh.

Eventually an agreement was concluded on 6 June 2003 in Pnom Penh between the United Nations and Cambodia on the jurisdiction and installation

30 The General Assembly addressed this request by adopting para. 16 of GA Res 52/135: "Requests the Secretary General to examine the request, including the possibility of appointment of a group of experts to evaluate the existing evidence and propose further measures, as a means of bringing about national reconciliation, strengthening democracy and addressing the issue of individual accountability".

31 "While the Articles of Cooperation (draft agreement, CP) may clarify certain nuances in the Law, and elaborate certain details, it is not possible for them to modify, let alone prevail over, a law that has just been promulgated".

of "Extraordinary Chambers in the Courts of Cambodia for the Prosecution of Crimes Committed during the Period of Democratic Kampuchea".[32] The agreement mainly regulates the jurisdiction of the Extraordinary Chambers, their composition and decision-making. It also contains issues normally catered for in host country agreements between an organisation and the host State such as immunities and privileges.

As an indication of the eventual consent to the agreement by the United Nations the Secretary-General wrote in his Report on Khmer Rouge trials:

> "The Secretary-General considers the draft agreement a considerable improvement over the draft that had been under discussion during his previous negotiations with the government of Cambodia, particularly the provisions on the status of the agreement and its provisions regarding the procedures that would have to be followed in prosecutions and trials.[33] The negotiations which resulted in the elaboration of the text of the draft agreement were protracted and, at times, difficult. There still remains doubt in some quarters regarding the credibility of the Extraordinary Chambers, given the precarious state of the judiciary in Cambodia. It is however the hope of the Secretary-General that the government, in the implementation of the Agreement, would carry out fully the obligations it would assume. It is worthwhile noting that, under the terms of the draft agreement, any deviation by the government from the obligations undertaken could lead to the United Nations withdrawing its cooperation and assistance of the process."[34]

The main difference between these trials and the Special Court is that the trials in Cambodia will be part of the national jurisdiction of Cambodia, not of a separate international jurisdiction. The Court is an independent international organization, with legal personality and the capacity to conclude treaties. While it remains true that Sierra Leone does have influence in practical matters, it cannot challenge the independence or affect the functioning of the Special Court:

---

32 *See* http:/ cambodia.gov.kh/krt/english/ chronology.html. The text of the agreement can be found in GA Res. 57/228B.

33 *See* UN Doc A/57/769 (2003), para. 25, on the formulation of the Agreement in such a manner that it would constitute an international agreement, which would fall to be implemented in accordance with the requirements of the law of treaties. The paragraph does not, however elaborate Cambodia's view on this issue. Further in para. 26 the number of instances is changed from 3 to 2, which makes the Chambers less cumbersome. In para. 27 reference is made to the international standards of justice to be applied (amongst others Arts. 14 and 15 of the International Covenant on Civil and Political Rights on fairness and due process of law) .

34 *Id.*, Executive Summary.

for instance, it does not provide the majority of judges. In Cambodia implementation of the agreement remains within the hands of the original parties. For instance, while the UN Secretary-General on 9 March 2006 nominated seven international judges, it remained within the Cambodian jurisdiction to appoint five of those judges.[35] Eventually on 5 May 2006, a list, in which also a Netherlands judge, Katinka Lahuis, is included, was promulgated by royal decree.[36]

A similarity with the Special Court is that, in spite of the opposition of the UN Secretary-General to financing based on voluntary contributions, the General Assembly still decided to use this basis. The Secretary-General in response clearly indicated that the setting up of the Extraordinary Chambers would only be started if enough funding would be available beforehand, meaning that commitments were needed for the full budget for the three years of operations (USD 57 million) , and that all commitments for the first year budget needed to be received. The Secretary-General pointed to experience with the Special Court for Sierra Leone. Neither the UN Resolution, nor the agreement on assistance to Cambodia contained such a mechanism as the Management Committee of the Special Court. Reasons given for this absence were, amongst others, that the Extraordinary Chambers were part of the Cambodian jurisdiction and that it would be improper for other States to interfere.

Cambodia appointed a national task force for the daily contacts with the UN on the Extraordinary Chambers. The UN from its side established a special unit within the Office of the Controller (the representative of the Secretary-General in the Management Committee for the Special Court is normally a high-ranking official in the Office of Legal Affairs). Interested States organised themselves informally in a group of interested States.

As described above, the cooperation between Cambodia and the UN was far from optimum. This lack of cooperation contributed to the inability of the UN and Cambodia for a long period, either jointly or individually, to collect enough voluntary contributions. The possible donors indicated that they might be interested in more organized contacts and information. In reaction, the coordinator for the United Nations Assistance to the Khmer Rouge Trials (UNAKRT) started to consult with the group of interested States.[37] Initially this contact was meant to keep potential donors informed of the state of develop-

35 *Annan nominates Seven Judges for Cambodia's Khmer Rouge Trials,* 9 March 2006, http://bloomberg.com/apps/news.

36 NS/RKT/0506/214 at http:/Cambodia.gov.kh/krt/english/judicial_officers.htm.

37 *Id.*, at 3. The first meeting of the Group of Interested States and UNAKRT took place on 23 February 2004.

ments and discussions with Cambodia. Later the discussion concentrated more on the progress in the process of establishment. Both sides (UNAKRT and the Cambodian task force) were encouraged to cooperate better. In addition, the budget levels were discussed and the part that Cambodia had to finance itself. These consultations led to a successful pledging conference at the United Nations in New York on 28 March 2005, which collected over USD 38 million. The first year budget for the Extraordinary Chambers was met, mainly because of a substantial gift from Japan of USD 21 million. The Netherlands pledged USD 1.9 million.[38]

3.4 Comparison with the Assembly of States Parties of the Rome Statute for the International Criminal Court

The International Criminal Court was not born from an agreement between the United Nations and another international legal person. It came into existence after the Rome Statute, which was negotiated in a diplomatic conference in July 1998 in that city and entered into force in 2002. It has its own "general assembly" called the Assembly of States Parties. All States that have ratified have one vote in the Assembly. Many of the functions, which can be found in the Management Committee, in one way or another, can also be found in the Rome Statute in Article 112(2): The Assembly shall:

(a) Consider and adopt, as appropriate, recommendations of the Preparatory Commission;
(b) Provide management oversight to Presidency, the Prosecutor and the Registrar regarding the administration of the Court;
(c) Consider the reports and activities of the Bureau established under paragraph 3 and take appropriate action in regard thereto;
(d) Consider and decide the budget for the Court;
(e) Decide whether to alter, in accordance with article 36, the number of judges;
(f) Consider pursuant to article 87, paragraphs 5 and 7, any question relating to non-cooperation;
(g) Perform any other function consistent with this Statute or the Rules of Procedure and Evidence.

38 *See* http:/ cambodia.gov.kh/krt/english/ chronology.html.

The reason for creating a Bureau (mentioned in (c) of the Assembly of States Parties functions) is that such an institution can maintain day-to-day oversight of the budgetary and other non-judicial aspects of the Court. The Assembly of States Parties as a rule only meets for annual meetings and elections.

The budget for both the International Criminal Court itself and the Assembly of States Parties is collected through assessed contributions for the States Parties (Articles 115 and 117 of the Statute). The International Criminal Court follows the same principles here, as does the UN. Financing can also take place by funds provided by the United Nations, subject to approval of the General Assembly, in particular in relation to the expenses incurred due to the referrals by the Security Council.

On 31 March 2005, the Security Council adopted Resolution 1593, referring the situation in Darfur, Sudan to the Prosecutor of the ICC. As a consequence of this referral, the Prosecutor received the documents and archives of the UN International Commission of Inquiry on Darfur, as well as a sealed list of individuals named by the Commission as suspects of grave international crimes in Darfur, Sudan. Following examination of the documents, and interviews with more than 50 experts, the Prosecutor of the ICC decided that there was reasonable basis to initiate an investigation on Darfur. In the referral of the Darfur situation to the International Criminal Court, the Security Council omitted use of Article 115 (b), which allows funds to be provided by the United Nations, subject to the approval of the General Assembly, in particular in relation to the expenses incurred due to the referrals by the Security Council. This was so mainly because of opposition of the United States. In paragraph 7 of Resolution 1593 the Security Council recognizes "that none of the expenses incurred to connection with the referral including expenses related to investigations or prosecutions in connection with that referral, shall be borne by the United Nations and that such costs shall be borne by the parties to the Rome Statute and those States that wish to contribute."[39] The Statute leaves open the possibility for such voluntary contributions in Article 116.

None of these mechanisms could prevent arrears from being incurred in the payment of contributions to the International Criminal Court. These arrears are however, incomparable to the level of arrears at the ICTY and the ICTR, where States, be it out of incapacity or unwillingness, did not contribute. Such

39 "Recognizes that none of the expenses incurred to connection with the referral including expenses related to investigations or prosecutions in connection with that referral , shall be borne by the United Nations and that such costs shall be borne by the parties to the Rome Statute and those states that wish to contribute."

principled unwillingness is not found in the International Criminal Court. In more practical terms the first years of the ICC budget suffered from "underspending", rather than overspending.

4 Conclusions

The last decade showed, together with the coming into being of the International Criminal Court, an exponential growth of the number of international and "mixed" tribunals. At the same time, the membership of the United Nations proved to be more and more critical of what it perceived as the unacceptably slow and expensive administration at the ICTY and the ICTR.[40]

This led to a call for more inventive, quicker and cost-effective administration of justice. It has been put forward that funding by voluntary contributions would contribute to more discipline and efficiency with the tribunals. In practice, the tribunals did not show this desired adaptability.[41] This is not simply a matter of unwillingness: also in national jurisdictions, where there has been much more time to discover best practices'', the demands of human rights standards and the rule of law cause criminal justice to be of a procedurally complex, and in practice, often slow nature. It is therefore understandable that the international adjudication of war crimes, crimes against humanity or genocide, is even much more complicated and time consuming. It has to be borne in mind that those cases from both a legal and factual perspective are far more complex than the average common crime. Often violations have taken place over a longer stretch of time, in a larger area.

There is, however, a lack of political will in the donor community to continue to donate substantial amounts to various tribunals for the whole period

40 The delay of justice is a danger which threatens the credibility of all international criminal tribunals. The clearest example is possibly the trials against the leadership of the Khmer Rouge in Cambodia. Crimes to be prosecuted in those trials in some cases took place more than 30 years ago (the temporal jurisdiction of the Extraordinary Chambers is 1975-1979). *See also* Nollkaemper & Nouwen, *supra* n. 13.

41 Also the Sierra Leone Special Court which was thought to become less expensive and shorter in duration originally had an approved budget of USD 57 million for the three year period 2002-2005, eventually in August 2006 it had cost the donor community USD 82 million, while the work of the Special Court is not yet finished. This adds to credibility of the earlier budget presented by the Secretary General of USD 114 million. (A rule of thumb seems to be that one year of operations of the Court will cost USD 20-25 million).

of their existence (which in practice always need more time than foreseen). The results are that the prolongation of the Special Court has already been uncertain, and that the Extraordinary Chambers in Cambodia have not even started. The proliferation of international and internationalized criminal tribunals such as the Mixed Panels in Kosovo and the Special Panels for Serious Crimes in East Timor only makes this situation more complicated.[42] It has to be borne in mind that while all these tribunals have their own budgets, procedures and institutions, financing at the end of the day depends on the same group of possible donor countries (and often the same type of budgets with those donors). Meanwhile, new ideas for mixed or international criminal tribunals pop up.[43] This adds to the call for more streamlining and moderation and brings the International Criminal Court clearly in the picture.[44]

The International Criminal Court cannot be a total substitute for all possible future tribunals. First, as explained before, it does not exercise jurisdiction retroactively before the entry into force of the Rome Statute, 1 July 2002. Furthermore, the International Criminal Court functions based on so-called complementarity: only when a State Party is unwilling or unable to investigate and prosecute crimes under the jurisdiction of the Court, the Court will start its own investigation and prosecution of such situation.[45] In addition, there is the lack of universality. 102 States of the 192 States at the UN have ratified the Rome Statute. Important States as Japan and Russia are reluctant to ratify. India and China are even further away from joining, while the United States still opposes the International Criminal Court.

In spite of all these downsides, the temporary international tribunals and their accompanying institutions like the Management Committee of the Sierra Leone Special Court, remain of vital importance for the development of international criminal law. Apart from the new case law, managerial experience is gathered which can benefit the International Criminal Court (or any other new international criminal tribunal).

---

42 Six other international or internationalized criminal tribunals function besides the International Criminal Court.

43 UN Secretary-General, Press Briefing of 29 March 2006: The Secretary-General recommended "[...] specifically the proposed tribunal of an international character, which would deal with the assassination of former Prime Minister Rafik Hariri. Following consultations on that subject, the Council decided to request the Secretary General to negotiate an agreement with the Government of Lebanon aimed at establishing such tribunal based on the highest international standards of criminal justice".

44 *See* Ingadottir, *supra* n. 16, at 289.

45 *See also* Nollkaemper & Nouwen, *supra* n. 13, at 41.

Structures such as the Management Committee and the Group of Interested States of the Extraordinary Chambers can help to raise awareness with the donor community on what is needed in terms of budget and procedure. The tribunals on their turn can learn that they do not operate in a vacuum. To be able to achieve their goals, a tribunal will have to show results, which can generate enough political will -and thus resources- to support the tribunals.

The difference between the situation of Special Court for Sierra Leone where a Management Committee has a day-to-day oversight of developments and the situation of the Extraordinary Chambers is remarkable.

An international or internationalised criminal tribunal based on voluntary contributions will have to struggle for survival in any case, but an institution as the Management Committee can help to raise the necessary profile of such a tribunal. The Management Committee is a new element in the development of internationalised tribunals, and therefore in the development of international criminal law. The direct involvement from the donor States has contributed considerably to the negotiations between Sierra Leone and the United Nations, and therefore to the establishment of the Special Court. This involvement also proved to be fundamental in helping to collect international support for the Court, politically and financially.

This is an important lesson for the International Criminal Court as well: it needs to maintain contact with the rest of the international community, represented in the Assembly of State Parties. While the independence of the International Criminal Court should never be challenged, and individual cases should not be discussed, the International Criminal Court should not shy away from maintaining a dialogue with the international community, represented in the Assembly of States Parties, on how it sees international justice best served on a budget which by definition will always be limited. International criminal tribunals cannot function in splendid isolation, but need both a general political and administrative-financial framework within which they can operate. In the absence of a *trias politica* as can only exist within States, the international community – and international criminal tribunals – had, and still have to find, by trial and error, appropriate checks and balances to maintain legitimacy and to manage these tribunals.

7

FEELING THE HEAT IN GENEVA AND NEW YORK

The Netherlands Before the UN Treaty Bodies in Individual Complaints Procedures

Roeland Böcker[*]

1 Fear of a Binding Commitment

It can't be easy for – say – a Madagascan, Qatari or Vanuatuan member of the one of the UN treaty bodies to have to decide on a complaint from an individual directed against one of those West European know-alls. Those countries that have seen it all and refer constantly to their Strasbourg Court as the standard for everything they say and do. And then treat your non-binding views[1] with disdain, and try to fob you off with excuses.

It can't be easy – but is this in fact really the case? As often happens, the truth lies somewhere in the middle: Strasbourg Court, yes. Disdain, no. Non-

* Legal counsel at the International Law Division of the Ministry of Foreign Affairs of the Kingdom of the Netherlands, Agent of the Kingdom of the Netherlands to the European Court of Human Rights and the United Nations treaty bodies. The opinions in this essay are solely the author's and do not necessarily represent those of the Kingdom of the Netherlands. The author extends his gratitude to Neda Oliai for her preparatory contribution and to Julie Love for her linguistic comments.
An earlier overview of the UN treaty body case law concerning the Netherlands, entitled *Zweten in Genève (Nederland voor de VN-verdragscomités in individuele zaken)*, was submitted by the author to the conference 'Progressive supervision' held by the Dutch Human Rights Research School on 25 and 26 April 2000 in Woudschoten, the Netherlands.

1 In the relevant UN treaties, several terms are used to denote the final documents issued by the various treaty bodies in individual complaints proceedings. For the purposes of this article, the term 'views' is understood to encompass all of those.

N. Blokker, R. Lefeber, L. Lijnzaad & I. van Bladel (eds.), *The Netherlands in Court. Essays in Honour of Johan G. Lammers*, © 2006 Koninklijke Brill NV. Printed in the Netherlands, pp. 125-140.

binding, yes and no. Know-alls, sometimes. Excuses: a question of interpretation.

The status of the opinions given by the various UN treaty bodies is a sensitive subject that has now been documented in detail a number of times.[2] In a nutshell, they are non-binding in terms of international law, but they *are* morally binding. Now lawyers trained in domestic law usually regard international law as a fairly elusive subject, and their feelings on moral law are even stronger. And that is the problem in its entirety: in what way are we bound by the moral force of the UN treaty bodies' opinions? Anyone who knows should tell us now. In practice, a latent fear of a binding commitment can be detected here and there.

The following is intended to set out practice of the UN treaty bodies in cases against the Netherlands. Before that, a few comments will be made on the position of the Netherlands *vis-à-vis* the individual right of complaint under the UN human rights treaties in general.

2 In the Netherlands too?

The explanatory memorandum accompanying the Act approving the Optional Protocol to the International Covenant on Civil and Political Rights, which introduced the individual right of complaint under the Covenant, contains the following passage:

> "The procedure leads not to a binding decision but to the Committee communicating its views to the State Party and the individual in question. It is hoped that these views will nevertheless carry so much weight that all the parties involved will act accordingly."[3]

Similar considerations apply to the other conventions that provide for an individual right of complaint. This country too, therefore, fears binding commitment. On the other hand, the government of the Netherlands, hereafter referred to

2 *Inter alia*: M. Nowak, UN Covenant on Civil and Political Rights: CCPR Commentary, (2005) at XXIV *et seq.*; I. Boerefijn, *Follow-up of the views of the United Nations treaty bodies*, *in* T. Barkhuysen *et al.* (eds.), The execution of Strasbourg and Geneva Human Rights Decisions in the National Legal Order (1999) at 101 *et seq.*

3 TK, 1975-1976, 13932 (R 1037), No. 4, at 39.

as 'the government', takes the second sentence of the above quotation seriously, and for good reason. After all:

- the Constitution[4] obliges the government to promote the development of the international legal order; promotion of a uniform interpretation of human rights conventions at international level can be seen as part of the fulfilment of that obligation;
- the government is in most cases[5] a strong advocate of the individual right of complaint;
- the government regularly reminds other States of their obligations arising from the relevant conventions;
- if a State fails to act on the views of one of the committees, there is always a very real risk that the domestic courts will overrule the government; this may happen in a case already dealt with by the relevant committee or in any comparable case;
- parliament and non-governmental organisations will, where necessary, call the government to account in the event of violations of the conventions;
- last but not least, if a complaint has been upheld, its author must be able to have confidence in his government's willingness to respect the committee's views.

The scope for a government to ignore an opinion stating that a violation has taken place is therefore very limited. Only in exceptional cases would this be a proper course of action, if for example a treaty body had reached its conclusions on the basis of incorrect or incomplete information or if the opinions of the treaty body were incompatible with binding international law, for instance case law of the Court of Justice of the European Communities or of the European Court of Human Rights. With regard to the latter Court, the following is relevant here.

Article 35 of the European Convention on Human Rights provides that the European Court of Human Rights shall not deal with any application that is substantially the same as a matter that has already been submitted to another procedure of international investigation or settlement and contains no relevant new information. A matter which has been examined by the Human Rights Committee under the Optional Protocol to the International Covenant on Civil and Political Rights, for instance, is no longer admissible under the European

4 Art. 90.

5 The position of the government in the ongoing debate on an individual right of complaint under the International Covenant on Economic, Social and Cultural Rights constitutes a noteworthy exception.

Convention for that reason. Article 5 of the Optional Protocol, however, corresponds only in part to this provision of the European Convention, where it states that the Committee shall not consider any communication from an individual unless it has ascertained that the same matter *is not being examined* under another procedure of international investigation or settlement. This means that *after* such an examination – by the European Court, for instance – has been concluded, there is nothing to prevent the matter being put before the Human Rights Committee.

In order to safeguard symmetry between the regional and the global right of individual complaint, many European States, urged by the Committee of Ministers of the Council of Europe,[6] have become parties to the Optional Protocol to the International Covenant on Civil and Political Rights on the condition that the prohibition of the examination of the same matter should extend to cases already settled by another international authority, such as the European Court. In fact, the Netherlands was the first European State to ratify the Optional Protocol without entering such a reservation.[7] One of the government's arguments for doing so was the belief that a general practice by States of entering reservations might be imitated in other regions, thus undermining the universal system for the protection of individual human rights. The added value of the UN complaints procedures *vis-à-vis* regional mechanisms, after all, lies precisely in the fact that the former embody the universal validity of human rights.

Be that as it may, the government will obviously inform the Human Rights Committee, in any appropriate case, of the fact that the same matter has been examined by another body, in particular the European Court of Human Rights, thereby intending as much as possible to avoid diverging case law in the international arena and the ensuing uncertainty about the State's obligations under international law.[8]

6 UN Res. (70) 17 of 15 May 1970.

7 *See* M. Nowak, UN Covenant on Civil and Political Rights: CCPR Commentary, (2005) at 881. Only a limited number of European States adopted the same approach.

8 ICCPR Communication No. 977/2001, Brandsma *v.* the Netherlands; ICCPR Communication No. 1192/2003, M. de Vos *v.* the Netherlands.

3 The National Record

3.1 Introductory Remarks

The Netherlands may be confronted with individual complaints pursuant to the International Covenant on Civil and Political Rights,[9] the Convention against Torture and Other Cruel, Inhuman or Degrading Treatment or Punishment[10] and the International Convention on the Elimination of All Forms of Racial Discrimination,[11] the supervisory committees of which reside in Geneva, as well as the Convention on the Elimination of All Forms of Discrimination against Women,[12] the supervisory committee of which resides in New York.[13] Individual complaints have in fact been brought against the Netherlands under all of the treaties mentioned.

In answering the question as to what consequences should be drawn by the State from the views of the respective committees in individual cases in which a violation is found, attention should be paid to the wording of the views themselves, as well as to general principles of international law,[14] while not losing sight of the level to which the views are considered binding.[15] Adding up these sources, the State will normally be obliged, first of all, to translate and publish the views. Secondly, the State will be required to take measures for the benefit of the individual concerned, which may take the form of *restitutio*

9 Art. 1 of the Optional Protocol to the International Convention on Civil and Political Rights 1976, ratified by the Netherlands on 11 December 1978.

10 Art. 22 of the Convention against Torture and Other Cruel, Inhuman or Degrading Treatment or Punishment and Declaration by the Netherlands with respect to Artikel 22 of 21 December 1988.

11 Art. 14 of the International Convention on the Elimination of All Forms of Racial Discrimination and Declaration by the Netherlands with respect to Artikel 14 of 10 December 1971.

12 Art. 22 of the Optional Protocol to the Convention on the Elimination of All Forms of Discrimination against Women, ratified by the Netherlands on 22 May 2002.

13 Discussions are pending within the United Nations on a transfer of the Committee from New York to Geneva. This would emphasize the human rights relevance of the fight against discrimination against women, but would at the same time mean a shift away from 'mainstream' United Nations.

14 *See, in particular*, Draft articles on State Responsibility, Report of the International Law Commission, UN Doc. A/51/10 and Corr. 1, Parts 125-151., in particular Arts. 41 *et seq*.

15 *See also* Barkhuysen & Van Emmerik, *Improving the implementation of Strasbourg and Geneva decisions in the Dutch legal order: reopening of closed cases or claims of damages against the State*, *in* T. Barkhuysen *et al.* (eds.), *supra* n. 2., para. 7.2.

in integrum or compensation, according to the circumstances of the case and the nature of the violation found. Thirdly, the views may reveal deficiencies in domestic law or practice, in which case the State is required to take general measures, for instance to adopt new legislation, in order to avoid similar violations in the future. Finally, the State is normally requested to report back to the Committee on any measures taken.

In the following, the numbers of complaints lodged with each of the committees will be given,[16] as well as an overview of all cases in which the supervisory committees were of the view that the State of the Netherlands had violated one or more treaty provisions, including the consequences of those views, if any, at the national level.

3.2 The International Covenant on Civil and Political Rights

3.2.1 Number of Complaints

The Human Rights Committee, which supervises compliance with the International Covenant on Civil and Political Rights, has to date dealt with seventy-seven complaints against the Netherlands. twenty-two of these were declared inadmissible *ex officio*, that is to say, without being submitted to the government for comments. Thirty were declared inadmissible after the government had had the opportunity to submit comments on the complaint. The remaining twenty-five were assessed on their merits. In eighteen of those cases, no breach of the Covenant was established and in seven cases, or 9% of the total, the Committee found that violations had taken place. Finally, four cases are currently pending.

3.2.2 Social Security Issues

The first reprimand from the Human Rights Committee came on 9 April 1987 in the *Broeks*[17] and *Zwaan-de Vries*[18] cases. At the time, women applying for benefit under the Unemployment Benefits Act had to be breadwinners. That condition did not apply to men. The Committee considered this to be a violation of the principle of equality before the law, laid down in Article 26 of the

16 Where reference is made to pending cases, the situation as at 1 September 2006 is reflected.

17 ICCPR Communication No. 172/1984, Broeks *v.* the Netherlands.

18 ICCPR Communication No. 182/1984, Zwaan-de Vries *v.* the Netherlands.

Covenant. Following these two cases the legislation was amended with retroactive force, thus nullifying the violations.

On 26 July 1999, the Human Rights Committee found that the Netherlands had committed a violation of the Covenant in the *Vos* case.[19] In its views, the Committee again came to the conclusion that the principle of equality before the law as enshrined in Article 26 of the Covenant had been violated in the case of a married male former public servant who had received less pension from the Public Servants' Superannuation Fund (ABP) than a married female former public servant. The background of this case was as follows.

In the Netherlands public servants are eligible for both a public service or ABP pension and a general or AOW pension. The latter is linked to the minimum wage and is paid out in full after an insurance period of fifty years. An ABP pension is equal to 70% of the last salary and is paid out in full after a period of service of forty years. Before 1985 a married man was entitled to a general pension for a married couple, which was equal to 100% of the minimum wage. Single people of either sex were entitled to a general pension equal to 70% of the minimum wage. A married woman had no independent entitlement. To prevent overlapping of the two pensions, the AOW pension was incorporated into the ABP pension, that is to say, it was deemed to form part of the ABP pension. In practice, the amount of the general pension was deducted from the ABP pension. The maximum amount that could be incorporated was 80%, 2% for each year of service. For married female public servants the amount was calculated on the basis of the AOW entitlement of a single woman, and was therefore up to 80% of 70% of the minimum wage. On 1 April 1985 married women became entitled in their own right to a general pension. Since that date, each partner has been entitled to an amount equal to 50% of the minimum wage. The ABP scheme was amended accordingly, so that the amount incorporated was the same for men and for women. However, and here lies the crux of the problem, the old rules still applied to entitlements built up before the amendment was introduced.

Mr Vos filed an objection to this state of affairs on 29 November 1990. The Central Appeals Tribunal asked the European Court of Justice for a preliminary ruling on the issue. The Court of Justice held that the old method of calculation was indeed discriminatory and therefore incompatible with Article 119 of the EC Treaty, but that the restitution on the grounds of discrimination of rights in respect of entitlements built up in the past could be limited to those

19 ICCPR Communication No. 786/1997, Vos *v.* the Netherlands.

who had filed a claim before 17 May 1990. Mr Vos was not among the latter group. 17 May 1990 was the date on which the Court of Justice had published its Judgment in the *Barber* case.[20] In what is known as the Barber protocol,[21] the EU Member States agreed that payments made under a company or sector-wide social insurance scheme could not be considered as wages if and insofar as they could be attributed to periods of work preceding 17 May 1990, except in respect of claims submitted before that date. At national level, therefore, Mr Vos's claim was dismissed.

Things turned out differently though in Geneva, where the Human Rights Committee agreed with the European Court of Justice that the old arrangement was discriminatory, but did not accept the time restriction imposed by the Court. The Committee's succinct conclusion was that the author had to date received less pension than a woman in similar circumstances, which was regarded as incompatible with Article 26 of the Covenant. In a nutshell, the government should have equalised the pensions in 1985. The State was required to provide the author with an effective legal remedy, to take measures to prevent similar violations in the future, to translate and publish the Committee's views and to inform the Committee within ninety days of the measures taken.

The government rapidly complied with the last two requests from the Committee[22] and, in addition, offered the author to reimburse any costs he had made in relation to the proceedings before the Committee. The issue of providing an effective remedy and preventing future violations, however, was much less straightforward. On 25 October 1999, the government informed the Committee that it would not act upon its opinion in that regard. It put forward a number of arguments to justify this decision in its written response to the Committee. First, the government referred to the nature of the Dutch pension system, which is a 'funded system' (*opbouwstelsel)*. This means that entitlements to pension are built up during the years of employment and not, as in assessment systems, calculated at the moment of retirement. As a consequence, differences in the building up of pension entitlements, even if they are discriminatory, may lead to different levels of pension years later. The fact that in the meantime the funding system has been changed to bring it into line with modern views on the equality of the sexes and therefore with international law, makes no difference to the way in which the old system was funded.

20 European Court of Justice C-262/88, Barber, 1990 ECR I-1889.

21 Protocol No. 2 to Artikel 119 of the EC Treaty, concluded by the Member States in December 1991 at the same time as the Maastricht Treaty.

22 Stcrt. No. 214, 5 November 1999.

The government argued that in its interpretation the European Court of Justice had taken into account the funded nature of the ABP pension and other supplementary pension schemes in several Member States. The Court had also appreciated the disruption to the pension system that would be caused by giving the principle of equality of treatment unlimited retroactive force. At the same time, it aimed to safeguard the rights of those who had taken legal action on their own initiative before the date of the *Barber* Judgment. This application of the principle of equal treatment balances the interests of all those concerned: public servants and other employees, public authorities and other employers, pension claimants and pension funds. Putting the Committee's views into practice would lead, *de facto*, to the abolition of the funded system, since taken to their logical conclusion, they imply that pensions should be calculated on the basis of what is considered equitable at the moment they are paid out. But the funded system was not in itself called into question in the Committee's views. Disrupting that system would also seriously undermine legal certainty: pension claimants who up to now have been sure of their entitlements would suddenly have them called into doubt. In this situation the government did not wish to draw such far-reaching conclusions. It justified its decision by referring to the requirements of legal certainty and the uniform application of the law in relation to the law of the European Community.

The *Derksen & Bakker* case,[23] of 1 April 2004, is the most recent Dutch case in which a treaty body found a violation. The complainants are mother and daughter. The father died in 1995. Since both parents were not married, no pension rights existed on the basis of the Widows and Orphans Benefits Act (AWW). That situation was not in contradiction with the human rights conventions. According to legal doctrine, difference in treatment between married and unmarried couples may be justified, as it is up to the persons involved to make a choice for or against marital status. In 1996, the Surviving Dependants Act (Anw) replaced the AWW. The Anw lifted the difference in treatment with a view to developments in society. This amendment, however, did not have retroactive force. Under the old law, the married surviving parent received an additional benefit for care of a child. Under the new law, the unmarried surviving parent became equally entitled to a benefit. It is important to note that under both laws it is the parent who receives the benefit, not the child, the 'half-orphan'.

---

23 ICCPR Communication No. 976./2001, Derksen & Bakker *v.* the Netherlands. The Committee's views are annotated by Prof. Manfred Nowak in 2005 (No. 2) NJCM-Bull., at 186-192.

Although the Anw was not introduced to repair a human rights violation – as there was none, which is acknowledged by the Committee – and although the Anw system itself *a fortiori* does not amount to a human rights violation, the Committee nevertheless finds unjustified discrimination in the lack of a transitional rule in favour of children, one of whose parents died before the entry into force of the new law. There is thus no discrimination of the latter with respect to children born from married parents, but with respect to children one of whose unmarried parents died after the entry into force of the law. The Committee requested the government to grant a half-orphan's pension to the child and to take the necessary measures to avoid similar violations in the future.

In its response,[24] the government indicated that it was unable to agree with the Committee's views. The government failed to see how there can be unequal treatment in a situation in which none of the groups compared can derive entitlements from the legislation concerned. It stated that no half-orphans can claim entitlement in their own right to surviving dependants' benefit, not even those who were born from a relationship, marital or otherwise, which ended after 1 July 1996 with the death of one of the parents. The government furthermore observed that one can only speak of a victim of direct or indirect discrimination, when someone is denied certain rights that are accorded to others in the same situation. In the case at issue this would be the surviving parent. It is the surviving parent to whom the benefit – including the extra amount – is awarded, and who may dispose of it entirely as he or she sees fit. Although the additional benefit is awarded to help pay for the maintenance of minor children, the State does not possess any instrument to guarantee or verify that it is used in this way. However, precisely in relation to the person entitled to benefit, the surviving parent, the Committee had determined that the failure to apply the new legislation to old cases does *not* amount to discrimination within the meaning of Article 26.

Besides the dissenting opinions of two members of the Committee,[25] the government derived support for its opinion from the Judgment of the European Court of Human Rights in a comparable case,[26] which dealt with half-orphans'

24 Stcrt. No. 165, 30 August 2004.

25 Nisuke Ando and Sir Nigel Rodley.

26 European Court of Human Rights, Van den Bouwhuijsen & Schuring *v.* the Netherlands, Decision of 16 December 2003, Appl. No. 44658/98. According to the Court, this case was different from the cases of Gaygusuz *v.* Austria, Appl. No. 17371/90, Judgment of 16 September 1996, and Wessels-Bergervoet *v.* the Netherlands, Decision of 3 October 2000, Appl. No. 34462/97, in which the applicants did fulfil the conditions for entitle-

benefit under the old legislation, the AWW. In that Judgment, the Court pointed out that benefit for the half-orphan had been refused not because the child had been born out of wedlock, but because the AWW did not provide for entitlement to benefit for half-orphans.

3.2.3 Other Issues

On 23 July 1990, the Human Rights Committee found that a violation of the Covenant had occurred in the *Van Alphen* case.[27] The Committee considered that the author had been held in pre-trial detention in order to compel him to talk; this qualified as arbitrary detention and therefore constituted a breach of Article 9, paragraph 1 of the Covenant. Although the government was unable to share the Committee's opinion, an *ex gratia* payment of 5,000 Dutch guilders was made to the author out of respect for the Committee.

On 31 October 1994, the Human Rights Committee gave its opinion in the *Coeriel & Aurik* case.[28] The authors had wanted to change their family names to Hindu names in order to be able to train as Hindu priests. The Committee believed that Article 17 of the Covenant regarding the right to privacy offers protection against arbitrary or unlawful interference in the right to choose or alter one's family name. It held that the refusal to change the names was arbitrary because it was not based on "grounds that are reasonable in the specific circumstances of the case". The Committee held the view that the State was obliged to offer the authors an "appropriate remedy" and if necessary to take measures to prevent similar violations in the future. In response, the government offered the authors the opportunity to change their names, with the customary fees being waived. The government's view was that the law on names as it stood offered sufficient guarantees that no future violations would occur.

On 14 May 2000, the Human Rights Committee found a violation of the Covenant in the case of *Jansen-Gielen*.[29] In domestic proceedings before the Central Appeals Tribunal, the complainant had submitted a document in support of her case only two days before a hearing. Although the Central Appeals Tribunal did not deny the importance of the document, it had refrained from examining it, since it was lodged out of time, thereby leaving insufficient time

---

ment to benefit under the relevant social security schemes. In those cases, the refusals to grant benefit were based on nationality and sex, respectively.

27 ICCPR Communication No. 305/1988, Hugo van Alphen *v.* the Netherlands.

28 ICCPR Communication No. 453/1991, Coeriel & Aurik *v.* the Netherlands.

29 ICCPR Communication No. 846/1999, Jansen-Gielen *v.* the Netherlands.

for the other party to respond to it. The Committee did not follow this reasoning. The submission of documents was not limited by law to a specific term. The Central Appeals Tribunal should have admitted the document in the proceedings and, if considered necessary, postpone the hearing in order to give an opportunity to the other party to react to it. The principle of fair trial, laid down in Article 14 of the Covenant, was thus violated. The Committee was of the opinion that the complainant was entitled to an adequate compensation. Consequently, the government offered the complainant an amount of 8,500 Dutch guilders, of which an amount of 5,000 Dutch guilders was offered *ex gratia*.

3.3 The Convention against Torture and Other Cruel, Inhuman or Degrading Treatment or Punishment

3.3.1 Number of Complaints

The Committee against Torture has dealt with fifteen cases against the Netherlands. They all related to the ban on *refoulement* to a country where the person threatened with expulsion faced a serious risk of torture. One of the cases was declared inadmissible *ex officio*. In twelve cases the Committee found no evidence of violations while in one case it did. In the fifteenth case the author disappeared before the Committee could reach its opinion, and the case was discontinued. I shall return to this last case in greater detail for reasons set out below. No cases against the Netherlands are currently pending before the Committee.

3.3.2 Specific Cases

The Committee against Torture held on 13 November 1998 in the case of *A v. the Netherlands*[30] that the proposed expulsion of the author to Tunisia constituted a violation of the ban on *refoulement* as referred to in Article 3 of the Convention. The government therefore decided not to expel the author.

Since then, no further violations by the Netherlands have been found by the Committee. An issue that nevertheless merits attention is the power of the Committee to request a State to suspend the expulsion of an author while his

30 CAT Communication No. 91/1997, A *v.* the Netherlands.

or her communication is being dealt with by the Committee.[31] After two such requests from the Committee on previous occasions[32] and regular requests to the same end from the European Court of Human Rights[33] in expulsion cases – with which the government invariably complied – in the *Rajendram* case,[34] the Minister of Foreign Affairs and the State Secretary for Justice saw no reason to comply with a request not to expel the author to Sri Lanka. A factor affecting this decision was that his application for admission as a refugee, settled by a court review in the light of Article 3 of the European Convention on Human Rights, had been declared manifestly ill-founded. In addition, the importance of effective control of the external Schengen borders was taken into account since the author had been refused entry to the Netherlands and had ended up in the border detention centre at Schiphol Airport on the basis of Section 7a of the Aliens Act. Following a storm of protest,[35] and criticism of the government's attitude by the Committee in its opinion on admissibility of the communication,[36] the author was admitted to an asylum centre for a medical examination requested by the Committee in the same opinion. In the summer of 1999 the author disappeared. In its opinion of 19 November 1999, the Committee regarded that disappearance as a reason to discontinue the hearing of the case, and stated that it could be resumed if there were grounds for doing so. To date there have been no grounds for resuming the hearing.

31 Rule 108, para. 9 of the Rules of Procedure of the Committee against Torture.

32 CAT Communication No. 36/1995, X *v.* the Netherlands and CAT Communication 96/197, A *v.* the Netherlands.

33 By virtue of rule 39 of the Rules of the European Court of Human Rights.

34 CAT Communication No. 124/1998, Joseph Rajendram *v.* the Netherlands.

35 TK, appendix to Parliamentary Proceedings Nos. 897 and 1207, 1998-1999, questions put by member of parliament Halsema and answers given by State Secretary for Justice Cohen; E. Rieter, T. van Boven & C. Flinterman, *Nederland wil asielzoeker uitzetten in strijd met een interim-maatregel van het VN-Comité tegen Folteringen* ("The Netherlands wants to expel an asylum seeker contrary to an interim measure requested by the UN Committee against Torture"), 20 NJB 908 (1999); letter from the AIV of 13 July 1999 (ref. AIV-066/99) and reply from the Minister of Foreign Affairs of 19 August 1999.

36 Dated 12 May 1999.

3.4 The International Convention on the Elimination of All Forms of Racial Discrimination

3.4.1 Number of Complaints

The Committee on the Elimination of Racial Discrimination has dealt with three complaints against the Netherlands and in two of those found that breaches of the International Convention on the Elimination of All Forms of Racial Discrimination had occurred. No cases are currently pending before the Committee.

3.4.2 Specific Cases

On 10 August 1988, the Committee on the Elimination of Racial Discrimination held in the *Yilmaz-Dogan* case[37] that a Turkish employee had been dismissed on discriminatory grounds and that this constituted a violation of the ban on discrimination in respect of the right to work as laid down in Article 5(e)(i) of the Convention. The author received 10,000 Dutch guilders from the State in compensation.

On 16 March 1993 the Committee found once again that there had been a violation of the Convention, this time in the *Karim* case.[38] The author, who was of Moroccan origin, had been the victim of racial threats from local people in the area in which he had been assigned a house. The Committee considered these threats to constitute "incitement to racial discrimination and to acts of violence against persons of another colour or ethnic origin" as referred to in Article 4(a) of the Convention. It held that the State had failed to provide "effective protection and remedies" as required by Article 6 of the Convention. The Committee recommended that the State should review its policy on the prosecution of racial discrimination and offer the author compensation for non-material damage. The entry into force on 1 September 1993 of new and more stringent Discrimination Guidelines complied with the first recommendation, while fair compensation of 8,500 Dutch guilders and the same amount to cover legal costs was paid to the author in fulfilment of the second.

37 CERD Communication No. 1/1984, A. Yilmaz-Dogan *v.* the Netherlands.
38 CERD Communication No. 4/1991, Larbi Karim *v.* the Netherlands.

3.5 The Convention on the Elimination of All Forms of Discrimination Against Women

Last but not least, the Committee on the Elimination of Discrimination Against Women has so far given its views concerning one complaint against the Netherlands, which it considered to be unfounded.[39] A second complaint is currently pending.

4 Conclusions and Final Remarks

The first conclusion to be drawn from the above summary is the fairly limited number of cases against the Netherlands in which a human rights violation was found, in light of the fact that the Netherlands has – decades ago or very recently – accepted all available individual complaints mechanisms. In a total of ten cases a treaty body found one or more violations.[40]

A second conclusion is that the output of the more specialised procedures, focusing on torture, racial discrimination and discrimination against women, is, at best, marginal in relation to the output of the procedure under the Optional Protocol to the International Covenant on Civil and Political Rights. The extremely limited number of complaints under the former procedures which were considered to be founded, three in total, does not point at significant added value of those mechanisms.

A third and final conclusion is that the only part of the case law of the committees which has proved to be more than casuistry, is the Human Rights Committee's case law on social security issues. It is in the latter area that the State was confronted with views that had potentially far-reaching impact. However, two considerations concerning that impact are of paramount importance. First, it cannot be denied that the Committee's views either concerned issues that had already been settled at the domestic level,[41] or were not accepted by the government, *inter alia* for being incompatible with other international case law.[42] The Committee's views in the latter cases, although duly translated and published, together with the government's response, did not lead to any political

39 CEDAW Communication No. 3/2004, Dung Thi Thuy Nguyen *v.* the Netherlands.

40 By way of comparison: the European Court of Human Rights, in recent years, has found some seven violations by the Netherlands *per year*.

41 Broeks *v.* the Netherlands, *supra* n. 17; Zwaan-de Vries *v.* the Netherlands, *supra* n. 18.

42 Vos *v.* the Netherlands, *supra* n. 42; Derksen & Bakker *v.* the Netherlands, *supra* n. 42.

debate at the domestic level. Second, since the last views of the Committee were issued, the Netherlands has become a party to Protocol No. 12 to the European Convention on Human Rights. This Protocol introduces a general prohibition of discrimination, no longer restricted to discrimination in relation to the other rights set out in the Convention and its Protocols, as was the case beforehand. The conclusion is justified that the entry into force of Protocol No. 12 in respect of the Netherlands will render obsolete the added value of the relevant provision in the International Covenant on Civil and Political Rights.

8

THE NETHERLANDS BEFORE THE EUROPEAN COURT OF HUMAN RIGHTS

Jolien Schukking[*]

1 INTRODUCTION

Judge Rolv Ryssdal, one of the great Presidents of the European Court of Human Rights, described in a public lecture in 1995 the birth and the growth of the Convention for the Protection of Human Rights and Fundamental Freedoms ('the Convention') in these terms:

> "The arrival on the scene of international law of what was a new species of international instrument aroused little more than polite curiosity at the time. Its infancy was difficult and for many years its role and future were uncertain. Almost exactly forty-five years later, it has developed into a regional system of unparalleled effectiveness. Its scope, its influence and the number of States that have agreed to abide by its standards have grown far beyond the most optimistic predictions of its founders. It is ... no exaggeration to say that, at least as far as the democratic protection of individuals and institutions is concerned, the Convention has become the single most important legal and political common denominator of the States of the continent of Europe in the widest geographical sense."

---

* Legal counsel at the International Law Division of the Ministry of Foreign Affairs of the Kingdom of the Netherlands, Agent of the Kingdom of the Netherlands to the European Court of Human Rights and the United Nations treaty bodies. The opinions in this essay are solely the author's and do not necessarily represent those of the Kingdom of the Netherlands.

N. Blokker, R. Lefeber, L. Lijnzaad & I. van Bladel (eds.), *The Netherlands in Court. Essays in Honour of Johan G. Lammers*, © 2006 Koninklijke Brill NV. Printed in the Netherlands, pp. 141-164.

Since that speech was delivered, the influence of the Convention has continued to spread: the number of Contracting States has grown to forty-six, stretching from the Atlantic to the Pacific, with a total population well above 800 million.[1]

This book is entitled *The Netherlands in Court*. The international court that has adjudicated in more cases involving the Netherlands than any other is, without a doubt, the European Court of Human Rights ('the Court') in Strasbourg. This Court has handed down approximately 120 judgments on the merits in Dutch cases, as well as countless decisions. At present, the Court receives an average of 500 applications per year against the Netherlands. The Court's case law has had an enormous impact on the Dutch legal system, leading to the amendment of many laws and policies. This article provides examples of this process.

Does all this give cause for concern about the human rights situation in the Netherlands? No, that conclusion would be unjustified. One should not forget that only a very small proportion of the individual applications result in a judgment against the Netherlands, as shown by the above mentioned figures. From the number of applications it can be deduced that those who feel that the Netherlands has violated their rights have found their way to Strasbourg. From the relatively low number of judgments one can at the same time conclude – in view of the subsidiary nature of the legal protection offered by the Court – that the Convention forms an integral part of the legal framework used by national courts when hearing cases.

Within the scope of this article, it would be impossible to cover all the judgments in cases involving the Netherlands, or even all the influential judgments. I have therefore chosen to highlight a selection of cases that illustrate the impact of the Court on the development of the law in the Netherlands. In doing so, I will make a distinction between judgments delivered in the period before 1998 and judgments delivered in the period 1999-2005. In late 1998, a constitutional change in the monitoring system took place: the new, permanent and full-time European Court of Human Rights came into being, replacing the part-time Commission and Court. Let me begin, however, by setting the scene with some introductory remarks on the Convention.

1 Philip Leach, Taking a Case to the European Court of Human Rights (2001), Foreword by Sir Nicolas Bratza.

2 The European Convention on Human Rights

2.1 Historical Background

Partly in response to the atrocities suffered and the serious human rights violations encountered during the Second World War, ten Western European States founded the Council of Europe on 5 May 1949.[2] A year later, three more countries acceded to this organization.[3] Like the Charter of the United Nations, the preamble to the Statute of the Council of Europe refers to human rights without defining them.[4] And like the UN, the Council of Europe felt the need to supplement the treaty establishing the organization with a legally binding text to ensure respect for human rights in practice. Its members very soon reached agreement on a catalogue of fundamental rights and a mechanism for their protection. The result, the Convention for the Protection of Human Rights and Fundamental Freedoms, was opened for signature in Rome on 4 November 1950 and entered into force on 3 September 1953. The Netherlands ratified the Convention on 31 August 1954. Over time, the membership of the Council of Europe grew, and with it the number of contracting parties to the Convention. After the fall of the Berlin Wall on 9 November 1989, the countries of the former Soviet bloc were quick to join the organization, and in 1996 Russia too became a member. This increase in membership led to an enormous upsurge in the number of applications to the Court, which in turn prompted far-reaching reforms of the Court's organization. Today, the Council of Europe has forty-six Member States, and in 2005 the Court received more than 40,000 applications, including 511 complaints against the Netherlands.

2.2 The Substantive Rights of the Convention and its Protocols

The Convention lays down civil and political rights and freedoms: the right to life (Article 2), the prohibition of torture (Article 3), and of slavery and forced labour (Article 4), the right to liberty and security (Article 5), and to

---

2 Belgium, Denmark, France, Ireland, Italy, Luxembourg, the Netherlands, Norway, Sweden and the United Kingdom.

3 Germany, Iceland and Turkey.

4 In the preamble to the Statute of the Council of Europe, its founders refer to 'the spiritual and moral values which are the common heritage of their peoples and the true source of individual freedom, political liberty and the rule of law, principles which form the basis of all genuine democracy'.

a fair trial (Article 6), the principle of legality (Article 7), the right to respect for private and family life (Article 8), of freedom of thought, conscience and religion (Article 9), of freedom of expression (Article 10), and of assembly and association (Article 11), the right to marry (Article 12) and the right to an effective remedy (Article 13). Article 14 prohibits discrimination, but only in connection with securing the enjoyment of the other rights and freedoms set forth in the Convention. These substantive rights have been supplemented by additional protocols to the Convention. In current legal practice, Article 1 of Protocol No. 1, on the protection of property, is the most important of the additional provisions. The most politically significant additional protocols to have been adopted are No. 6, on the abolition of the death penalty, and, as an extension thereof, No. 13, on the abolition of the death penalty in all circumstances, even in times of war. Protocol No. 12 could become of great importance in the coming decades, since it prohibits discrimination in general, not only in relation to other Convention rights as Article 14 of the Convention does.

2.3 The Right of Individual Petition

The Convention created a right of individual petition – the right of individuals and organizations to challenge their governments through the Strasbourg process, by taking their case to the European Commission of Human Rights and the European Court of Human Rights. The Court's judgments are legally binding on the States Parties to the Convention. Although at first the acceptance of this right of individual petition was optional and it could therefore be exercised only against those States which had accepted it, it was in many ways revolutionary, given the strength of notions of State sovereignty at the time of the creation of the Convention. Protocol No. 11 to the Convention made it compulsory to recognise this right.

2.4 Enforcement Mechanism

The original monitoring system

Under the Convention in its original version, three institutions were entrusted with responsibility for enforcing the obligations entered into by the Contracting

States: the European Commission of Human Rights ('the Commission'),[5] the European Court of Human Rights,[6] and the Committee of Ministers of the Council of Europe, which is composed of the Ministers of Foreign Affairs of the Member States or their representatives. The acceptance of the Court's jurisdiction was optional. Complaints were first subject to preliminary examination by the Commission, which determined their admissibility. Where an application was declared admissible, the Commission placed itself at the parties' disposal with a view to reaching a friendly settlement. If no settlement was forthcoming, it drew up a report establishing the facts and expressing an opinion on the merits of the case. The report was transmitted to the Committee of Ministers. Where the respondent State had accepted the compulsory jurisdiction of the Court, the Commission and/or the Contracting State concerned could, within a period of three months following the transmission of the report to the Committee of Ministers, bring the case before the Court for a final, binding adjudication. Individuals were not entitled to bring their cases before the Court. If a case was not referred to the Court, the Committee of Ministers decided whether there had been a violation of the Convention and, if appropriate, awarded 'just satisfaction' to the victim. The Committee of Ministers also had responsibility for supervising the execution of the Court's judgments.[7]

The current monitoring system

From 1980 onwards, the steady growth in the number of cases brought before the Convention organs made it increasingly difficult to keep the length of the proceedings within acceptable limits. The problem was aggravated by the accession of new Contracting States from 1990. The number of complaints submitted annually to the Commission rose from 404 in 1981 to over 12,000 in 1997. The Court's statistics reflected a similar story: 7 cases were referred to it in 1981 and 119 cases in 1997. A new system had to be introduced. After a lengthy debate, Protocol No. 11 to the Convention was adopted, abolishing the two-tier system of the Commission and the Court, and creating a single, full-time, permanent Court. There were a number of other procedural changes; for example, the possibility of a second hearing before the Grand Chamber of the Court (a kind of internal appeals procedure) was introduced and the Committee of Ministers ceased to play a quasi-judicial role. The Committee continues,

5 Set up in 1954.

6 Set up in 1959.

7 *See* Information document issued by the Registrar of the European Court of Human Rights, http://www.echr.coe.int.

however, to supervise the execution of judgments. Furthermore, the jurisdiction of the Court is accepted *de jure* by all Contracting States and it is no longer optional to recognise the right of individual petition. This new system came into effect on 1 November 1998.

The future monitoring system

Unfortunately, the system introduced by Protocol No. 11 proved insufficient to enable the Court to manage the ever-increasing flow of cases. In 2000, negotiations were therefore started on further changes, such as the streamlining of procedures and further legislative reform. This resulted in Protocol No. 14 to the Convention, which was opened for signature on 13 May 2004. The main innovations it proposes are a single-judge formation assisted by rapporteurs, extending the competence of the three-judge committees to include repetitive cases and a new admissibility criterion under which applications are to be declared inadmissible if the applicant has not suffered a significant disadvantage. This Protocol has not yet entered into force. In the meantime, new activities have already been initiated, such as the installation of a Group of Wise Persons whose task is to brainstorm on the future structure of the monitoring system.

3 The Netherlands before the Court

3.1 The Period until 1998

In this period the Court delivered about thirty judgments on the merits in Dutch cases. This number is relatively low because most cases were dealt with only by the Commission. Some of these early judgments are referred to as 'leading cases' (also for other Member States), because it was the first time that the Court gave an interpretation of a given article of the Convention in a specific context; other judgments led to changes in the Dutch legal and judicial system. The first Judgment in a Dutch case was:

Engel and others v. *the Netherlands, 8 June 1976*[8]

All applicants were conscript soldiers serving in the Netherlands armed forces. On separate occasions, various penalties had been passed on them by their commanding officers for offences against military discipline. One of the legal

8 Ser. A, Judgments and Decisions, Vol. No. 22.

issues the Court had to examine was whether these penalties were in conformity with the right to liberty and security under Article 5 of the Convention, which requires that any arrest or detention be lawful. The Court considered, first of all, that the Convention applies, in principle, to members of the armed forces and not only to civilians. It added that the fact of confining soldiers to their dwellings or to military buildings or premises as a disciplinary measure ('light arrest' and 'aggravated arrest'), does not constitute deprivation of liberty within the meaning of Article 5 of the Convention. In contrast, it considered that 'strict arrest' and 'committal to a disciplinary unit' involve deprivation of liberty. The Court concluded that the provisional arrest inflicted on Engel in the form of strict arrest was, despite its short duration (two days), not compatible with Article 5(1) because it did not come within the ambit of one of the sub-paragraphs. Another question that arose was whether the proceedings before the Supreme Military Court were in conformity with the right to a fair trial in Article 6 of the Convention. The Court concluded that to the extent that the hearings had taken place in camera – and given that the government did not plead, nor did it emerge from the file, that the circumstances of the case warranted an exception from the principle of public hearings – there had been a violation of Article 61) of the Convention.

The government had to pay Engel a sum of 100 Dutch guilders. The consequences of this Judgment included the acceptance of the notion that Convention rights are also applicable to persons who have a special legal relationship with the State, such as civil servants, prisoners, or psychiatric patients; the acceleration of the reform process of the Dutch system of military discipline; and the 'discovery' of the Convention by Dutch lawyers.[9]

Winterwerp v. *the Netherlands, 24 October 1979*[10]

Winterwerp had been admitted to a psychiatric hospital by direction of the local burgomaster and later confined to the same hospital under an order made by the District Court. He submitted a complaint concerning the procedure followed in his case, invoking Articles 5 and 6 of the Convention. The Court emphasised that sub-paragraph (e) of Article 5(1) obviously cannot be taken as permitting the detention of a person simply because his views or behaviour deviate from

9 Art. 6 of the Convention, in particular, has been invoked almost as a matter of course in national criminal proceedings ever since.

10 Ser. A, Judgments and Decisions, Vol. No. 33.

the norms prevailing in a particular society.[11] It emphasised that this paragraph sets out an exhaustive list of exceptions calling for a narrow interpretation. In the case in question, the Court concluded that Winterwerp's confinement, during all the various phases under consideration, constituted 'the lawful detention of [a person] of unsound mind', within the meaning of the said provision and that he had been detained 'in accordance with a procedure prescribed by law'. It thus ruled that Article 5(1) had not been violated. As regards the applicant's complaint under Article 5(4) of the Convention that he was not entitled to take proceedings before a court, the Court considered that mental illness may entail restricting or modifying the manner of exercise of the right to have access to a court, but cannot justify impairing the very essence of that right. It considered that special procedural safeguards may prove called for in order to protect the interests of mentally disabled persons. In the case in question the Court concluded that the guarantees demanded by Article 5(4) of the Convention were lacking both in law and in practice. The applicant finally complained that insofar as his detention automatically divested him of the capacity to administer his property, there had been a 'determination of his civil rights and obligations' without the guarantees of a judicial procedure as laid down in Article 6(1) of the Convention. The Court agreed with the applicant on both points.

Winterwerp is seen as one of the Court's leading cases because it was the first time the Court dealt with the issue of deprivation of liberty in connection with psychiatric patients. The Dutch government was instructed to pay the applicant a sum of 10,000 Dutch guilders in compensation for non-pecuniary damage. As a general measure preventing breaches of the Convention in future, the government replaced the Dutch Mentally Ill Persons Act with new legislation.

X & Y v. *the Netherlands, 26 March 1985*[12]

Y, a mentally-handicapped girl of sixteen, was sexually abused while residing in a home for mentally-handicapped children. Her father X filed a complaint with the police, because she was mentally and legally, unable to do so. No proceedings were instituted, however, because according to Dutch legislation a victim of sexual abuse of sixteen or older had to file a complaint on her own behalf. X claimed that the authorities had failed to protect his and his daughter's rights under Articles 3 (prohibition of torture) and 8 (right to respect for private

11 In the 1970s there were many stories about psychiatric 'treatment' of Soviet dissidents by the former Soviet Union.

12 Ser. A, Judgments and Decisions, Vol. No. 91.

life) of the Convention. The Court recalled that in addition to the primarily negative undertaking of abstaining from interference with the right guaranteed by Article 8, there may be positive obligations inherent in an effective guarantee of respect for private or family life. The Court found that the protection afforded by the civil law in the event of wrongdoing of the kind inflicted on Y was insufficient; effective deterrence could be achieved only by criminal-law provisions. The Court concluded that the Criminal Code did not provide Y with practical and effective protection, and that she was therefore the victim of a violation of Article 8 of the Convention.

The importance of this Judgment from a legal perspective is that the Court developed its case law by accepting that a government may be obliged to adopt measures in order to secure respect for private life even in the sphere of relations between private parties. The Dutch government was instructed to pay the applicants a sum of 3,000 Dutch guilders and the procedural obstacle in the Dutch Criminal Code was eliminated by the legislature.[13]

Benthem v. *the Netherlands, 23 October 1985*[14]

Benthem, a garage owner, was granted a licence for the installation of aliquid petroleum gas storage tank. In subsequent proceedings, however, the highest administrative authority, the Crown, quashed the decision to grant him this licence. Benthem claimed that the proceedings violated Article 6 of the Convention, in that he had no access to an independent tribunal. The first point which the Court had to settle was whether Article 6 was applicable in this case. The Court considered that a 'genuine and serious' contestation as to the 'actual existence' of the right to a licence had arisen between the applicant and the authorities. It added that since the grant of that licence was one of the conditions for the exercise of part of his activities as a businessman and, in addition, a licence of this kind has a proprietary character in that it can be assigned to third parties, a 'civil' right within the meaning of Article 6(1) was at stake. That provision was therefore applicable to the proceedings in the appeal to the Crown. Six judges dissented on this issue. They felt that the dispute in question did not have as its object a civil right or obligation at all. As regards compliance with Article 6, the Court considered that the Administrative Litigation Division of the Council of State had merely tendered an advice from which, in principle, the Crown could depart as it saw fit. It concluded that the proceedings before the Division thus did not provide the 'determination by a tribunal of the matters

13 Act of 27 February 1985; Stb. 1985, 115.

14 Ser. A, Judgments and Decisions, Vol. No. 97.

in dispute' which is required by Article 6(1) of the Convention. The Court furthermore considered that, as head of the executive, the Crown, which ruled in the appeal proceedings, did not have the features of an independent and impartial tribunal as required by Article 6.[15]

In this Judgment the Court developed its case law on the scope of Article 6, but it did not give an abstract definition of the concept of 'civil rights and obligations'. The Court held that the finding of a violation in itself constituted sufficient just satisfaction for the applicant. The Judgment had a great impact on Dutch law. As an initial response, the Crown Appeals (Interim Measures) Act (*Tijdelijke Wet Kroongeschillen*) was adopted in 1987. The Act assigned the authority to settle such disputes to the Administrative Litigation Division of the Council of State. In 1994 the new Administrative Jurisdiction Division, also referred to as the Administrative Law Division, of the Council of State replaced the former division.

Berrehab v. *the Netherlands, 21 June 1988*[16]

Berrehab, a citizen of Morocco living in the Netherlands, had married a Dutch citizen. They had divorced shortly before their first child was born. As a result of the divorce, his residence permit had not been renewed and he had been deported by the Dutch authorities. Berrehab claimed that this constituted a breach of his right to respect for family life as laid down in Article 8 of the Convention. The Court emphasized that Berrehab had already lawfully lived in the Netherlands for several years, having a job and a home there, without any complaint from the authorities. The refusal of an independent residence permit and the ensuing expulsion threatened to break the very close ties between Berrehab and his very young daughter. In view of these circumstances, the Court held, by six votes to one, that a proper balance had not been achieved. Article 8 of the Convention had thus been violated.

In the *Berrehab* case, the Court interpreted the concept of 'family life' broadly, not regarding cohabitation as a *sine qua non* for the applicability of Article 8. It considered that there was a rebuttable presumption that spouses

15 A similar issue was at stake in the Van de Hurk *v.* the Netherlands case (19 April 1994). Van de Hurk argued that the Industrial Appeals Tribunal was not 'independent', as required by Art. 6(1) of the Convention, since the Crown had the power to deprive the Tribunal's decision of its effect. Although the Dutch government maintained that this possibility was merely theoretical, the Court agreed with the applicant and held, by six votes to three, that there had been a violation of this Article.

16 Series A, Judgments and Decisions, Vol. No. 138.

or former spouses have a bond constituting 'family life' with the children born of their marriage, and that subsequent events *may* break that tie.[17]

Not Dutch legislation, but the relative importance assigned to different arguments, had led to a breach with the Convention; in response to the Judgment, the government therefore provided assurances that its immigration policy would 'henceforth be applied in such a manner as to avoid violations of the kind found in the *Berrehab* case'.[18] The Dutch government had to pay the applicant a sum of 20,000 Dutch guilders by way of just satisfaction.

Kostovski v. the Netherlands, 20 November 1989[19]

Mr Kostovski had been convicted of armed robbery and sentenced to six years' imprisonment. His conviction had mainly been based on statements made by two anonymous witnesses. Mr Kostovski claimed under Article 6 of the Convention that he had not received a fair trial, as the defence was not given the opportunity to examine these witnesses or contest their credibility. The Court noted that in principle all the evidence must be produced in the presence of the accused at a public hearing with a view to adversarial argument. An accused should be given an adequate and proper opportunity to challenge and question a witness against him, either at the time the witness made his statement or at some later stage of the proceedings. The Court was of the view that the use of anonymous statements subsequent to the investigation stage as sufficient evidence to found a conviction, as in the present case, involved limitations on the rights of the defence which were irreconcilable with the guarantees contained in Article 6, especially given that the applicant's conviction had been based 'to a decisive extent' on these anonymous statements. It concluded that Article 6 had been violated.

The Dutch government offered to pay Kostovski the impressive sum of 150,000 Dutch guilders, the amount he had claimed, as just satisfaction for the non-pecuniary damage resulting from his detention in the Netherlands. Kostovski accepted that offer, and a friendly settlement was thus reached. The implications of this case were much wider: in an Act of 11 November 1993, the Witness Protection Act,[20] the Code of Criminal Procedure was amended, introducing

17 R.A. Lawson & H.G. Schermers, Leading Cases of the European Court of Human Rights (1999).

18 Resolution DH (89) 13, adopted by the Committee of Ministers of the Council of Europe, 27 April 1989.

19 Ser. A, Judgments and Decisions, Vol. No. 166.

20 *Wet getuigenbescherming*, Stb. 1993, 603, entered into force on 1 February 1994.

a set of conditions for using the statements of anonymous witnesses in evidence.[21] Many cases regarding the use of anonymous witnesses have since been brought before the Court, including the following Dutch cases: *Doorson* v. *the Netherlands* in 1996,[22] *Van Mechelen and others* v. *the Netherlands* in 1997, *Kok* v. *the Netherlands* in 2000, *Visser* v. *the Netherlands* in 2002,[23] and *Bocos-Cuesta* v. *the Netherlands* in 2005.[24] Among these cases, the most important were *Van Mechelen and others* and *Kok*.

In the *Van Mechelen and others* case, three persons were convicted of armed bank robbery and attempted manslaughter and sentenced to fourteen years' imprisonment. Before the Court, they claimed to be victims of a violation of Article 6 of the Convention, because the anonymous testimony of police officers had played an essential role in their conviction. The Court, by Judgment of 23 April 1997, agreed with the applicants for the following reasons. Firstly, the defence was not allowed to openly confront the witnesses. Secondly, the Court was not persuaded that sufficient effort had been made to assess the threat of reprisals against the police officers and their families. Finally, the conviction of the applicants had been based to a decisive extent on these anonymous statements. In the absence of the option of reopening domestic proceedings, the Dutch Minister of Justice released the applicants immediately after the Court's Judgment. The Dutch public reacted with shock. As a consequence of this Judgment, the Code of Criminal Procedure has been amended (Article 457,

---

21 Arts. 226(a)-226(f) of the Code of Criminal Procedure provide, in essence, that the identity of a witness may remain secret if there is reason to believe that the disclosure of his identity may threaten his life, health, safety, family life or socioeconomic welfare. The decision is made by the investigating judge, who must first hear the prosecution, the defence and the witness. Appeal lies to the trial court. The investigating judge may order that the witness be heard in the absence of the accused and his counsel; in that case the prosecution may not attend the questioning of the witness either.

22 In the *Doorson* case, which was instituted before the amendment of the Dutch legislation, the Court's Judgment of 26 March 1996 argued that the principles of fair trial also require that an appropriate balance be struck between the interests of the defence and those of witnesses and victims called upon to testify. The Court acknowledged that in the case in question the Dutch courts were entitled to consider that the safety of the witnesses required that their anonymity be maintained. Moreover, in this case the conviction was also based on corroborating evidence; no violation of Art. 6 was found.

23 In the *Visser case*, the Court found in its Judgment of 14 February 2002 that the conviction was based to an decisive extent on the statements of a anonymous witness and concluded, in line with its reasoning in *Van Mechelen and others*, that Art. 6 of the Convention had been violated.

24 In the *Bocos-Cuesta* case, the Court again concluded that Art. 6 had been violated (Judgment of 10 November 2005), Appl. No. 54789/00.

paragraph 1(b)), making it possible to reopen a criminal case at national level after the Court renders judgment.

In the *Kok* case, the Dutch legislation amended as a consequence of *Kostovski* was challenged before the Court. The Court noted that although it is true that the precise grounds of the anonymous witness's fears were never made known to the defence or the public, the seriousness and well-foundedness of his or her apprehensions were investigated by the Investigating Judge, who did not rely solely on the information provided by the witness him- or herself but also on background information obtained from a police source. It appeared that the anonymous witness was a person who needed to be protected and whose evidence could not be obtained if sufficient protection was not forthcoming. The Court also observed that in the case in question the applicant's conviction was not based exclusively or to a decisive extent on the evidence of the anonymous witness. The Court concluded that the rights of the defence had been sufficiently respected in the light of Article 6 of the Convention and declared the application, by decision of 4 July 2000, inadmissible.

Lala v. *the Netherlands, 22 September 1994*[25]

After a trial *in absentia*, a District Court convicted Lala of the offence of forgery. Lala filed an appeal. Summoned to the hearing, he failed to appear. The reason given for this failure was that Lala was still liable to pay a fine, which he was unable to do. He therefore ran the risk of being arrested immediately to serve the term of detention to which he would be liable in the event of failure to pay. In its default Judgment, the Court of Appeal again convicted Lala. The Supreme Court noted that it appeared from the official record of the hearing before the Court of Appeal that the lawyer had stated the reasons for his client's absence, but not that he had acted as counsel during his client's trial. Consequently, it had to be assumed that he had not so acted. Lala complained that at the appeal hearing before the Court of Appeal his counsel had not been allowed to conduct the defence in his absence. He relied on Article 6 of the Convention. The Court considered that, in the interests of a fair and just criminal process, it is of capital importance that the accused should appear at his trial. As a general rule, this is equally true for an appeal by way of rehearing. However, it is also of crucial importance for the fairness of the criminal justice system that the accused be adequately defended, both at first instance and on appeal, the more so if, as is the case under Netherlands

25 Ser. A, Judgments and Decisions, Vol. No. 297.

law, no objection may be filed against a default judgment given on appeal. In the Court's view the latter interest prevailed. Consequently, the fact that the defendant, in spite of having been properly summoned, had not appeared could not – even in the absence of an excuse – justify depriving him of his right under Article 6(3) of the Convention to be defended by counsel. The Court concluded that there had been a violation of Article 6(1) and (3)(c) of the Convention.

The Court held that the finding of a violation in itself constituted sufficient just satisfaction for the applicant. The Supreme Court of the Netherlands adapted its case law,[26] and the Code of Criminal Procedure was amended (Articles 278-280).[27]

3.2 The Period 1999-2005

In this period, 2,320 applications were submitted to the Court alleging violations by the Netherlands, of which 1,735 were declared inadmissible. In relation to this group of applications, fifty-two judgments were delivered, in twenty-nine of which the Court held that the Convention had been violated. In twelve judgments, it held that there had been no violation; the other eleven judgments related to friendly settlements or were struck from the list because, for instance, the problem had been solved or, in the Court's view, there were other reasons not to pursue the case. In some instances, for example, the government had already unilaterally offered just satisfaction. Some leading cases from this period are summarised below.

Ciliz v. *the Netherlands, 11 July 2000*[28]

Ciliz separated from his Dutch wife, thereby losing the right to reside in the Netherlands *ex jure* from the moment of separation. During court proceedings at which he contested the refusal to prolong his residence permit, he requested the court to establish an arrangement concerning parental access to his minor son. Before the court had ruled on this request, the applicant was expelled to Turkey. In Strasbourg, he complained of a violation of the right to respect for his family life under Article 8. The Court took the view that the Dutch authorities not only prejudged the outcome of the proceedings relating to the question of access by expelling the applicant when they did, but also denied the applicant

26 *See, e.g.*, the Judgment of 3 January 1995, NJ (1995) 517.

27 Act of 15 January 1998 (Stb. 1998, No. 33).

28 Reports of Judgments and Decisions 2000-VIII.

all possibility of any meaningful further involvement in those proceedings for which his availability for trial meetings in particular was obviously of essential importance. In sum, the Court considered that the decision-making process concerning both the question of the applicant's expulsion and the question of access did not afford the requisite protection of the applicant's interests as safeguarded by Article 8. There had, accordingly, been a breach of that provision. As a consequence of this Judgment, the Dutch authorities issued guidelines clarifying the policy applicable to cases like the one in question, which stressed the importance of striking an appropriate balance among the interests involved in the context of Article 8 of the Convention.[29]

Zoon v. *the Netherlands, 7 December 2000*[30]

The *Zoon* case concerned the practice in Dutch criminal proceedings of issuing a judgment in abridged form (*kop-staart vonnis*). A general practitioner was convicted of taking another person's life at that person's request. The District Court gave Judgment in public and in the presence of the applicant's defence counsel. In Strasbourg, the applicant complained that he had not had available a copy of the complete written Judgment of the first-instance court at the time when he had to decide whether or not to lodge an appeal. He alleged a violation of Article 6(1) and (3)(b) of the Convention. The Court noted, among other things, that in Netherlands criminal procedure an appeal is not directed against the Judgment of the first-instance court but against the charge brought against the accused. An appeal procedure thus involves a completely new establishment of the facts and a reassessment of the applicable law. The Court concluded that in the circumstances of the present case, it could not be said that the applicant's defence rights were unduly affected by the absence of a complete judgment. There had been no violation of Article 6(1) of the Convention taken in conjunction with Article 6(3)(b).

For the Dutch judiciary, this Judgment was of great importance, because the practice of issuing abridged judgments allows the necessary efficiency and speed in criminal procedures. If the outcome of the Judgment had been different, it would have had a major impact on the organization of the judiciary.

---

29 *Tussentijds Bericht Vreemdelingencirculaire* 2000/12, Stcrt. No. 75, 18 April 2001, at 8.

30 Reports of Judgments and Decisions, 2000-XII.

Banković and others v. *17 NATO Member States, 19 December 2001 (Decision)*[31]

Close relatives of the victims and a number of survivors of the bombing by NATO forces of Radio-Televizija Srbije in Belgrade, submitted to the Court an application against those Contracting States that also belong to NATO, invoking, *inter alia*, the right to life under Article 2 of the Convention. The governments involved disputed the admissibility of the case. Their main contention was that the application was incompatible *ratione personae* with the provisions of the Convention because the applicants did not fall within the jurisdiction of the respondent States within the meaning of Article 1 of the Convention. The Court noted that the Convention is a multilateral treaty operating in an essentially regional context and notably in the legal space (*espace juridique*) of the Contracting States, and that the Federal Republic of Yugoslavia clearly did not fall within this legal space at that time. It considered that the Convention was not designed to be applied throughout the world, even in respect of the conduct of Contracting States. Accordingly, the desirability of avoiding a gap or vacuum in human rights' protection had so far been relied on by the Court in favour of establishing jurisdiction only when the territory in question was one that, but for the specific circumstances, would normally be covered by the Convention. The Court concluded that the impugned action of the respondent States did not engage their Convention responsibility and that it was therefore unnecessary to consider the other admissibility issues raised by the parties. The application was declared inadmissible.

With regard to the legal issues of State responsibility and extraterritorial jurisdiction, the importance of this decision is evident. The decision was also important from a political perspective; not all extraterritorial acts by States (e.g. activities of their armed forces abroad) were automatically deemed to fall within their extraterritorial jurisdiction.[32]

A.B. v. *the Kingdom of the Netherlands, 29 January 2002*[33]

This was a case against the Netherlands Antilles. The applicant was detained in the Point Blanche Penitentiary on the island of St. Maarten and later transferred to Koraal Specht Prison on the island of Curaçao. The applicant alleged

31 Reports of Judgments and Decisions, 2001-XII.

32 However, *see also* Issa and others *v.* Turkey, 16 November 2004, Appl. No. 31821/96; Saddam Hussein *v.* 21 European countries, Decision of 14 March 2006, Appl. No. 23276/04.

33 Appl. No. 37328/97.

that the penitentiary authorities had interfered with his correspondence with, *inter alia*, the former European Commission of Human Rights, in violation of his rights under Article 8 of the Convention and, relying on Article 13 taken in conjunction with Articles 3 and 8 of the Convention, he claimed not to have had any effective remedy in respect of the conditions of his detention and the control of his correspondence. The Court rejected the government's preliminary objection that the applicant had failed to exhaust domestic remedies, in this case summary civil proceedings. It concluded that, in the absence of convincing explanations from the government for their failure to take the necessary measures within a reasonable time to repair the structural problems criticised in the reports of the European Committee for the Prevention of Torture and Inhuman Treatment, and to observe the domestic court orders to repair serious structural shortcomings in prison facilities, there were special circumstances which dispensed the applicant from the obligation to exhaust the remedy suggested by the government. On these grounds, the Court found a violation of Article 13. Furthermore, the Court concluded that there had been a violation of Article 8 of the Convention in so far as the prison authorities interfered with the applicant's correspondence with the Commission and his representative in the proceedings before the Commission.

The government was required to pay the applicant € 3,500 for immaterial damages. Furthermore, reparation of structural shortcomings in the prison facilities in this part of the Kingdom took place.

Wessels-Bergervoet v. *the Netherlands, 4 June 2002*[34]

The applicant and her husband had always lived in the Netherlands. At the age of retirement, the applicant's husband was granted a married man's old age pension under the General Old Age Pensions Act, reduced by 38% because neither he nor the applicant had been insured under the Act during periods (nineteen years in total) when he had worked in Germany and had had old-age insurance under the German social security legislation. After the applicant reached the age of 65, she was granted an old age pension which was also reduced by 38%. Before the Court, she claimed that the reduction in her pension constituted discrimination on the ground of sex, prohibited by Article 14 of the Convention taken in conjunction with Article 1 of Protocol No. 1, in that at the relevant time a married woman was only insured under the Act for periods when her husband was insured, whereas there was no equivalent rule for married

34 Reports of Judgments and Decisions, 2002-IV.

men. The Court was not convinced by the government's argument that at the material time social attitudes were different in that most of the bread-winners were married men, so that the difference in treatment was justified. It considered it relevant that the Convention and Protocol No. 1 had already come into force in the Netherlands by 31 August 1954 and that the inequality in treatment inherent in the former legal rules materialised in 1989 when, given the prevailing social attitudes at that time, the aim pursued by the legal provisions concerned could no longer be upheld. The Court therefore held that the difference in treatment between married women and married men as regards entitlement to benefits under the AOW was not based on any 'objective and reasonable justification' and concluded that there had been a violation of Article 14 of the Convention taken in conjunction with Article 1 of Protocol No. 1.

The State paid the applicant € 45,040.08 to compensate for the reduction of her pension and compensated others who had been in the same position.

Lorsé v. *the Netherlands, 4 February 2003 and Van der Ven* v. *the Netherlands, 4 February 2003*[35]

Lorsé and van der Ven, both serving long prison sentences in the extra security institution (*Extra Beveiligde Inrichting*, 'EBI') in Vught, complained that the prison regime in this institution was in violation of Articles 3, 8 and 13 of the Convention. The Court rejected the complaints under Articles 8 and 13. However, it observed that for many years the applicants had been subjected to a strip-search, including an anal inspection, at the time of the weekly cell inspection, even if in the week preceding that inspection they had had no contact with the outside world and despite the fact that they would already have been strip-searched had they received an 'open' visit or visited the clinic, dentist or hairdresser's. This strip-search had thus been a matter of routine, and the Court therefore held that it amounted to inhuman or degrading treatment in violation of Article 3 of the Convention.

The applicants were paid the financial compensation they had requested. Furthermore, the EBI rules regarding routine strip searches were altered. Lorsé instituted successful civil proceedings against the State for further compensation.[36]

35 Reports of Judgments and Decisions, 2003-II.

36 Judgment, President of the District Court of The Hague, 12 February 2003.

Kleyn and others v. *the Netherlands, 6 May 2003*[37]
The applicants, a large group of individuals and companies, saw their objections against the *Betuweroute* Routing Decision (*Tracébesluit*) rejected by the national authorities at first instance and by the jurisdiction of last resort, the Administrative Jurisdiction Division of the Council of State. Before the Court they invoked Article 6 of the Convention, questioning the independence and impartiality of the Administrative Jurisdiction Division and pointing out that the Council of State, in its capacity as adviser to the government, had in an earlier stage presented an advisory opinion on the Transport Infrastructure Planning Bill (*Tracéwet*). They relied on the *Procola* v. *Luxembourg* Judgment, in which the Court criticised a similar combination of functions within the *Conseil d'Etat* in Luxembourg. The Court rejected the complaint. It considered that although the notion of the separation of powers between the political organs of government and the judiciary had assumed growing importance in the Court's case law, neither Article 6 nor any other provision of the Convention requires States to comply with any theoretical constitutional concepts regarding the permissible limits of the powers' interaction. The Court is faced therefore solely with the question whether, in the circumstances of the case, the Administrative Jurisdiction Division had the requisite 'appearance' of independence, or the requisite 'objective' impartiality.

The Court was of the opinion that, unlike the situation examined by it in *Procola*, the advisory opinions given on the Transport Infrastructure Planning Bill and the subsequent proceedings on the appeals brought against the routing decision could not be regarded as involving 'the same case' or 'the same decision'. In these circumstances, the Court concluded that the applicants' fears as to a lack of independence and impartiality of the Administrative Jurisdiction Division could not be regarded as being objectively justified and held, by twelve votes to five, that there had been no violation of Article 6(1) of the Convention.

Volkert van der Graaf v. *the Netherlands, 11 March 2003 (Decision)*[38]
On 6 May 2002, the applicant was arrested and taken into custody on suspicion that earlier that day he had shot and killed Pim Fortuyn, a well-known Dutch politician and the first candidate on the list of the LPF party for the parliamentary elections on 15 May 2002. The applicant was placed in solitary confinement and under permanent camera surveillance. He submitted a complaint about the latter under Articles 3 and 8 of the Convention. Although the Court recognised

37 Reports of Judgments and Decisions 2003-VI.
38 Appl. No. 8704/03.

that being permanently observed by a camera for a period of about four and a half months may have caused the applicant feelings of distress because he was deprived of any form of privacy, it found that it had not been sufficiently established through objective and concrete evidence that this measure had in fact subjected the applicant to mental pain and suffering of at least the minimum level of severity which constitutes inhuman or degrading treatment within the meaning of Article 3 of the Convention. Consequently, it rejected the complaint as manifestly ill-founded. As regards the complaint under Article 8, the Court acknowledged that the applicant's detention placed an exceptionally heavy responsibility on the penitentiary authorities to prevent the applicant from escaping or from being harmed, either by himself or otherwise, stemming directly from the fact that the authorities rightly considered it to be of the utmost importance that, in order to appease and prevent the great public unrest caused by the killing of Fortuyn, the applicant be brought to trial. The Court therefore concluded that the balance struck in deciding to put the applicant under permanent camera observation had not been unreasonable, and that the interference complained of could be regarded as necessary in a democratic society in the interests of public safety and the prevention of disorder and crime.

Saïd v. *the Netherlands, 5 July 2005*[39]

Saïd complained that on account both of his criticism of the military and of his desertion, he would be exposed to a real risk of being executed and/or exposed to torture or inhuman or degrading treatment contrary to Articles 2 and 3 of the Convention if he were expelled from the Netherlands to Eritrea. The Dutch administrative and judicial authorities considered that the applicant's alleged desertion had not been made sufficiently plausible, pointing out that it was unlikely the army had still been mobilised at the time of the applicant's escape in April 2001, given that the war had ended in June 2000. The Court decided otherwise. It held that a strong indication that the applicant was indeed a deserter lay in the fact that he applied for asylum in the Netherlands in May 2001, at a time when demobilisation had not yet begun and would not begin for another year. It considered that, although the war had ended in June 2000, the information available suggested that the authorities in Eritrea had not proceeded to demobilise the troops. On the contrary, it appeared that the Eritrean authorities had been eager to keep their army at full strength. In those circumstances it is difficult to imagine by what means other than desertion the ap-

39 Appl. No. 2345/02.

plicant might have left the army. Even if the account of his escape may have appeared somewhat remarkable, the Court considered that it did not detract from the overall credibility of his claim that he was a deserter. The Court found that, since public sources indicated that deserters had been ill-treated in Eritrea, the expulsion of the applicant would be in violation of Article 3 of the Convention.

This is a remarkable Judgment in that it was the first time the Court found that the Netherlands had violated Article 3 in an expulsion case. As a consequence of this Judgment, the applicant was granted a residence permit and the policy regarding conscripts and deserters from Eritrea was changed.

Üner v. *the Netherlands, 5 July 2005*[40]

The applicant, who was of Turkish nationality, came to the Netherlands with his mother and brothers at the age of twelve to join his father, who had already established residence there. He eventually received a permanent residence permit. The applicant had a partner and two children, all of Dutch nationality. After he was convicted of manslaughter and serious assault, his residence permit was revoked. Once he had served his prison sentence, he was required to remain outside the Netherlands for ten years pursuant to an exclusion order (*ongewenstverklaring*). Before the Court, the applicant invoked Article 8 of the Convention, arguing that the exclusion order was in conflict with the right to respect for family life. In the Court's view, the central issue was whether the Dutch authorities had struck a fair balance, when issuing the exclusion order, between the applicant's interest in contact with his family and the public interest of maintaining public safety and preventing crime. Although a number of members of the Court had taken a stand against exclusion orders in general in earlier cases, in this case the majority (6 to 1) of the Court concurred with the government's view that, given the specific circumstances in this case, the authorities had struck a fair balance. Accordingly, the Court concluded that the State had not violated Article 8 of the Convention. One of the seven judges, Judge Baka, issued a dissenting opinion expressing the view that Article 8 of the Convention had been violated. At the applicant's request, the case has now been referred to the Grand Chamber (composed of seventeen judges). This is an internal appeal procedure and will involve re-examining the case on the merits.

40 Appl. No. 46410/99.

4 CONCLUSIONS

The Court has heard a tremendous variety of cases; those discussed here are just the tip of one of the 46 "icebergs" in the Council of Europe. Its case law has undergone profound development over the past fifty years, a process which is bound to continue. It is clear why we call the Convention a living instrument.

Looking at Dutch cases from the first period, I note a striking emphasis on criminal law. Many applications invoking Articles 5 and 6 were brought before the Court, which in some cases were indeed found in favour of the applicant. Alongside the cases described above, there were also complaints under Article 6 of the Convention, that the 'reasonable time' limit had been exceeded, especially in criminal cases.[41] Such complaints became infrequent in the second period. This is because the national courts, in view of Strasbourg case law, reduced sentences on their own initiative in cases where invocation of Article 6 as regards the length of the procedure seemed justified. If ever another application regarding 'undue delay' finds its way to Strasbourg, the government will be inclined to reach a settlement with the applicant. The issue of anonymous witness statements demands ongoing attention, as was recently reconfirmed by the Judgment in the *Bocos-Cuesta* case.[42] A relevant development in connection with this issue, is the current draft legislation to amend the Code of Criminal Procedure which would make it easier to use information provided by the General Intelligence and Security Service (*Algemene Inlichtingen- en Veiligheidsdienst*) and the Military Intelligence Service (*Militaire Veiligheidsdienst*) in criminal cases, both to guide the investigation and as evidence.[43] The source of this type of information will, given its national security character, not be disclosed. Employees of the Intelligence Services could, under restrictions, be heard by the investigation judge in the course of criminal proceedings. The question will arise whether, in concrete cases, these restrictions would not disproportionate limit the rights of the defence. No doubt this bill will one day prompt applications to the Court against the Netherlands.

In the second period we see the emphasis in Dutch cases shift from topics in criminal law to aliens law. Applications claiming that an expulsion will be in conflict with Article 3 or Article 8 nowadays make up more than 75 percent of all cases in which the government must mount a defence. To date, the Court

41 *See, e.g.*, Abdoella *v.* the Netherlands, 25 November 1992, Appl. No. 12728/87; Bunkate *v.* the Netherlands, 26 May 1993, Appl. No. 13645/88.

42 *See supra* n. 24.

43 TK, 2003-2004, 29 743.

has found only one violation of Article 3 in an alien case. In addition, a number of settlements have been reached in cases of this type,[44] and the Court has regularly declared such applications inadmissible.[45] In these cases, and also when Article 8 of the Convention is invoked, the specific circumstances of the case are of crucial importance.[46] The case law thus focuses very much on the specifics of individual cases. Another striking feature of such cases is the difference between *ex tunc* review by the national courts, in which the question is whether the authorities were justified in refusing residence rights at the moment of the decision, and *ex nunc* review by the Court, in which the central issue is whether at the time of the Court's Judgment the applicant should be regarded as a victim of a violation of the articles invoked. This time difference sometimes leads the Court to conclude that circumstances in the applicant's country of origin have improved to such an extent that there is no longer any obstacle to returning;[47] however, it could also lead to an opposite conclusion. It is difficult to say on what type of cases applications against the Netherlands will concentrate in the near future. To a great extent, it will depend on political decisions and the legislation based on them.

---

44 *See, e.g.*, Incedursun *v.* the Netherlands, 22 June 1999, Appl. No. 33124/96; K.K.C. *v.* the Netherlands, 21 December 2001, Appl. No. 58964/00.

45 *See, e.g.*, the following decisions of the Court: S.N. *v.* the Netherlands, 4 May 1999, Appl. No. 38088/97; Solhan *v.* the Netherlands, 16 January 2001, Appl. No. 48784/99; Cicek *v.* the Netherlands, 28 August 2001, Appl. No. 49866/99; Tekdemir *v.* the Netherlands, 1 October 2002, Appl. Nos. 46860/99 and 49823/99; Arcila Henao *v.* the Netherlands, 24 June 2003, Appl. No. 13669/03; Meho and others *v.* the Netherlands, 20 January 2004, Appl. No. 76749/01; Taheri Kandomabadi *v.* the Netherlands, 29 June 2004, Appl. Nos. 6276/03 and 6122/04; Amegnigan *v.* the Netherlands, 25 November 2004, Appl. No. 25629/04; I.N.N. *v.* the Netherlands, 9 December 2004, Appl. No. 2035/04; Shikpohkt and Shole *v.* the Netherlands, 27 January 2005, Appl. No. 39349/03; Ramadan and Ahjredini *v.* the Netherlands, 10 November 2005, Appl. No. 35989/03; Paramsothy *v.* the Netherlands, 10 November 2005, Appl. No. 14492/03.

46 *See, e.g.*, the following Court decisions on admissibility in Art. 8 cases: Afonso and Antonio *v.* the Netherlands, 8 July 2003, Appl. No. 11005/03; Chandra and others *v.* the Netherlands, 13 May 2003, Appl. No. 53102/99; I.M. *v.* the Netherlands, 25 March 2003, Appl. No. 41226/98; Ismail Ebrahim and Serhan Ebrahim *v.* the Netherlands, 18 March 2003, Appl. No. 59186/00; Adnane v. the Netherlands, 6 November 2001, Appl. No. 50568/99; Kaya *v.* the Netherlands, 6 November 2001, Appl. No. 44947/98; Mensah *v.* the Netherlands, 9 October 2001, Appl. No. 47042/99; Javeed *v.* the Netherlands, 3 July 2001, Appl. No. 47390/99; J.M. *v.* the Netherlands, 9 January 2001, Appl. No. 38047/97.

47 *See, e.g.*, Venkadajalasarma *v.* the Netherlands, 17 February 2004, Appl. No. 58510/00; Thampibillai *v.* the Netherlands, 17 February 2004, Appl. No. 61350/00.

Many people in Europe, including many in the Netherlands, have found their way to the Court and had the opportunity to air their complaints about perceived violations of their human rights. The Court is a great force for good, the only institution of its kind in Europe; we should be proud, but also sparing of it. We must make sure that it does not become a victim of its own success. In the words of Judge Luzius Wildhaber, current President of the Court, in the Court's 2004 Annual Report:

> "The history of the Convention system has been a history of expansion and success, shorn of its earlier optional features; a geographical expansion, across Western Europe to Central, Eastern, Baltic and Caucasian Europe and Turkey; a widening of the safeguards of the Convention through an evolving case-law and additional Protocols; and, last but not least, a confirmation of the Court's central position in the European constitutional architecture through the projected accession of the European Union to the Convention. As a logical consequence of such developments, however, there has been a huge increase in the Court's caseload, so much so that today the system's effectiveness remains seriously jeopardised, despite the remarkable progress the Court has achieved in its output. Further measures, going beyond a constant search for improvements in working methods and internal organisation, are therefore likely to be necessary if the human rights protection system set up by the Convention is to remain effective in the long term. Governments are faced with a choice about the nature of the international protection machinery which must be provided to individuals in the 21st-century Europe."[48]

Let's hope that the governments of the European countries will make the 'right' choice without 'undue delay'!

48 2004 Annual Report of the Court, June 2005.

9

THE LAST JUDGMENT: LEGAL EFFECTS OF THE DECISIONS OF INTERNATIONAL COURTS AND ARBITRAL TRIBUNALS IN THE PROCEEDINGS OF NATIONAL COURTS

René Lefeber[*]

1 INTRODUCTION

Johan Lammers has devoted a significant part of his academic and diplomatic career to a dispute between France and the Netherlands with respect to the pollution of the Rhine with chlorides.[1] The discharge of waste salts by the *Mines de Potasse d'Alsace*, a French state-owned company, contributed in a considerable amount to the high salinity levels in the Rhine that caused damage downstream in the Netherlands to market gardeners and other water consumers.[2] In the early 1970s, a group of market gardeners initiated proceedings against the French Potassium Mines before a court in the Netherlands. They substantiated their claim with reference to, amongst others, the arbitral award rendered in the *Trail Smelter* case.[3] This award addressed a dispute between

* Legal counsel at the International Law Division of the Ministry of Foreign Affairs of the Kingdom of the Netherlands. The opinions in this essay are solely the author's and do not necessarily represent those of the Kingdom of the Netherlands.

1 *See* Award of 12 March 2004 of the Arbitral Tribunal *in* Affaire concernant l'apurement des comptes entre le Royaume des Pays-Bas et la République Française en application du protocole du 25 septembre 1991 additionel à la convention relative à la protection du Rhin contre la pollution par les chlorures du 3 décembre 1976 (Netherlands/France), in which Johan Lammers acted successfully as the Agent for the Netherlands.

2 *See*, on the pollution of the Rhine by chlorides, J.G. Lammers, Pollution of International Watercourses (1984) at 166 *et seq.*; R. Lefeber, Transboundary Environmental Interference and the Origin of State Liability (1996) at 254-258.

3 *See* Trail Smelter (Canada/United States), Award of 11 March 1941, II UNRIAA 1905.

N. Blokker, R. Lefeber, L. Lijnzaad & I. van Bladel (eds.), *The Netherlands in Court. Essays in Honour of Johan G. Lammers*, © 2006 Koninklijke Brill NV. Printed in the Netherlands, pp. 165-197.

Canada and the United States with respect to damage caused in the United States by fumes originating in a lead and zinc smelter in Canada. Thus, the market gardeners invoked an interstate arbitral award in national proceedings between private parties, in particular the finding of the tribunal that "no State has the right to use or permit the use of its territory in such a manner as to cause injury by fumes in or to the territory of another or the properties or persons therein".[4] The District Court of Rotterdam accepted this argument and founded the unlawfulness of the discharge of waste salts by the Potassium Mines on unwritten rules of international law as well as national tort rules.[5] However, this reasoning was rejected by the Court of Appeal of The Hague. This Court considered it "incorrect to apply, as the District Court did, the unwritten rules of international law, which have no direct effect but which apply exclusively to States as subjects of law, in a dispute between private persons as is the case here".[6] Instead, it applied national tort rules and found that the discharges constituted a tort under the law of the Netherlands. Although the supremacy of international law, at least of treaties and binding decisions of international organizations, over national law is well-established in the legal order of the Netherlands, Johan Lammers has always pointed to the procedural hurdles that would have to be overcome by a litigant who invokes international law in national court proceedings in the Netherlands. The case above is a perfect illustration of his point.

The objective of this chapter is to determine whether a national court is bound by and must apply an international judicial decision that addresses the State of which that court is a judicial organ. The term 'international judicial decision' refers in this chapter to a judgment or an opinion rendered by an international court or arbitral tribunal. It should be noted that it is only the operational part of the international judicial decision that may be binding for national courts and not the reasoning of the international court or arbitral tribunal underlying such operational part. The reasoning may provide an interpretation of international law, but is as such not binding for national courts.

4 *Id.*, at 1965.

5 *See* Decision of 16 December 1983, reproduced *in* 15 NYIL 471 (1984) at 479 (para. 8.10) and 481 (para. 9.8) respectively; *see also* Interlocutory Judgment of 8 January 1979, reproduced *in* 11 NYIL 326 (1980).

6 *See* Decision of 10 September 1986, reproduced *in* 19 NYIL 497 (1988) at 497-498 (para. 5.3); endorsed by the Netherlands Supreme Court in its Decision of 23 September 1988, reproduced *in* 21 NYIL 434 (1990).

The international judicial decisions discussed have been randomly selected to illustrate the issue from different perspectives.

The chapter commences with some general observations on the relation between international law and national law (Section 2). This will be followed by an analysis of the legal effects of judgments (Section 3) and opinions (Section 4) of international courts and arbitral tribunals in national court proceedings. Finally, some conclusions will be drawn on the basis of the discerned trends in national court proceedings (Section 5).

2 The Coexistence of International Legal Orders and National Legal Orders

International law does not contain any rules on the effect and status of international law in national legal orders, with the exception of rules that have been laid down in or can be derived from a treaty. Accordingly, it would seem that a State has the exclusive right to determine the effect and status of international law in its own legal order. If, as a result, national law would prevail over international law, the supremacy of national law over international law could result in non-compliance of such State with its international obligations. However, it is a well-established rule of international law that a State cannot invoke its national law to justify non-compliance with its international obligations.[7] Such non-compliance constitutes an internationally wrongful act. In such case, the State concerned is required by international law to make reparation and it is also well established in international law that that State cannot invoke its national law to justify non-compliance with its obligation to make such reparation.[8] Accordingly, it would seem that international law ultimately prevails over national law. However, national courts continue to deploy legal techniques to withhold the full effect of international law in national legal orders and the restricted access to international courts and arbitral tribunals limit their exercise of jurisdiction to correct national courts. The legal techniques that are deployed by national courts to withhold the full effect of international law in national legal orders include (a) rules for such courts on the application of international

---

7 *See* Art. 3 of the 2001 Articles on Responsibility of States for Internationally Wrongful Acts and the commentary to that Article, UN Doc. A/56/10, at 74-80; *see also* Art. 27 of the 1969 Vienna Convention on the Law of Treaties.

8 *See* Art. 32 of the 2001 Articles on Responsibility of States for Internationally Wrongful Acts and the commentary to that Article, *id.*, at 231-233.

law in the national legal order, (b) rules for litigants to invoke international law in national court proceedings, and (c) rules on the status of international law in the national legal order.

First, the rules for national courts on the application of international law in the national legal order may limit the competence of national courts to apply rules of international law in national court proceedings. These rules for national courts may originate either in acts of the legislative branch or in case law of the judicial branch, or in both. The extreme positions adopted by States are reflected in a dualistic and a monistic approach to this issue. In a dualistic national legal order, rules of international law incumbent on a State must first be incorporated or transformed into national law before they can be applied by national courts. In a monistic national legal order, rules of international law incumbent on a State can be applied by national courts as rules of international law irrespective whether a State decides to implement such rules into national law or not. A national legal order may also be a hybrid, for example a national legal order could be monistic as regards written rules of international law, including treaties and binding decisions of international organizations, and dualistic as regards unwritten rules of international law. Another hybrid is the exception that could be made in a dualistic national legal order for specific rules of international law, such as the law of the European Union.

An international judicial decision could qualify as a binding decision of an international organization. This would seem obvious for a judgment of an international court, for instance a judgment of the International Court of Justice is a binding decision of an organ of the United Nations. It would equally seem to hold true for an award rendered by an arbitral tribunal, in which case the arbitral tribunal itself constitutes an international organization. If a national legal order is monistic in relation to binding decisions of international organizations, national courts are not restricted in the application of an international judicial decision. However, if a national legal order is dualistic in relation to binding decisions of international organizations, a national court will not be competent to apply the international judicial decision without a specific mandate from the legislative branch. When a national court is not competent to apply an international judicial decision, it could, instead, resort to the application of the rules of international law, as incorporated or transformed into national law, to which the international judicial decision relates and which it interprets or applies.

Second, the rules for litigants to invoke international law in national court proceedings may limit the possibility for a litigant to assert an individual right. At the national level, the right of a litigant to invoke a specific rule of international law will generally be determined on the basis of tests developed by the judicial branch in case law, but the opinion of the executive branch or the legislative branch is a factor that is given weight, albeit in varying degrees in different States. The right of a litigant to invoke a specific rule of international law may differ from State to State as a result of differences in these national tests. Pursuant to these tests, a national court may examine whether a specific rule of international law confers rights on individuals; whether the rule requires intervention by the legislative or the executive branch to further specify the rule in order to make it operational in the national legal order (self-executing effect); or whether the rule is unconditional and sufficiently clear and precise to be applied by a court, in the light of the object and purpose of the body of international law of which the rule is part (direct effect). An international judicial decision will often not address rights or obligations of individuals. This is only different if the international judicial decision originates in a dispute where an individual can appeal to an international court or tribunal, or where one of the parties to the dispute has exercised its right of diplomatic protection, in the case of a State, or functional protection, in the case of an international organization, and has brought an international claim on behalf of one or more of its nationals or officials respectively.

Third, the rules on the status of international law in the national legal order may result in the supremacy of national law over international law at the national level. In a monistic national legal order, international law, including an international judicial decision, is supreme and prevails over national law. In a dualistic legal order, international law is incorporated or transformed into national law and will be henceforth subject to rules of national law on the hierarchical relationship between rules of national law. A rule of international law may thus become subordinate to particular rules of national law, such as the constitution, or national laws adopted after the rule of international law was incorporated or transformed into national law. Since the application of an international judicial decision is less likely in a dualistic national legal order (see above), a national court may have to resort to the application of the incorporated or transformed rules of international law to which the international judicial decision relates and which it interprets or applies. Even if the national court is willing to give effect to the international judicial decision, it may be required by national law to subordinate it to rules of national law that may prevent it to give full effect to the international judicial decision.

The 1992 Treaty on the European Union and related treaties, including the 1957 Treaty Establishing a European Economic Community (EEC Treaty), are part of international law and, hence, a legal order of international law. In principle, the effect and status of the law of the European Union in the legal orders of the Member States could therefore be the same as for other treaties. However, the Court of Justice of the European Communities dismissed in two landmark cases the application by national courts of legal techniques that limit the effect of the EEC Treaty in the legal orders of the Member States.[9] Pursuant to this case law, the EEC Treaty must be applied as an integral part of the legal orders of the Member States and prevails over national law. The Court has only acknowledged that there may be limitations for litigants to invoke provisions of the EEC Treaty in national court proceedings because they do not have direct effect, but the application of any such limitations is subject to review by the Court. The Court's findings were based on an interpretation of the provisions of the EEC Treaty in their context, in particular the spirit, scheme and the wording of the relevant provisions. At the same time, it emphasised the contrast between the EEC Treaty and ordinary treaties, in particular the real powers of the EEC stemming from a limitation of sovereignty or a transfer of powers from the Member States to the EEC. Yet, in principle, this would not seem to prevent a competent international court or arbitral tribunal to arrive at similar conclusions in whole or in part in respect of other treaties.

3 Judgments of International Courts and Arbitral Tribunals

3.1 Introduction

An international judicial decision rendered in a particular case is only binding on the parties to a dispute if those parties have given their consent to the jurisdiction of the international court or arbitral tribunal on that basis. The decision is furthermore only binding between those parties in respect of that case.[10] Thus, for an international judicial decision to be binding for a national court, the international court or arbitral tribunal must have the authority to make decisions binding on the parties to a dispute and the national court must be a judicial organ of one of the parties involved in the dispute.

9 *See* Case 26-62, NV Algemene Transport- en Expeditie Onderneming van Gend en Loos *v.* Netherlands Inland Revenue Administration, Judgment of 5 February 1963, 1963 ECR 1; Case 6/64, Flaminio Costa *v.* ENEL, Judgment of 15 July 1964, 1964 ECR 585.

10 *See e.g.* Art. 59 of the 1945 Statute of the International Court of Justice; Art. 46(1) of the 1950 European Convention for the Protection of Human Rights and Fundamental Freedoms as amended by Protocol No. 11.

A binding international judicial decision becomes international law incumbent on the parties to the dispute. Since national courts are State organs, the failure to observe the international judicial decision would constitute an act of the State of which that court is a judicial organ.[11] A decision of a national court that conflicts with an international judicial decision binding on the State of which that court is a judicial organ would amount to a violation of the international obligations incumbent on that State and may therefore entail the responsibility of that State for an internationally wrongful act. It remains to be seen, however, whether the failure of a national court to apply an international judicial decision will always result in a violation of the international obligations incumbent on the State of which that court is a judicial organ.

3.2 The Practice of National Courts

(a) United States. The legal effect for a national court of a decision of the International Court of Justice was addressed for the first time in the United States after the Court's Judgment in the case concerning military and paramilitary activities in and against Nicaragua. Following reports of the involvement of the Nicaraguan government in logistical support for guerrillas in El Salvador, the US government became involved in military and paramilitary activities in and against Nicaragua in the early 1980s. These activities comprised (a) the provision of support to groups fighting against the Nicaraguan government (*Contras*); (b) military activities in which the United States itself was involved, such as the mining of ports; attacks on infrastructure, including ports, oil installations and naval bases; overflights of Nicaraguan territory for purposes of intelligence gathering, supply to the *Contras* in the field, and the intimidation of the population; and (c) economic measures, such as the withdrawal of economic aid, the reduction of import quota, the imposition of a general trade embargo, and the blocking of the provision of loans from international institutions.

In its Judgment on the merits, the International Court of Justice found that the United States had violated several customary international obligations as

11 *See* Art. 4(1) of the 2001 Articles on Responsibility of States for Internationally Wrongful Acts.

well as provisions of a bilateral treaty.[12] The Court found in particular that the acts of the United States amounted to breaches of the obligation not to intervene in the affairs of another State; the obligation not to use force against another State; the obligation to respect the sovereignty of another State; the obligation not to interrupt peaceful maritime commerce; the obligation to make known the existence and the location of the mines laid by it; and general principles of humanitarian law. It decided that the United States was under an obligation immediately to cease and to refrain from all such acts as may constitute breaches of these obligations, and to make reparation for all injury caused to Nicaragua by the breaches of these obligations.

The United States did not participate in the consideration of the case by the International Court of Justice on the merits, reserved its rights in respect of any decision of the Court regarding Nicaragua's claims, terminated the bilateral treaty, withdrew from the Court's general compulsory jurisdiction, and refused to comply with the Judgment after it was rendered.[13] Unhappy with the refusal of the United States to comply with the Judgment and believing that the continued funding of the *Contras* injured their own interests, several plaintiffs jointly filed suit in a State court in the United States for injunctive and declaratory relief. These plaintiffs included organizations that sought to strengthen the influence of and respect for the United Nations, organizations that sent aid and volunteers to Nicaragua, organizations that represented US citizens living in Nicaragua, and named individuals living in Nicaragua. Their complaint was rejected at first instance on the ground that it involved non-justiciable political questions and on appeal on the ground that it failed to state a claim on which relief can be granted.[14] The US Court of Appeals for the District of Columbia Circuit found that

> "[n]either individuals nor organizations have a cause of action in an American court to enforce ICJ judgments. The ICJ is a creation of national governments, working through the U.N.; its decisions operate between and among such governments and are not enforceable by individuals having no relation to the claim that the ICJ has adjudicated".[15]

12 *See* Case Concerning Military and Paramilitary Activities in and Against Nicaragua (Nicaragua *v.* United States of America) , Merits, Judgment of 27 June 1986, 1986 ICJ Rep. 14, para. 292.

13 *Id.*, paras. 10 and 36.

14 *See* Committee of United States Citizens Living in Nicaragua *et al. v.* Ronald Wilson Reagan, Decision of 14 October 1988, 859 F.2d 929, 938 (D.C. Cir. 1988).

15 *Id.*, Section II.A.

It also found that the International Court of Justice "does not aspire to regulate actions of the United States towards its own citizens" and that its "judgments thus resist importation into American law as substantive legal standards". It added that, in theory, a national law could supersede these limitations in the 1945 Statute of the International Court of Justice and provide for the transformation of decisions of the International Court of Justice into legal standards for national judicial review.[16] However, no such national law was in force in the United States.

To overcome this difficulty, the plaintiffs argued that the funding of the *Contras* by Congress violated Article 94 of the 1945 UN Charter that requires members of the United Nations to comply with decisions of the International Court of Justice in any case to which they are a party. The Court of Appeals pointed out that this argument could only succeed if the plaintiffs could prove that a prior treaty, in this case the UN Charter, pre-empts a subsequent statute, in this case the legislation that funded the *Contras*. The argument could, in the opinion of the Court of Appeals, not succeed in the United States, because of "the principle that treaties and statutes enjoy equal status and therefore that inconsistencies between the two must be resolved in favor of the *lex posterior*". The Court of Appeals, furthermore, stressed that Article 94 does not confer rights on individuals, but only calls upon governments to take certain action.[17]

The plaintiffs also argued that it is a rule of customary international law that States must obey the rulings of an international court to whose jurisdiction they submit. The Court of Appeals observed in this respect that

> "[s]tatutes inconsistent with principles of customary international law may well lead to international law violations. But within the domestic legal realm, that inconsistent statute simply modifies or supersedes customary international law to the extent of the inconsistency".[18]

According to the plaintiffs, this rule of customary international law had become a peremptory norm of international law (*jus cogens*) and, therefore, it was absolutely binding as a matter of national law and had risen to the level of a constitutional obligation which cannot be overridden by statute. However, the Court of Appeals found that there is no evidence that a decision of the Inter-

16 *Id.*, Section II.C.
17 *Id.*, Section II.B.2.
18 *Id.*, Section II.B.3.

national Court of Justice, at least in a case of general compulsory jurisdiction as the present one, represents a peremptory norm of international law.[19]

The legal effect for a national court of a decision of the International Court of Justice was subsequently addressed by several US courts in cases concerning the treatment of foreign nationals who had been charged, tried, convicted and sentenced to death in criminal proceedings in the United States. The foreign nationals had not been informed of their right to consular assistance under Article 36 of the 1963 Vienna Convention on Consular Relations ("Vienna Convention"), including their right to request a consular post of the State of their nationality, *i.e.* the sending State, to be notified of their arrest so that consular assistance could be rendered. The United States admitted the violation of the Convention and apologised to the sending States. These remedies did not satisfy these States, because they did not allow for the review and reconsideration of the convictions and sentences. In spite of many diplomatic protests, the competent US authorities consistently refused to provide relief adequate to put an end to these violations and to ensure that they will not reoccur in the future. Several States – Paraguay, Germany and Mexico – initiated proceedings before the International Court of Justice against the United States.[20]

In the case involving the national from Paraguay, the International Court of Justice issued an order on 9 April 1998 indicating as provisional measures that the United States should take all measures at its disposal to ensure that he is not executed pending the final decision.[21] The Paraguayan national then sought to 'enforce' the order of the International Court of Justice before the US Supreme Court. On 14 April 1998, the Supreme Court ruled that

> "while [it] should give respectful consideration to the interpretation of an international treaty rendered by an international court with jurisdiction to interpret such, it has been recognized in international law that, absent a clear and express statement to the contrary, the procedural rules of the forum State govern the implementation of the treaty in that State".[22]

---

19 *Id.*, Section II.B.4.

20 *See* Case Concerning the Vienna Convention on Consular Relations, n. 21 *infra*; LaGrand Case (Germany *v.* United States of America), n. 24 *infra*; Case Concerning Avena and Other Mexican Nationals, n. 24 *infra*.

21 *See* Case Concerning the Vienna Convention on Consular Relations (Paraguay *v.* United States of America), Order of 9 April 1998, 1998 ICJ Rep. 426, para. 41; the case was removed from the list of cases before a judgment on the merits was rendered.

22 Breard *v.* Greene, 523 U.S. 371 (1998) at 375.

Since the Paraguayan national had not timely asserted his right to consular assistance in a State court, these procedural rules prevented the Paraguayan national to claim a violation of this right in a federal court. Furthermore, the Supreme Court ruled that an Act of Congress is "on a full parity with a treaty, and that when a statute which is subsequent in time is inconsistent with a treaty, the statute to the extent of conflict renders the treaty null".[23] Since several statutes require claims based on the violation of a treaty to be filed in a State court, this rule also prevented the Paraguayan national to assert his right to consular assistance in a federal court. The Supreme Court, however, did confirm the power of the executive branch, in this case the Governor of Virginia, to stay the execution and wait for the final decision of the International Court of Justice, but it stressed that nothing in the existing case law allowed it to make that choice for him. The Paraguayan national was executed on 14 April 1998.

In its Judgments in the cases involving the German and Mexican nationals, the International Court of Justice found that the Convention confers rights on foreign nationals as well as sending States and that the United States had violated the Convention in relation to both the foreign nationals and the sending states by not informing the foreign nationals of their right to consular assistance.[24] It is the national law of the receiving State that must give full effect to the purposes for which the rights accorded under Article 36 are intended.[25] It added in the case involving the Mexican nationals that the procedural rules of the United States as they are applied at present effectively bar the defendant from raising the violation of his rights under Article 36.[26] It also found in these cases that the appropriate reparation in these cases consisted of the obligation of the United States to provide, by means of its own choosing, review and reconsideration of the convictions and sentences of the foreign nationals.[27]

Following the Judgment of the International Court of Justice in the case involving Mexico, several Mexican nationals initiated proceedings for review and reconsideration of their convictions and sentences. In one of these cases, the Governor of Oklahoma commuted the sentence of one of the Mexican

23 *Id.*, at 376.

24 *See* LaGrand Case (Germany *v.* United States of America), Judgment of 27 June 2001, 2001 ICJ Rep. 466, para. 77; *see also* Case Concerning Avena and Other Mexican Nationals (Mexico *v.* United States of America), Judgment of 31 March 2004, 2004 ICJ Rep. 12, para. 40.

25 *Id.*, para. 91, and para. 112, respectively.

26 *See* Case Concerning Avena and Other Mexican Nationals, *supra* n. 24, para. 134.

27 *See* LaGrand Case, *supra* n. 24, para. 125; Case Concerning Avena and Other Mexican Nationals, *supra* n. 24, paras. 121 and 131.

nationals to life without the possibility of parole. In the press release, the Governor referred to the finding of the International Court of Justice that the rights of the Mexican national were violated and, then, noted that "[u]nder agreements entered into by the United States, the ruling of the ICJ is binding on U.S. courts".[28] On the same day, the Oklahoma Court of Criminal Appeals issued an order staying the execution and remanding the case for an evidentiary hearing to consider, amongst others, whether the Mexican national had been prejudiced by the violation of the Convention. The Court to which the case had been remanded for the hearing found that it is bound by the Convention and, hence, that it is "bound to give full faith and credit" to the Judgment of the International Court of Justice in the case concerning the Mexican nationals.[29] Subsequently, it found that the Mexican national was prejudiced because he was not adequately informed of his rights under the Convention.[30] On the basis of the hearing, the Court of Criminal Appeals concluded that the Mexican national only had suffered actual prejudice in the context of his capital sentence, but not for his conviction of murder.[31] It considered that Mexico would have offered its national assistance to avoid the imposition of the death penalty and in fact did offer such assistance when it learned that he was facing the death penalty. However, any assistance Mexico could have given at an earlier stage had become moot following the grant of clemency. The Mexican national had not shown that Mexico would have assisted him in other respects during his trial. The Court of Criminal Appeals made a point of stressing that the test it applied to establish prejudice is consistent with the direction of the Judgment of the International Court of Justice in the case concerning the Mexican nationals.

In another case, the Supreme Court decided to take up the question whether a federal court (a) "is bound by the International Court of Justice's (ICJ) ruling that the United States courts must reconsider [the] claim for relief under the

---

28 Office of Governor Brad Henry, Press Release: Governor Henry Grants Clemency to Death Row Inmate Torres (13 May 2004), reported *in Implementation of Avena Decision by Oklahoma Court*, 98 AJIL 581 (2004), at 582.

29 Torres *v.* Oklahoma, Decision of 13 May 2004, reported *in Implementation of Avena Decision by Oklahoma Court*, 98 AJIL 581 (2004) at 583.

30 *See* Torres *v.* Oklahoma, Decision of 18 March 2005, reported *in Oklahoma Court Finds Accused Was Prejudiced by Lack of Consular Notification in Death Penalty Case*, 99 AJIL 695 (2005) at 696.

31 *See* Torres *v.* Oklahoma, Decision of 6 September 2005, reported *in Oklahoma Court Addresses Proof of Prejudice for Failure to Provide Consular Access*, reported *in* 100 AJIL 462 (2006).

Vienna Convention on Consular Relations" and (b) "should give effect, as a matter of judicial comity and uniform treaty interpretation, to the ICJ's judgment".[32] Subsequently, President Bush issued a memorandum in which he determined that the United States would discharge its international obligations under the Judgment of the International Court of Justice by having State courts give effect to the Judgment in accordance with general principles of comity in the cases filed by the Mexican nationals addressed in that Judgment.[33] Since competent State courts are to provide the Mexican nationals with the review they seek pursuant to the Judgment of the International Court of Justice and the President's memorandum, the Supreme Court declined to answer the questions at this stage of the proceedings.

In a brief as *amicus curiae* in this case, the US government presented its view on the enforcement of decisions of the International Court of Justice in US courts.[34] It recognised that the Convention is self-executing in the sense that government officials can provide foreign nationals with access to consular officers without the need for implementing legislation and can give effect to provisions that were intended to be judicially enforced, such as those relating to consular privileges and immunities, but then argued that Article 36 of the Vienna Convention does not give a foreign national a private right to challenge his conviction and sentence based on an alleged denial of consular assistance.[35] According to the US government, the International Court of Justice had not stated that Article 36 gives a foreign national domestically enforceable private rights, but only that, when there has been a denial of a foreign national's rights under Article 36, a State may seek relief from the International Court of Justice.[36] While the US government acknowledged that

> "the ICJ's understanding of the Convention's requirements is entitled to respectful consideration, it is ultimately the responsibility of [the Supreme Court] to interpret the meaning of a federal treaty. Moreover, the level of 'consideration' is at its nadir when the Executive Branch, whose views on treaty interpretation are entitled to

---

32 Medellín *v.* Dretke, Decision of 23 May 2005, 544 U.S. 660 (2005).

33 *See* President George W. Bush: Memorandum for the U.S. Attorney-General Regarding Compliance with the Decision of the International Court of Justice *in* Avena of 28 February 2005, 44 ILM 96 (2005).

34 Brief for the United States as *Amicus Curiae* Supporting Respondent, *in* Medellín *v.* Dretke, No. 04-5928.

35 *Id.*, at 32.

36 *Id.*, at 37.

> at least 'great weight,' has considered the ICJ's decisions and determined that its own longstanding interpretation of the treaty is the correct one".[37]

In the brief, Article 94 of the UN Charter is identified as the source of the United States' obligation to comply with decisions of the International Court of Justice, "[b]ut as the text and background of Article 94 demonstrate, it does not make an ICJ decision privately enforceable in court".[38] According to the US government, "[i]n particular circumstances, the President may decide that the United States will not comply with an ICJ decision and direct a United States veto of any proposed Security Council enforcement measure".[39] This approach was followed by the United States after the Judgment of the International Court of Justice in the case concerning military and paramilitary activities in and against Nicaragua. However, in the case involving the Mexican nationals,

> "the President has determined that the foreign policy interests of the United States in meeting its international obligations and protecting Americans abroad required the ICJ's decision to be enforced without regard to the merits of the ICJ's interpretation of the Vienna Convention".[40]

In a subsequent case involving a Honduran national and a Mexican national, the Supreme Court addressed several questions relating to the availability of judicial relief for the violation of Article 36 of the Vienna Convention.[41] Since none of these individuals had been the subject of the decisions of the International Court of Justice relating to Article 36, these decisions did not bind the United States in respect of these individuals. Yet, the reasoning of the Supreme Court is relevant as it addressed the question whether the interpretation of international law by the International Court of Justice, in this case Article 36, is binding on US courts. The Supreme Court did not find it necessary to resolve the question whether Article 36 grants rights that individuals may invoke in a criminal trial or in a postconviction proceeding in spite of the finding of the International Court of Justice in that regard[42] and in spite of divided

37 *Id.*, at 38.

38 *Id.*, at 43.

39 *Id.*, at 51.

40 *Id.*, at 60.

41 *See* Sanchez-Llamas *v.* Oregon / Bustillo *v.* Johnson, Decision of 28 June 2006, 548 U.S. ____ (2006).

42 *Id.*, Section II.

opinions of lower federal and State courts on this question.[43] The Mexican national sought to suppress statements he had made to the police before trial. In this respect, the Court found that suppression of evidence would be "a vastly disproportionate remedy" for a violation of Article 36 that is neither supported by the Convention nor by precedents in its case law.[44] The Honduran national challenged a procedural rule that barred him from raising the violation of Article 36 because he had failed to raise such violation at trial or on appeal. In this respect, the Court found that this question was controlled by its decision in the case involving the Paraguayan national in spite of the subsequent finding of the International Court of Justice that the procedural rules of the United States as they are applied at present effectively bar the defendant from raising the violation of his rights under Article 36. According to the Supreme Court, "[n]othing in the structure or purpose of the ICJ suggests that its interpretations were intended to be conclusive on our courts".[45] It argued that the interpretation of the law by the International Court of Justice is not even binding precedent for itself according to Article 59 of its Statute; Article 94 of the UN Charter provides for international remedies for non-compliance with decisions of the International Court of Justice; the United States had agreed to discharge its international obligations in having State courts give effect to the decision of the International Court of Justice in the case involving the Mexican nationals, but has not taken the view that the interpretation of Article 36 of the Vienna Convention by the International Court of Justice is binding; and that "it is doubtful that our courts should give decisive weight to the interpretation of a tribunal whose jurisdiction in this area is no longer recognized by the United States".[46] Although it found that the interpretation of Article 36 by the International Court of Justice is thus not conclusive, it reaffirmed that such interpretation is entitled to 'respectful consideration'. However, even according such consideration, the Supreme Court rejected the interpretation of Article 36 by the International Court of Justice, because it overlooked the importance of the challenged procedural rule in the adversary legal system of the United States.

43 For an overview of diverging decisions of US courts on this issue, *see* Sanchez-Llamas *v.* Oregon / Bustillo *v.* Johnson (dissenting opinion of Justice Breyer), 548 U.S. ____ (2006).

44 Sanchez-Llamas *v.* Oregon / Bustillo *v.* Johnson, *supra* n. 41, Section II.A.

45 *Id.*, Section II.B.

46 *Id.*, Section II.B. For the withdrawal from the 1963 Optional Protocol to the Vienna Convention on Consular Relations concerning the Compulsory Settlement of Disputes, *see* the letter of the US Secretary of State to the UN Secretary-General of 7 March 2005.

The finding of the Supreme Court in the case involving the Paraguayan national that 'respectful consideration' shall be given to international judicial decisions did not provide sufficient guidance, as evidenced by diverging opinions of State courts, federal courts, the federal government, and State governors above. One governor said that decisions of the International Court of Justice are binding on US courts, other governors chose not to comply with orders of that Court. The federal government argued that the President has the option not to comply with a decision of the International Court of Justice. A State court considered itself bound to give 'full faith and credit' to a decision of the International Court of Justice, but that was in one of the cases where the President had decided to comply with that decision. The Supreme Court refused to apply a decision of the International Court of Justice and, instead, confined itself to the 'respectful consideration' of the interpretation of a treaty in that decision. This enabled the Supreme Court to subordinate that treaty to national legislation that was adopted subsequent to the incorporation of the treaty in the national legal order. The international judicial decision, which was adopted subsequent to that national legislation, could have prevailed over the national legislation if the decision itself was transformed into the national legal order of the United States. However, a State court had already found that that would require a specific national law and the Supreme Court has not addressed this question. The Supreme Court subsequently clarified that interpretations of international law by an international court or tribunal are not conclusive for US courts and that 'respectful consideration' could result in the rejection of such interpretation. As called for by the US government, the Supreme Court has thus assumed the power to render the last judgment on the interpretation of international law and its effect in the national legal order.

(b) Germany. The legal effect for a national court of a decision of the European Court of Human Rights was the subject of legal proceedings in Germany in a case concerning the right to respect family life under Article 8 of the 1950 European Convention for the Protection of Human Rights and Fundamental Freedoms. A child was given up for adoption by its unmarried mother. When the father learned of the child's birth, he moved to acquire custody and access rights. Following the exhaustion of local remedies, he instituted proceedings before the European Court of Human Rights.

In its Judgment, the Court found a violation of Article 8 in respect of the refusal of custody and access rights.[47] It also awarded compensation to the father for non-pecuniary damages resulting from the separation from his child and also in view of the restriction on his access rights. In its reasoning, it pointed out that

> "a judgment in which the Court finds a breach imposes on the respondent State a legal obligation not just to pay those concerned the sums awarded by way of just satisfaction, but also to choose [...] the general and/or, if appropriate, individual measures to be adopted in their domestic legal order to put an end to the violation found by the Court and to redress so far as possible the effects".[48]

It added that the father should at least have access to his child.

After the Judgment of the European Court of Human Rights, the case returned to the German courts for a decision on the custody and access rights. Decisions granting such rights were reversed on appeal and resulted in constitutional complaints challenging the unsatisfactory enforcement of the Judgment of the European Court of Human Rights. In the proceedings on access rights, the Federal Constitutional Court addressed the opinion of the Court of Appeals that "[t]he judgment of the ECHR remained a judgment that at all events for the domestic courts was not binding without any influence on the finality and non-appealability of the decision appealed against".[49] The Federal Constitutional Court annulled the decisions of the Court of Appeals and found that German courts were under an obligation to take the Judgment of the European Court of Human Rights into account, but it added that this does mean enforcement "without reflection".[50] According to the Court, "[t]he authorities and courts of the Federal Republic of Germany are obliged, *under certain conditions* [emphasis added], to take account of the European Convention on Human Rights as interpreted by the ECHR in making their decisions" and

---

47 *See* Görgülü *v.* Germany, Judgment of 26 February 2004, Appl. No. 74969/01.

48 *Id.*, para. 64.

49 Order of the Second Senate of 14 October 2004, para. 17. *Cf.*, similarly, in the proceedings on custody rights, Order of the First Chamber of the First Senate of 5 April 2005, para. 4.

50 Order of the Second Senate of 14 October 2004, para. 68. This decision was confirmed in the proceedings on custody rights; *see* Order of the First Chamber of the First Senate of 5 April 2005, para. 12.

> "[t]he binding effect of a decision of the ECHR extends to all state bodies and *in principle* [emphasis added] imposes on these an obligation [...] to end a continuing violation of the Convention and to create a situation that complies with the Convention".[51]

The Federal Constitutional Court explained that, in the German legal system, the Convention has the status of a federal statute resulting from its transformation by the federal legislature into German law. On this basis, the Federal Constitutional Court subordinated the Convention and the decisions of the European Court of Human Rights to prior-ranking law, in particular the German Basic Law. On the one hand, it noted that

> "[t]he text of the Convention and the case-law of the European Court of Human Rights serve, on the constitutional level, as *guides* [emphasis added] to interpretation in determining the content and scope of fundamental rights and constitutional principles of the Basic Law, *provided* [emphasis added] that this does not lead to a restriction or reduction of protection of the individual's fundamental rights under the Basic Law"

and that

> "the Basic Law encourages both the exercise of state sovereignty through the law of international agreements and international cooperation, and the incorporation of the general rules of public international law, and therefore is, *if possible* [emphasis added], to be interpreted in such a way that no conflict arises with duties of the Federal Republic of Germany under public international law".[52]

On the other hand, it concluded that the Basic Law

> "aims to integrate Germany into the legal community of peaceful and free states, but does not waive the sovereignty contained in the last instance in the German constitution. There is therefore no contradiction with the aim of commitment to international law if the legislature, exceptionally, does not comply with the law of international agreements, provided this is the only way in which a violation of fundamental principles of the constitution can be averted".[53]

51 Order of the Second Senate of 14 October 2004, paras. 29 and 30.

52 *Id.*, paras. 32 and 33; *see also* para. 62.

53 *Id.*, para. 35.

With respect to international judicial decisions, this meant that

> "the legal effect of the decisions of an international court that was brought into existence under an international agreement is determined according to the content of the incorporated international agreement and the relevant provisions of the Basic Law as to its applicability".[54]

As for decisions of the European Court of Human Rights, the Federal Constitutional Court concluded that

> "appropriate Convention provisions in conjunction with the consent Act and constitutional requirements [...] bind all organizations responsible for German public authority *in principle* [emphasis added] to the decisions of the ECHR".[55]

However,

> "[t]he binding effect of decisions of the ECHR depends on the area of competence of the state bodies and the relevant law. [...] Both a failure to consider a decision of the ECHR and the 'enforcement' of such a decision in a schematic way, in violation of prior-ranking law may therefore violate fundamental rights in conjunction with the principle of the rule of law".[56]

The Court nevertheless stressed the need to reconcile national law with international law:

> "[a]s long as applicable methodological standards leave scope for interpretation and weighing of interests, German courts must give precedence to interpretation in accordance with the Convention. The situation is different only if observing the decision of the ECHR, for example because the facts on which it is based have changed, clearly violates statute law to the contrary or German constitutional provisions, in particular also the fundamental rights of third parties. 'Take into account' means taking notice of the Convention provisions as interpreted by the ECHR and applying it to the case, provided the application does not violate prior-ranking law, in particular constitutional law".[57]

---

54 *Id.*, para. 37.
55 *Id.*, para. 45.
56 *Id.*, para. 47.
57 *Id.*, para. 62.

The changing of facts, to which the Court alluded in this case, was the emergence of family ties between the child and the foster parents during the years of litigation.

Thus, the Federal Constitutional Court reserved it right of last judgment on the legal effect of an international judicial decision in the German legal order. Yet, it did not claim – as the US Supreme Court did – the right of last judgment over the interpretation of international law, but over its application in the national legal order. When an international judicial decision violates prior-ranking law, in particular constitutional rights, national law prevails over international law in spite of the fact that this would result in a violation of international law by Germany at the international level. Although the Federal Constitutional Court emphasised that this is not likely to happen and that German courts must endeavour to interpret national law in accordance with international law, it did reserve its right and did give an example where it could happen, namely where the relevant factual position has changed due to the passage of time.

(c) The Netherlands. As yet, international judicial decisions have not been invoked in national court proceedings in the Netherlands. Hence, there is no case law of national courts on the binding nature of an international judicial decision for a national court. However, the parliamentary debate on the approval of the *compromis* for the submission of a dispute between Belgium and the Netherlands to an arbitral tribunal sheds some light on the position of the Netherlands government on this matter. The dispute concerned the reactivation of a railway on Netherlands territory.[58] The 1839 Treaty of Separation attributes a right of passage to Belgium over Netherlands territory and the 1873 Iron Rhine Treaty lays down the route for a railway line.[59] The right of passage as such was not in dispute nor was the trajectory of the passage, but the application of Netherlands law and the allocation of costs of environmental and safety measures required by Netherlands law to the reactivation of the railway, including national law implementing directives of the European Community, were.

---

58 For a contribution in this book on the *Iron Rhine* case (n. 63, *infra*), *see* I. van Bladel, *The Iron Rhine Case and the Art of Treaty Interpretation. The Application of Nineteenth Century Obligations in the Twenty-first Century.*

59 *See* 1839 Treaty between Belgium and the Netherlands relative to the Separation of their Respective Territories, 88 CTS (1838-1839) at 427; and 1873 Convention between Belgium and the Netherlands relative to the Payment of the Belgian Debt, the Abolition of the Surtax on Netherlands Spirits, and the Passing of a Railway Line from Antwerp to Germany across Limburg, 145 CTS (1872-1873) at 447.

In the Lower House of Parliament, the debate focused on the powers of national courts following an international judicial decision. On this matter, the Minister of Transport, Public Works and Water Management stressed that States Parties to a dispute are bound by an international judicial decision. Accordingly, national courts do not have the power to render a decision that conflicts with such an international judicial decision; and the remaining power for Netherlands courts in the *Iron Rhine* case would depend on the content and purpose of the decision of the arbitral tribunal.[60] In the Upper House of Parliament, the debate focused on the question whether citizens could still challenge the trajectory of the 1873 Iron Rhine Treaty before a national court and whether that national court could annul the related decision of the competent authorities on the basis of national law after the arbitral tribunal had rendered its decision. In his reply, the Minister of Foreign Affairs assumed that a national court would *take into account* a binding decision of the arbitral tribunal. Obviously with the separation of powers in mind, he then pointed out that he could not encroach on the prerogative of national courts to uphold the law. When pressed, he proceeded to state that the decision of the arbitral tribunal would not bind national courts and that national courts are only bound by Netherlands law.[61]

The arbitral tribunal had not been asked to determine whether Belgium is entitled to a right of passage or to the route specified in the 1873 Iron Rhine Treaty.[62] Yet, the arbitral tribunal did confirm the existence of the right of passage of Belgium over the historic line and concluded that a modification of the historic line would require the consent of Belgium.[63] It also found that the Netherlands may apply its national legislation to the reactivation of the Iron Rhine, but this entitlement may not amount to a denial of the right of passage of Belgium or render the exercise of this right unreasonably difficult.[64]

However, the law of the European Union complicates this state of affairs. Pursuant to Article 307 of the EC Treaty, the law of the European Community prevails over bilateral treaties between Member States that conflict with that law. A Netherlands court and the Court of Justice of the European Communities would therefore still be competent to address the compatibility of the bilateral

---

60 *See* TK, 2004-2005, 29 579, No. 15, at 4; *see also* EK, 2004-2005, 29 579 E, at 7.

61 *See* EK, Handelingen 26 April 2005, 24-1062.

62 *See* para. 3 of the 2003 Arbitration Agreement between the Kingdom of Belgium and the Kingdom of the Netherlands.

63 *See* Arbitration Regarding the Iron Rhine ("IJzeren Rijn") Railway (Belgium/Netherlands), Award of 24 May 2005 (http://www.pca-cpa.org), para. 232; *see also* para. 201.

64 *Id.*, para. 239; *see also* para. 163.

treaties between Belgium and the Netherlands with the law of the European Community.[65] If it were established that the trajectory of the 1873 Iron Rhine Treaty conflicts with the law of the European Community, a national court would be obliged to annul a decision of the competent authorities that designates such trajectory. In order to arrive at its conclusions, the arbitral tribunal found that it was not necessary to interpret the law of the European Community. However, the arbitral tribunal made clear that, in respect of the law of the European Community, it considered itself in a position analogous to a national court within the European Union and, hence, subordinate to the Court of Justice of the European Communities.[66] The arbitral tribunal thus acknowledged that this Court is competent to render the last judgment on this matter.

An arbitral award can be regarded as a decision of an international organization, as discussed in Section 2 above. Pursuant to the Netherlands Constitution, a decision of an international organization, which may be binding on all persons by virtue of their contents, is binding after it has been published (Article 93). Statutory regulations in force shall not be applicable if such application would be in conflict with a decision of an international organization (Article 94). On the basis of Article 94, national courts may thus not render a decision that conflicts with an arbitral award – see also statement of the Minister of Transport, Public Works and Water Management above. However, an arbitral award such as the one rendered in the *Iron Rhine* case between two States on treaty provisions not directly related to rights of individuals would not seem to be binding on all persons by virtue of their contents. This would mean that the arbitral award is not binding in the national legal order pursuant to Article 93 and, hence, not for national courts – see also statement of the Minister of Foreign Affairs above. Accordingly, in a case in which individuals challenge a decision of the competent authorities that designates the trajectory of the 1873 Iron Rhine Treaty, national courts may not invoke the arbitral award to reject the case. They will have to deal with the case on the basis of Netherlands law that includes treaties in accordance with Articles 93 and 94 of the Netherlands Constitution – these provisions of the Constitution do not only apply to decisions of international organizations, but also to provisions of treaties. The arbitral award may thus still be relevant in national court proceedings. The

---

65 *See also* EK, 2004-2005, 29 579 E, at 8.

66 *See* Arbitration Regarding the Iron Rhine Railway, *supra* n. 63, para. 232; *see also* para. 103. *See further* I. van Bladel, "*The Iron Rhine Arbitration Case: on the Right Legal Track? An Analysis of the Award and of its Relation to the Law of the European Community*", 18 Hague Yearbook of International Law 3 (2005).

interpretation of the 1839 Treaty of Separation and the 1873 Iron Rhine Treaty by the arbitral tribunal is likely to guide national courts in their interpretation of these treaties and the adjudication of the case.

4 Opinions of International Courts and Arbitral Tribunals

4.1 Introduction

Some international courts and arbitral tribunals have the power to render opinions. An example is the power of the International Court of Justice to render advisory opinions on any legal question at the request of entities that are eligible to request such an opinion.[67] In principle, such opinions are not binding. They are of an advisory nature and only provide guidance to the requesting entity or entities. Since States are not bound by such opinions, national courts are also not bound by such opinions. Yet, such opinions contain authoritative interpretations of international law that may be relevant in national court proceedings. Consideration will therefore be given in this Section to the application of such opinions by national courts and to the question whether litigants can invoke them in national court proceedings.

A party to a dispute may agree for the dispute to be submitted to an international court or arbitral tribunal for an opinion and for the opinion to be binding upon the parties. The binding nature of such opinions is to be derived from a treaty. An example is the 1946 Convention on Privileges and Immunities of the United Nations which provides for a compulsory mechanism to settle disputes between the United Nations and a member on differences arising out of the interpretation or application of that Convention (Section 30). Pursuant to this provision, differences shall be referred to the International Court of Justice through a request for an advisory opinion. The opinion given by the Court shall be accepted as decisive by the parties to a dispute.[68] It would seem that the legal effect of an opinion rendered on the basis of such a provision does not differ from that of a judgment of an international court or arbitral tribunal in a contentious case (see Section 3.1).

---

67 *See* 1945 UN Charter, Art. 96; 1945 Statute of the International Court of Justice, Art. 65(1).

68 For another example, *see* 1986 Vienna Convention on the Law of Treaties between States and International Organizations or between International Organizations, Art. 66.

4.2 The Practice of National Courts

(a) Malaysia. The legal effect for a national court of an advisory opinion of the International Court of Justice that is binding on the basis of a treaty was addressed by a Malaysian court in the case concerning immunity from process of Dato' Param Cumaraswamy. This Malaysian national was a Special Rapporteur of the UN Commission on Human Rights on the Independence of Judges and Lawyers. He gave an interview to a magazine, *International Commercial Litigation*, in which he commented on certain litigations in Malaysian courts. In the article published on the basis of that interview, a critical appraisal was given of the Malaysian judicial system in relation to a number of court decisions. Several commercial companies in Malaysia asserted that the article contained defamatory words that amounted to accusations of corruption. They filed lawsuits against Cumaraswamy claiming damages for slander and libel. The UN Secretary-General determined that Cumaraswamy was interviewed in his official capacity as Special Rapporteur and that the quoted passages related to allegations concerning the independence of the judiciary and therefore requested Malaysia to promptly advise the Malaysian courts of the Special Rapporteur's immunity from legal process with respect to that particular complaint. However, a Malaysian court concluded that Cumaraswamy was not absolutely protected by immunity and that it had jurisdiction to hear the case on the merits, including determining whether Cumaraswamy was entitled to immunity. Noting that a difference had arisen between the United Nations and Malaysia, the UN Economic and Social Council requested an advisory opinion from the International Court of Justice on the applicability of the 1946 Convention on Privileges and Immunities of the United Nations to Cumaraswamy and the legal obligations of Malaysia in this case.[69]

In its advisory opinion,[70] the International Court of Justice found that the Convention was applicable to Cumaraswamy and that he was entitled to immunity from legal process of every kind for the words spoken by him during the interview. Second, it found that the Malaysian courts had the obligation to deal with the question of immunity from legal process as a preliminary issue to be expeditiously decided before it proceeds with the consideration of the case. Third, it found that Cumaraswamy was to be held financially harmless

---

69 *See* UN ECOSOC Decision 1998/297.

70 *See* Difference Relating to Immunity from Legal Process of a Special Rapporteur of the Commission on Human Rights, Advisory Opinion of 29 April 1999, 1999 ICJ Rep. 62, para. 67.

for any costs imposed upon him by the Malaysian courts. Finally, it found that the Malaysian government was under an obligation to transmit the finding of the Secretary-General to the national courts involved.

Pending the consideration of the case by the International Court of Justice, the proceedings in Malaysia had been stayed. Following the advisory opinion, Cumaraswamy applied to the competent court to have the lawsuits dismissed. The Kuala Lumpur High Court noted that the United Nations and Malaysia had agreed to accept the opinion given by the International Court of Justice as decisive by the parties. It stated that

> "[t]his is a serious consequence which parties had willingly entered into and it is therefore a matter of grave concern for this court to be called upon to rule otherwise. Whilst this court might disagree with certain aspects of the decision of the ICJ, the decisive acceptance of the ICJ's ruling by the parties will in my view prevail in respect of this case because the parties had specifically agreed to refer this case for an advisory opinion from the ICJ."[71]

The Court concluded that it is "bound to give binding effect to the advisory opinion".[72]

The conclusion of the Kuala Lumpur High Court was preceded by criticism of the advisory opinion of the International Court of Justice and followed by criticism of Cumaraswamy's behaviour. The Court found that it was not "appropriate for the ICJ to hold that the question of immunity ought to be decided as a preliminary issue and then to take upon itself the right to decide that the defendant enjoyed such immunity".[73] It also decided that each party ought to bear its own costs. In this respect, it stated that Cumaraswamy

> "who is supposed to be a special rapporteur relating to the independence of judges and lawyers, was able to make damaging and disparaging statements of the plaintiffs, their lawyer, and the judiciary in most unpalatable terms".[74]

Apparently, the Kuala Lumpur High Court did not feel itself bound to give effect to the part of the advisory opinion of the International Court of Justice relating to costs. The UN Secretary-General protested against the part of the

---

71 Insas Bhd and Another *v.* Dato' Param Cumaraswamy, 121 ILR 464 (2002) at 470.

72 *Id.*, at 471.

73 *Id.*

74 *Id.*

Judgment relating to costs, yet Cumaraswamy decided not to appeal against it.[75]

In spite of a critical appraisal of the international judicial decision, the Malaysian court considered itself bound by it and applied it, albeit only on the merits of the case. It recognised that another ruling would be a 'matter of grave concern' as it would result in the violation of international obligations incumbent on Malaysia. It also accepted by implication that the entitlement of Cumaraswamy to immunity from legal process implied that the Convention creates individual rights that can be enforced in a national court and that prevail over national law.

(b) Israel. The legal effect for a national court of an advisory opinion of the International Court of Justice was addressed by the Israeli Supreme Court in a case concerning the construction of a major complex of ditches, walls and fences (wall/fence or barrier) on the West Bank in Occupied Palestinian Territory. According to Israel, the construction of the barrier is a necessary physical obstruction to prevent the illegal entry of Palestinian suicide bombers into Israel. In accordance with the construction plan in some sections, the barrier runs along the Green Line – the 1949 Armistice Line between Israel and Jordan, currently the internationally recognised border between Israel and the West Bank. In other sections, the barrier complex enters into the West Bank, cutting across land and isolating Palestinian communities. Only a small percentage of the barrier's length runs along the Green Line; the rest of the barrier – including the sections both already constructed and planned – will run up to several kilometres deep into the West Bank. The barrier includes a limited number of gates to allow the crossing of people and goods, and a number of agricultural gates to facilitate access by Palestinians to agricultural land. According to the estimates, the route of the planned barrier, along with the depth barriers, would result in the isolation of approximately 128,500 Palestinians from the rest of the West Bank and from each other in enclaves and double-walled areas on the eastern side of the barrier. The completed sections of the barrier have resulted in the destruction of thousands of olive and other fruit trees, irrigated agricultural lands, including greenhouses, water networks, and agricultural roads in different areas of the West Bank. The UN General Assembly requested the International Court of Justice to render an advisory opinion on the legal consequences arising from

75 *See* UN Doc. E/CN.4/2001/165, at 33, paras. 145-149.

the construction of the wall being built by Israel in the Occupied Palestinian Territory.[76]

In its Advisory Opinion,[77] the International Court of Justice found first that the construction of the wall by Israel in the Occupied Palestinian Territory and its associated regime are contrary to international law. In particular,

> "the Court, from the material available to it, is not convinced that the specific course Israel has chosen for the wall was necessary to attain its security objectives. The wall, along the route chosen, and its associated régime gravely infringe a number of rights of Palestinians residing in the territory occupied by Israel, and the infringements resulting from that route cannot be justified by military exigencies or by the requirements of national security or public order".[78]

Second, Israel is under an obligation to terminate its breaches of international law, to cease the works of construction of the wall being built in the Occupied Palestinian Territory, to dismantle the structure therein situated, and to repeal or render ineffective forthwith all legislative and regulatory acts relating thereto. Third, Israel is under an obligation to make reparation for all damage caused by the construction of the wall in the Occupied Palestinian Territory.

After the International Court of Justice had rendered its Advisory Opinion, residents of the West Bank challenged the construction of the fence before the Israeli Supreme Court. This Court had already concluded in an earlier case that there is a military necessity to erect the fence, but also that some discussed segments of the fence route violate the Palestinian residents' rights disproportionately.[79] In one of the cases filed in the aftermath of the advisory opinion, the Israeli Supreme Court considered the legality of an enclave of Palestinian villages created by the separation fence on the western side of the fence.[80] The Israeli Supreme Court addressed in this case the legal status of the advisory opinion to which reference had been made by the residents of the Palestinian villages who had brought the case before the Court. It noted not only that the opinion does not bind States and is not *res judicata*, but also that it is "an

---

76 *See* UN Doc. A/Res/ES-10/14.

77 *See* Legal Consequences of the Construction of a Wall in the Occupied Palestinian Territory, Advisory Opinion of 9 July 2004, 2004 ICJ Rep. 136, para. 163.

78 *Id.*, para. 137.

79 *See* Beit Sourik Village Council *v.* the Government of Israel, Judgment of the Israeli Supreme Court sitting as the High Court of Justice of 30 June 2004, HCJ 2056/04.

80 *See* Mara'abe *v.* the Prime Minister of Israel, Judgment of the Israeli Supreme Court sitting as the High Court of Justice of 15 September 2005, HCJ 7957/04.

interpretation of international law, performed by the highest judicial body in international law" and that "[t]he ICJ's interpretation of international law should be given its full appropriate weight".[81]

The Israeli Supreme Court found that the normative foundation of both the International Court of Justice and the Israeli Supreme Court was a common one.[82] Yet, it avoided taking positions on some of the conclusions of the International Court of Justice regarding the law of belligerent occupation[83] and even became critical of some of the conclusions regarding the right of self-defence. In respect of the latter conclusions, it stated that the approach of the International Court of Justice was "not indubitable" and "hard to come to terms with".[84] However, with respect to the consideration of the case before it, the Israeli Supreme Court pointed out that the interpretation of international law by the International Court of Justice coincided with its own. Both Courts agree that the Occupied Palestinian Territory is held by Israel in belligerent occupation and is, therefore, not governed by Israeli law but by international law regarding belligerent occupation. Furthermore, in the words of the Israeli Supreme Court, "[a]ccording to international law, the legality of the wall/fence route depends upon an appropriate balancing between security needs on the one hand and the impingement upon the rights of the local residents on the other".[85]

The Israeli Supreme Court then explained with painstaking effort why both Courts had reached different conclusions as regards the legality of the fence. It found that the main difference between the legal conclusions stems from the difference in the factual bases laid before the courts.[86] As a result, before the International Court of Justice

> "full weight was placed on the rights-infringement side; no weight was given to the security-military needs, and therefore the questions of proportionality of the impingement or of the margin of appreciation were not discussed at all".[87]

It furthermore found that the difference in the factual bases was affected by the difference between the proceedings which took place before the International Court of Justice and those before the Israeli Supreme Court. The injured parties

81 *Id.*, para. 56.
82 *Id.*, para. 57.
83 *Id.*, paras. 14, 17, 19 and 23.
84 *Id.*, para. 23.
85 *Id.*, para. 68.
86 *Id.*, para. 60; *see also* paras. 61, 68 and 73.
87 *Id.*, para. 68.

in the case before it, that is residents of the Palestinian villages, did not participate in and Israel was not party to the proceedings before the International Court of Justice. It observed that "[t]here was no adversarial process, whose purpose is to establish the factual basis through a choice between contradictory factual figures".[88] As a result, the International Court of Justice had to accept figures presented by the UN Secretary-General and UN special rapporteurs as objective factual figures. The Israeli Supreme Court then noted that the entire route of the fence was up for examination by the International Court of Justice. Having regard to the factual basis before the International Court of Justice and the model of the proceedings, this "cast an unbearable task" upon the International Court of Justice.[89]

With respect to the effect of the advisory opinion of the International Court of Justice in the case concerning the legality of the barrier on the future approach of the Israeli Supreme Court on the question of the legality of the fence according to international law, the Supreme Court of Israel replied that it

> "shall give the full appropriate weight to the norms of international law, as developed and interpreted by the ICJ in its Advisory Opinion. However, the ICJ's conclusion, based upon a factual basis different than the one before us, is not *res judicata*, and does not obligate the Supreme Court of Israel to rule that each and every segment of the fence violates international law."[90]

In this case, it found that the chosen route of the segment of the fence did violate international law and, therefore, that it had to be reconsidered by the competent Israeli authorities.

From an academic point of view, the approach of the Israeli Supreme Court is almost exemplary. First, the Court did not have to apply the international judicial decision as such, because it was not binding and not *res judicata*. What it did apply were the relevant rules of international law, as it was obliged to do under the law of belligerent occupation. In this respect, it gave 'full appropriate weight' to the interpretation and development of international law by the International Court of Justice, albeit with some criticism that was not relevant for the disposition of the case before it. Second, it was beyond doubt that the law of belligerent occupation creates individual rights that can be enforced in

88 *Id.*, para. 69.
89 *Id.*, para. 70.
90 *Id.*, para. 74.

a national court. Third, since Israeli law was not applicable, international law was supreme in the absence of competing national law.

5 CONCLUSIONS

The failure to give effect to an international judicial decision by a national court is an act of State that may entail its responsibility for an internationally wrongful act. However, it appears from the review of practice that national courts are reluctant to give full effect to international judicial decisions in their national legal orders irrespectively. National courts continue to apply techniques to reject the application of such decisions in the national legal order or substitute them for their own interpretation of international law with the consequential risk in dualistic national legal orders that international judicial decisions are subordinated to national law. This approach to international judicial decisions by the judicial branch may originate in acts of the legislative branch or views expressed by the executive branch, or both.

A first such legal technique is based on the rules for national courts on the application of international law in the national legal order. In principle, German courts and US courts do not apply international judicial decisions, because they are not part of their dualistic national legal orders. It requires a legislative exception in such legal orders to apply international judicial decisions. In Germany, such an exception exists for decisions of the European Court of Human Rights. In the United States, courts refused to apply decisions of the International Court of Justice, but instead applied the rules of international law, as incorporated or transformed into national law, to which the decision relates and which it interprets or applies. The approach followed in Germany only impacts on compliance with international law, whereas the approach in the United States also impacts on the unity of international law. In legal orders that are monistic as regards decisions of an international organization, international judicial decisions can in principle be applied by national courts, for example in the Netherlands. The application of rules of international law by an Israeli court in the case concerning the construction of a wall in Occupied Palestinian Territory is special, because it was governed by the rules of international law regarding belligerent occupation and not by Israeli law. Finally, in the case relating to immunity from legal process of a UN Special Rapporteur, the decisive acceptance of the decision of the International Court of Justice by the parties to the dispute was sufficient reason for the Malaysian court to apply the international judicial decision. It simply did not address the question of the application of international law in the national legal order.

A second such legal technique is based on the rules for litigants to invoke international law in national court proceedings. An international judicial decision will often not address rights or obligations of individuals apart from disputes where an individual can appeal to an international court or tribunal, or where one of the parties exercises its right of diplomatic protection or functional protection. Rights of individuals were addressed by international courts in the cases relating to consular assistance, custody and access rights, and immunity from legal process of a UN Special Rapporteur. However, international judicial decisions in other cases may affect rights and obligations of individuals, as seen in the cases relating to military and paramilitary activities in Nicaragua, the right of passage of Belgium over Netherlands territory, and the construction of a wall in Occupied Palestinian Territory. To avoid non-compliance with international law, a national court cannot take a decision that conflicts with an international judicial decision or the rules of international law which it interprets or applies – but this has not barred national courts in dualistic national legal orders to take such decision while recognising the resulting non-compliance with international law at the international level. This situation must be distinguished from a refusal of a national court to enforce an international judicial decision or the rules of international law which the decision interprets or applies. In the absence of rules of international law on the effect and status of international law in national legal orders, such as the EEC Treaty, the rules for litigants to enforce an international judicial decision or the rules of international law which it interprets or applies in national court proceedings is solely governed by national law. Unless a rule of international law is crystal clear or has become crystal clear following its interpretation by an international court or tribunal in this respect, it is for a national court to decide whether such rule confers rights on individuals, is self-executing, or has direct effect. In the case relating to military and paramilitary activities in Nicaragua, a US court refused to apply the rules of international law that were invoked by the litigants with a view to enforcing a judgment of the International Court of Justice. In contrast, the Israeli Supreme Court applied rules of international law that were invoked by the litigants in the case concerning the construction of a wall in Occupied Palestinian Territory to enforce an advisory opinion of the International Court of Justice, but it should be added that it was required to do so by the rules of international law regarding belligerent occupation.

A third such legal technique is based on the rules on the status of international law in the national legal order. In dualistic national legal orders, such as those of Germany and the United States, prior-ranking national law, such as the constitution and legislation adopted subsequent to the incorporated or transformed rule of international law which the international judicial decision interprets or applies, may prevail over rules of international law. German and US courts are aware of the consequential violation of international law, accept this consequence and defer to international remedies to address that violation. In monistic legal orders, international judicial decisions and the rules of international law which they interpret or apply prevail over national law and cannot be subordinated to national law by national courts.

Although national courts thus continue to deploy techniques to prevent the full effect of international law in the national legal order, overall they demonstrate great respect for the interpretation and application of international law by international courts and arbitral tribunals despite occasional criticism. They may therefore be expected to interpret national law as far as possible in conformity with international judicial decisions or the rules of international law which they interpret or apply. However, as demonstrated, this does not warrant that international law, as interpreted or applied by an international judicial decision, prevails over national law. Although it is exceptional for a national court to reject the interpretation or application of international law by an international court or tribunal and to substitute it for its own (US Supreme Court), several national courts have claimed a margin of discretion to reassess the factual situation. Due to the passage of time (German Federal Constitutional Court) or to the lack of information (Israeli Supreme Court), a national court may appreciate the facts differently and this may result in a different ruling.

The consideration of international judicial decisions in national court proceedings is likely to increase and become even more controversial with findings in such decisions that specific rules of international law create individual rights. In the absence of an explicit recognition of the existence of such rights in the rule of international law itself, such findings are usually based on an interpretation of that rule in an international judicial decision. Nothing prevents international courts and arbitral tribunals to find that such rule can be enforced in a national court and that it prevails over national law. As a result, it will become more difficult for national courts to deploy the techniques discussed in this article to withhold full effect to an international judicial decision in the national legal order. In this perspective, the international judicial decisions discussed in this article in which it was found that a specific rule of international law creates individual rights, notably the international judicial decisions on the right to consular assistance, may become for international law what the landmark cases discussed in Section 2 were for the law of the European Union. Accordingly, international courts and arbitral tribunals will determine which rules of international law have legal effect in national legal orders, at least as long as access to such courts and tribunals is not curtailed by the withdrawal from their compulsory jurisdiction.

10

THE SUBMISSION OF *AMICUS CURIAE* BRIEFS TO UNITED STATES COURTS: THE PRACTICE OF THE NETHERLANDS

*Wim van Reenen**

1 INTRODUCTION

The purpose of this contribution to the Essays in Honour of Johan G. Lammers, whom I respect as a stimulating and inspiring head of the International Law Division I used to work for before my retirement, is to see how the submission by the Netherlands of *amicus curiae* briefs before United States federal courts, in particular the Supreme Court, as well as State courts of the United States fits in with the legal doctrine on the exercise of diplomatic protection and on taking diplomatic action in general. From the outset it must be recognized that Netherlands' State practice with regard to the submission of *amicus curiae* briefs is extremely limited. Yet I am confident that it will be possible to draw some conclusions that may be helpful in gaining insight into the Netherlands' position with regard to the use of this instrument in protecting the interests of the Netherlands in the United States. At the same time through the prism of the use of this instrument – or, as the case may be, of the decision to refrain from its use – it is also possible to gain insight into the position of the Netherlands in respect of certain issues arising in the following areas of international law: jurisdiction, human rights, antitrust law and consular relations.

* Former legal counsel at the International Law Division of the Ministry of Foreign Affairs of the Kingdom of the Netherlands.

N. Blokker, R. Lefeber, L. Lijnzaad & I. van Bladel (eds.), *The Netherlands in Court. Essays in Honour of Johan G. Lammers*, © 2006 Koninklijke Brill NV. Printed in the Netherlands, pp. 199-222.

2 *Amicus Curiae* Briefs

Submission of *amicus curiae* briefs is a well-known phenomenon in United States court procedure in both civil and criminal procedure. *Amicus curiae* means someone who is not a party to the litigation, but who believes that the court's decision may affect its interests.[1] *Amicus curiae* briefs may be filed in all courts, but in practice they are usually filed in appeals cases, including appeals to the Supreme Court, both at the State and the federal level.

It is the *amicus* – or *amici* as the case may be – *curiae* briefs filed in the proceedings of the United States Federal Supreme Court that draw most attention of legal scholars and the public at large, but also important are the briefs filed in proceedings of State Supreme Courts or appeals proceedings in general.

The persons and entities capable of filing *amicus curiae* briefs are manifold. The Federal Rules of Appellate Procedure explicitly mention *inter alia* the United States or its officer or agency, or a State, *i.e.* a constituent State of the United States, who may file an *amicus curiae* brief without the consent of the parties or leave of court. Other entities, such as foreign States, international organisations and foreign natural or legal persons, need the consent of the parties or leave of court.[2]

When a foreign State submits an *amicus curiae* brief, it often does so because it has adopted the cause of one of its nationals. This national may either be directly involved in judicial proceedings in the United States or indirectly affected by such proceedings.

The American authorities do not consider submission of *amicus curiae* briefs by foreign States and other entities as an unlawful intervention in the domestic affairs of the United States.

3 Diplomatic Protection – Diplomatic Action in General

The Report of the International Law Commission on the Work of its Fifty-Sixth Session contains in its Chapter 4 the following definition of diplomatic protection:

1 W.H. Rehnquist, The Supreme Court: How It Was, How It Is (1987) at 89.

2 Federal Rules of Appellate Procedure, Rule 29(a). The Supreme Court Rules contain comparable provisions (Rule 37(3)(a) and Rule 37(4)).

> "Diplomatic protection consists of resort to diplomatic action or other means of peaceful settlement by a State adopting in its own right the cause of its national in respect of an injury to that national arising from an internationally wrongful act of another State".[3]

In other words, the phrase "diplomatic protection" covers a wide range of State acts. Apart from making claims by a State on behalf of one of its nationals through diplomatic channels and direct communications and negotiations at ministerial level, diplomatic protection also embraces the concept of a State instituting judicial or arbitral proceedings.[4]

One may argue that the filing by a State of an *amicus curiae* brief in the proceedings of American courts (State trial courts and federal district courts, State and federal appellate courts, State Supreme Courts and the Federal Supreme Court) on a legal point affecting a national of that State is to a certain extent comparable to the instituting of judicial proceedings by that State in the context of exercising diplomatic protection. However, an important *caveat* must be made. Under international law the exercise of diplomatic protection will only be admissible once the injured national concerned will have exhausted local remedies in the State alleged to be responsible for the injury.[5] In other words, that State is offered a chance to remedy the alleged internationally wrongful act. If no effective remedy is available for the injured person, that State will also be responsible for a denial of justice, thereby compounding its earlier internationally wrongful act.

As long as the threshold of exhaustion of domestic remedies for the exercise of diplomatic protection has not been crossed, any intervention of the State of nationality on behalf of its injured national must be described as consular assistance or diplomatic action. Diplomatic action is a broader concept that comprises both diplomatic protection and action, which cannot be defined as diplomatic protection, for instance action aimed at the protection of nationals for humanitarian reasons which cannot be attributed to an internationally wrongful act of another State.

---

3 Draft Articles on Diplomatic Protection, Report of the International Law Commission on the Work of its Fifty-Sixth Session, UN Doc. A/59/10 (2004), Chapter IV, at 13 *et seq.*, 17.

4 *See id.*, at 26; J. Dugard, First Report of the Special Rapporteur for Diplomatic Protection of the International Law Commission, UN Doc. A/CN.4/506 (2000) at 15.

5 *See* Art. 14 of the Draft Articles on Diplomatic Protection, Report of the International Law Commission.

With regard to any action of the State of nationality vis-à-vis the United States, in light of the latter's practice of allowing *amicus curiae* briefs, the following comment may be made. Litigation with regard to which a foreign State submits an *amicus curiae* brief on a legal point affecting one of the nationals of that State who is directly involved in the proceedings – acting as petitioner, not as defendant – may by its nature be part of the process of exhaustion of local remedies as a prerequisite for the right of exercising diplomatic protection. Also in the situation where the State of nationality files an *amicus curiae* brief in proceedings indirectly affecting one or more of its nationals there can be no question of diplomatic protection. Therefore, submission of an *amicus curiae* brief is a form of diplomatic action.

4 Use made by the Netherlands of the Instrument of an *Amicus Curiae* Brief

4.1 In the Framework of the European Union

In its capacity as Member State of the European Union the Netherlands has always actively participated in the activities of the Union aimed at abolishing the death penalty. In 1998 the European Union's Member States adopted guidelines for joint action to prevent the execution of death sentences in countries outside Europe.[6] In practice the action of the Union is almost exclusively aimed at the United States. The European Union intervenes in death penalty cases in the United States if the offender was a juvenile at the time the crime was committed; if the offender is mentally retarded or if the United States has violated its obligation under the Vienna Convention on Consular Relations (Vienna Convention) to notify the consular post of the sending State of the arrest of a non-national, if the latter so requests.[7] The action of the Union in this field consists of diplomatic demarches made by the EU Presidency, together with the subsequent Presidency and the EU Commission, on behalf of the Union. In view of the fact that in matters like the death penalty the influence of the federal political authorities with the authorities of the constituent States is limited, the European Union normally intervenes directly with the State authority concerned (Governor, State Parole Board) and also with the US courts con-

6 Guidelines to EU Policy toward Third Countries on the Death Penalty, Council of the European Union, 3 June 1998.

7 1963 Vienna Convention on Consular Relations, 596 UNTS 261, Art. 36(1)(b).

cerned, in particular the Federal Supreme Court, by submitting *amicus curiae* briefs.

Strictly speaking, this action of the Union cannot be considered diplomatic protection. First of all, as we have seen in Section 3, there is no diplomatic protection as long as an effective judicial remedy remains still available for the person concerned. A second reason is that diplomatic protection as a legal concept only relates to protection exercised by States. Moreover, even if one would extend the concept of diplomatic protection to action taken by an international organisation such as the European Union, one must be aware that the persons who have been sentenced to death are not necessarily nationals of an EU Member State. In actual practice most offenders on whose behalf the European Union intervenes are US citizens or nationals of third countries. In the case of juvenile offenders or mentally retarded offenders intervention by the European Union takes place in the light of the EU policy to contribute to respect for human rights and fundamental rights and basic freedoms throughout the international community.[8] In death penalty cases where the US authorities had failed at the appropriate time to notify the consular post of the sending State of the arrest of one of its nationals, action by the European Union is motivated by its wish to ensure respect for treaty based rights. This may be illustrated by the *amicus curiae* brief the European Union filed with the US Supreme Court in the case of the Mexican national Medellín Rojas.[9] In its statement of interest the European Union – also on behalf of other *amici* such as the Council of Europe, Iceland, Liechtenstein, Norway and Switzerland – declared:

> "The European Union considers the respect for treaty based rights to be of vital importance both nationally and within the international community. [...] Like the United States all EU Member States are party to the Vienna Convention on Consular Relations ("Vienna Convention"). Article 36 of the Vienna Convention confers both individual and State rights. As such, the EU has an interest in securing compliance with rights guaranteed under article 36 [...]".[10]

---

8 *See* n. 6, *supra*.

9 Medellín *v.* Dretke on writ of certiorari to the United States Court of Appeals for the Fifth Circuit, 23 May 2005.

10 After the Supreme Court withdrew its earlier grant of certiorari in order to enable a State court, namely the Texas Court of Criminal Appeals, to consider the matter, the European Union re-submitted its brief.

4.2 Outside the framework of the European Union

As far as I was able to determine, the Netherlands submitted an *amicus curiae* brief outside the framework of the European Union only three times. The first case was in the area of antitrust law; the second and third in the field of the law on consular relations, namely the issue of lack of consular notification in case of arrest of a national of the sending State.

4.2.1 Antitrust Law

In 2004 the United Kingdom, Ireland and the Netherlands submitted a joint *amicus curiae* brief to the US Supreme Court in the case *Hoffmann-LaRoche Ltd. et al. (petitioners)* v. *Empagran S.A. et al. (respondents)* on a writ of certiorari to the United States Court of Appeals for the District of Columbia Circuit.[11]

This case concerned a worldwide operating vitamin cartel, in which, in addition to Hoffmann-LaRoche, BASF and Rhône-Poulenc, some Dutch companies were also involved. The cartel was prohibited both in the United States and European Union. Antitrust authorities in the United States and in the European Union impose fines on companies participating in a cartel. In the United States the victims of a cartel may also in civil proceedings claim treble damages from the participants in the cartel. In this particular case vitamin purchasers brought a class action lawsuit before the US District Court for the District of Columbia alleging that vitamin manufacturers and distributors had engaged in a price-fixing conspiracy, raising vitamin prices in the United States and foreign countries, in violation of the US Sherman Act. Among those purchasers were companies, such as Empagran S.A., which are located outside the United States. The defendants, including Hoffmann-LaRoche, moved to dismiss the suit as to the foreign purchasers of vitamins asserting that the court lacked subject matter jurisdiction under the federal antitrust laws, because the injuries plaintiffs sought to redress were sustained in transactions that lack any direct connection to United States commerce.[12]

---

11 Hoffmann-LaRoche Ltd. *et al.* (petitioners) *v.* Empagran S.A. *et al.* (respondents), No. 03-724. The brief was filed on 3 February 2004. The Supreme Court made its decision on 14 June 2004.

12 For the exercise of jurisdiction (both prescriptive or legislative and adjudicative or enforcement jurisdiction) international law makes a distinction between prohibitive rules and permissive rules. In the next Section I will return to this issue in more depth.

The District Court dismissed the claims of the foreign purchasers on the grounds that the Foreign Trade Antitrust Improvements Act (FTAIA), which aims at clarifying the Sherman Act, provides that the Sherman Act shall not apply to conduct involving trade or commerce with foreign nations. The District Court found that none of the exceptions contained in the FTAIA for conduct that significantly harms imports, domestic commerce or American exporters applied. The Court of Appeals for the District of Columbia Circuit reversed on the grounds that the Sherman Act's text, legislative history, and policy goal of deterring harmful price-fixing activity made the lack of connection between the foreign effect of the conduct (*i.e.* the cartel), namely higher foreign prices, and the domestic effect, namely higher domestic prices in the United States, inconsequential. The Supreme Court held that the adverse foreign effect of the price-fixing conduct was independent of any adverse domestic effect, and that therefore the FTAIA exception does not apply – and thus neither does the Sherman Act – to a claim based solely on the foreign effect. The Judgment of the Court of Appeals was vacated and the case was remanded.[13]

The brief of the *amici,* United Kingdom, Ireland and the Netherlands, was in support of the defendants, the participants in the cartel, who before the Supreme Court acted as petitioners. In view of the involvement of a number of Dutch companies in this case the Netherlands' government decided to join the United Kingdom and Ireland in drawing up this brief.

Although – as pointed out in Section 3 above – the filing of an *amicus curiae* brief is diplomatic action, but not diplomatic protection, it is interesting to see that in this case most conditions for the exercise of diplomatic protection were met,[14] namely (a) the fact that the injury to the national arose from an internationally wrongful act of the other State and (b) the adoption by the State of the cause of its national in its own right. As to the first condition, it is clear that the Netherlands, and, for that matter, the United Kingdom and Ireland, had good reasons to fear that a verdict by the Supreme Court in favour of the respondent vitamin purchasers, Empagran and others, thus upholding the Judgment of the Appeals Court for the District of Columbia, would have confirmed the exercise of a form of extraterritorial jurisdiction by the US judiciary incompatible with the requirements of international law and would therefore have constituted – or rather aggravated – an internationally wrongful act by the

13 On remand the Court of Appeals affirmed the Judgment of the District Court (No. 01-7115; decided 28 June 2005).

14 *See* Section 3, *supra.*

United States. According to the international rules on State responsibility the act of a State organ, such as a judicial organ, is attributable to the State.[15]

In accordance with the second condition referred to above, the Netherlands indeed adopted the cause of its nationals in its own right. The formal statement of the interest of the *amici* leaves no doubt that the three governments concerned were indeed asserting their own rights. It states, for example, that:

> "[t]he Governments in general are opposed to assertions of extraterritorial jurisdiction in private antitrust cases where foreign claimants seek to recover from foreign defendants solely for foreign injuries not incurred in the country in which the private suit is filed. Such litigation contravenes basic principles of international law and may impede trade and investment as well as undermine public enforcement by the Governments of their competition laws. It also would interfere with a sovereign nation's right to regulate conduct within its territory".

With regard to the enforcement of foreign and domestic competition laws and the provision of access to an independent judiciary for litigants, the three governments declare that they

> "are concerned that the Court of Appeal's expansive reading of the Foreign Trade Antitrust Improvements Act ("FTAIA") [...] will undermine their respective choices regarding the proper balance of public and private enforcement. Thus they have a substantial interest in this litigation and in the proper interpretation of the FTAIA".[16]

In their summary of argument the three governments stated that

> "the Court of Appeal's ruling [...] would wrongly expand the extraterritorial reach of the United States antitrust laws beyond this Court's or, to our knowledge, any foreign court's exercise of jurisdiction. International law principles recognize that a nation may prescribe laws and adjudicate claims beyond its own territory only

15 *See* Articles on Responsibility of States for Internationally Wrongful Acts, General Assembly Res. 56/83, UN Doc. A/RES/83 (2001), Chapter II (Attribution of Conduct to a State), Art. 4: "The conduct of any State organ shall be considered an act of that State under international law, whether the organ exercises legislative, executive, judicial or any other functions [...]".

16 *Amicus curiae* brief of the United Kingdom, Ireland and the Netherlands, *see* n. 11, *supra*, at 2.

> where its assertion of jurisdiction does not infringe the rights of other nations to determine the law applicable to conduct within their own territories".[17]

It is clear from all these statements that – in accordance with one of the elements of the definition of diplomatic protection – the three governments were primarily asserting their own rights.

4.2.2 Lack of Consular Notification

In Section 4.1 above reference has already been made to the interventions of the European Union in death penalty cases where the offender under death sentence had not been notified at the time of his/her arrest of his/her right, under article 36(1)(b) of the Vienna Convention, if he or she so requests, to be brought in contact with the nearest consular post of the State of his nationality. For obvious reasons, contact of arrested persons with the consulate or embassy may be useful in view of obtaining adequate legal representation.

The interventions of the Union in respect of nationals of a EU Member State are based on the EU policy with regard to the death penalty and cannot be seen in the context of diplomatic protection.

At the national level there have been in the recent past a number of cases where governments intervened with the US government and the US judiciary and instituted proceedings before the International Court of Justice on behalf of one or more of their respective nationals who had not benefited from the application of the Vienna Convention and were under death sentence. As effective domestic remedies in the United States no longer seemed available, these interventions may be considered examples of the exercise of diplomatic protection. I refer to the efforts made by the governments of successively Paraguay, Germany and Mexico to rescue their respective nationals from the execution of the death sentence. Apart from efforts through diplomatic channels both Paraguay and Germany started legal action before US courts, but to no avail.[18] All three governments instituted proceedings before the International

17 *Id.*, at 6.

18 In the final analysis Paraguay addressed the Supreme Court, both in the form of a petition for a writ of certiorari (to the US Court of Appeals for the Fourth Circuit) and in the form of an application for a temporary restraining order or preliminary injunction and a motion for leave to file a bill of complaint (Republic of Paraguay *et al. v.* James S. Gilmore, Governor of Virginia *et al.*, 97-1390 (A-738) and No. 125 Orig. (A-771), Supreme Court, 14 April 1998; Breard *v.* Greene, 97-8214 (A-732). Germany applied for a temporary restraining order or preliminary injunction and motioned for leave to

Court of Justice. Paraguay, after receiving a positive ruling of the Court on its request for the indication of provisional measures,[19] refrained from persisting in its complaint on the merits even though the United States had not obeyed the Court's Order to take all measures at its disposal to ensure that the Paraguayan national Angel Breard was not executed pending the final decision in the proceedings.

Similarly, Germany received a positive ruling on its request for provisional measures with regard to the imminent execution of its national Walter LaGrand.[20] Contrary to Paraguay, Germany proceeded with its legal action before the International Court of Justice. The commendable persistence of Germany led to a – in my view – very important Judgment of the Court which may turn out to be beneficial for all those arrested and prosecuted in a State which is not the State of their nationality and – as we will see below – might be helpful in the process of engaging diplomatic protection or taking diplomatic action in a broader sense on behalf of such persons.[21] On all scores the Court ruled in favour of Germany with large majorities. The Court found that the United States due to lack of the so-called consular notification had violated its obligations to Germany and the LaGrand brothers under article 36(1)(b) of the Vienna Convention.[22] At the same time the Court found that the United States by applying a rule of its domestic law, namely the procedural default rule which bars accused persons from raising a claim in a federal court if it has not been raised in court proceedings at State level, and thereby not per-

---

file a bill of complaint (Federal Republic of Germany *et al.* *v.* United States *et al.*, No. 127 Orig. (A-736) Supreme Court, 3 March 1999).

19 Case Concerning the Vienna Convention on Consular Relations (Paraguay *v.* United States of America), Request for the Indication of Provisional Measures, Order of 9 April 1998, 1998 ICJ Rep. 248.

20 Case Concerning the Vienna Convention on Consular Relations (Germany *v.* United States of America), Request for the Indication of Provisional Measures, Order of 3 March 1999, 1999 ICJ Rep. 9. Before Germany made its request to the International Court of Justice, another German national, Karl LaGrand, brother of Walter, had already been executed.

21 LaGrand Case (Germany v. United States of America), Judgment of 27 June 2001, 2001 ICJ Rep. 466.

22 "[B]y not informing Karl and Walter LaGrand without delay following their arrest of their rights under article 36, paragraph 1(b), of the Convention, and by thereby depriving the Federal Republic of Germany of the possibility, in a timely fashion, to render the assistance provided for by the Convention to the individuals concerned, the United States breached its obligations to the Federal Republic of Germany and to the LaGrand brothers under article 36, paragraph 1".; *id.*, para. 128.

mitting the review and reconsideration of the conviction and sentences of the LaGrand brothers had breached its obligations to Germany and the LaGrand brothers under Article 36(2) of the Vienna Convention.[23] Furthermore, particular attention should be drawn to the seventh paragraph of the operative part of the Court's Judgment in the *LaGrand* case, at which the Court found

> "that should nationals of the Federal Republic of Germany nonetheless be sentenced to severe penalties, without their rights under Article 36, paragraph 1(b), of the Convention having been respected, the United States of America, by means of its own choosing, shall allow the review and reconsideration of the conviction and sentence by taking account of the violation of the rights set forth in that Convention".[24]

The Court confirmed and further elaborated its conclusions in other proceedings instituted by Mexico against the United States with regard to fifty-one Mexicans on death row whose rights under Article 36 of the Vienna Convention had been violated (*Avena* case).[25] In the *Avena* case the International Court of Justice added *inter alia* that the review and reconsideration of convictions and sentences must also ascertain whether the violations of Article 36 caused actual prejudice to the defendant in the process of the administration of criminal justice.[26]

The Judgments of the International Court of Justice in the *LaGrand* and *Avena* cases have wide implications. Even though Article 59 of the Statute of the Court provides that the Judgment of the Court has no binding force except between the parties and in respect of that particular case, it may be argued that with these Judgments the Court has determined the law with regard to the consequences of a State's failure to comply with the provisions of the Vienna Convention as to consular notification. Its rulings therefore have a significance

---

23 Art. 36(2) reads as follows: "The rights referred to in paragraph 1 of this article shall be exercised in conformity with the laws and regulations of the receiving State, subject to the proviso, however, that the said laws and regulations must enable full effect to be given to the purposes for which the rights accorded under this article are intended". The United States had breached its obligations under Art. 36(2) because the procedural default rule, which requires exhaustion of remedies at the State level before a *habeas corpus* motion can be filed with federal courts, prevented the LaGrand brothers from effectively challenging their convictions and sentences other than on United States constitutional grounds; *supra* n. 21, paras. 81 and 91.

24 *Supra* n. 21, para. 128

25 Case Concerning Avena and Other Mexican Nationals (Mexico *v.* United States of America), Judgment of 31 March 2004, 2004 ICJ Rep. 12.

26 *Id.*, para.121 *et seq.*

extending far beyond the parties to the particular dispute arising out of the interpretation or application of the Convention. This is reflected in the Declaration appended to the Judgment in the *LaGrand* case by the then President Guillaume. The President declared that

> "[...] subparagraph (7) does not address the position of nationals of other countries or that of individuals sentenced to penalties that are not of a severe nature. However, in order to avoid any ambiguity, it should be made clear that there can be no question of applying an *a contrario* interpretation to this paragraph".[27]

The Judgments in the *LaGrand* and *Avena* cases should in principle make it easier for States in general – and not exclusively Germany and Mexico – to bring more pressure to bear on US authorities to comply with the provisions of the Vienna Convention concerning consular notification. Compliance with Article 36(1)(b), the consular notification *per se,* is the easy part. There are already ample indications that US authorities, primarily the State Department, but also local authorities are aware of the obligations of law enforcement officers under this provision of the Vienna Convention.[28] The difficult part may concern persons who have exhausted legal procedures and are on death row or serving long prison sentences, namely to remind the US judiciary of the obligation of the United States to respect the ruling of the International Court of Justice to allow review and reconsideration of the conviction and sentence if these have not met the requirements of Article 36(1) and (2), and to determine whether these violations of the Vienna Convention caused actual prejudice. In the first six months following the Court's decision in the *LaGrand* case, out of twenty reported US court judgments expressly addressing the Vienna Convention only three mentioned the decision, and none relied on it, except a dissenting judge in one case.[29]

Admittedly, the situation may have changed since 2001/2002. On 28 February 2005 the President of the United States issued a memorandum that stated that the United States would discharge its international obligations under the *Avena* Judgment by having State courts give effect to the decision in accordance with general principles of comity in cases filed by the fifty-one Mexican

27 Declaration of President Guillaume, LaGrand Case, *supra* n. 21, at 517.

28 *See* D. Cassel, *International Remedies in National Criminal Cases: ICJ Judgment in Germany v. United States*, 15 LJIL (2002) at 80.

29 *Id.*, at 79.

nationals addressed in that decision.[30] Since the statement of the President at least one State court has granted one of the fifty-one Mexican nationals a review of his conviction and sentence. The Oklahoma District Court Oklahoma County found that the Mexican national Osbaldo Torres had been prejudiced because he was not adequately informed of his rights under the Vienna Convention.[31] However, the problem remains whether federal judges would be prepared, on the basis of the *LaGrand* and *Avena* rulings, to refrain from applying the procedural default rule.[32] It is my impression that – at least until a recent date – the American federal judges seek guidance from US constitutional law rather than from international law, should a conflict arise between the two law systems. Whereas the Constitution of the United States recognizes that all treaties, *i.e.* self-executing treaties or self-executing provisions of treaties, have a direct effect in the American legal order,[33] in case of conflict such a treaty overrides only *previously* enacted congressional statutes.[34] As the procedural default rule has found a solid base in the Antiterrorism and Effective Death Penalty Act, American federal judges may still take the view that this federal statute dating from 1996 prevails over the 1963 Vienna Convention even though the Vienna Convention contains self-executing provisions. This was actually the line taken in 1998 by the US Federal Supreme Court in *Breard* v. *Greene*.[35] However, two dissenting justices took the view that more time for consideration of the issues was needed.

In 2003, when the Supreme Court denied the petition for certiorari of the Mexican national Torres[36] two justices dissented. One justice considered the application of the procedural default rule in direct violation of the Vienna

---

30 Cited *in* Opinion of the US Supreme Court, Medellín *v.* Dretke, *supra* n. 9.

31 Torres *v.* Oklahoma, No. PCD 2004-442 (Oklahoma District Court Oklahoma County, 18 March 2005. Reported *in* 99 AJIL 695 (2005). This case was on remand from the Oklahoma Court of Criminal Appeals (13 May 2004; *see* 42 ILM (2004) at 1227). At an earlier stage (1993) the same Oklahoma District Court had convicted Torres and sentenced him to death. The Oklahoma Court of Criminal Appeals had confirmed his conviction and sentence.

32 *See*, *supra*, this Section.

33 US Constitution, Art. VI, clause 2: "[...] all treaties [...] shall be the supreme Law of the Land [...]"

34 *See* D. P. O'Connell, International Law, Vol. 1 (1970) at 63.

35 Supreme Court on writ of certiorari to the United States Court of Appeals for the Fourth Circuit, 14 April 1998, Breard *v.* Greene, *supra* n. 18.

36 Osbaldo Torres *v.* Mike Mullin, Warden. On petition for writ of certiorari to the United States Court of Appeals for the Tenth Circuit (No. 03-5781; decided 17 November 2003). *See also* the last sentence of n. 31.

Convention. The other justice was in favour of deferring Torres' petition in light of the fact that this case raised important questions concerning the relation between the domestic law of the United States and decisions of the International Court of Justice.

In March 2005 the Supreme Court in *Medellín* v. *Dretke*[37], in deference to the statement of the President of the United States, dismissed its earlier writ of certiorari as improvidently granted. This allowed a State court, the Texas Court of Criminal Appeals, to consider Medellín's State *habeas corpus* action and thus provide Medellín with a review and reconsideration of his conviction and sentence on the basis of his claim under the Vienna Convention. Nevertheless, the Court presented an extensive analysis why a federal *habeas corpus* claim of Medellín on the basis of violation of the Vienna Convention may fail.

The latest development is the Supreme Court's combined Judgment in two consular notification cases, *Sanchez-Llamas* v. *Oregon* and *Bustillo* v. *Johnson.*[38] With a six to three majority the Court ruled that the *LaGrand* and *Avena* decisions of the International Court of Justice did not compel the Court to reconsider the Court's understanding of the Vienna Convention as laid down in *Breard* v. *Greene*. Ignoring the statement of the President of the International Court of Justice in the LaGrand case[39] the Court *inter alia* noted that judgments of the International Court of Justice have no binding force except between the parties and in respect of that particular case. Also the Court held that the interpretation of the International Court of Justice of Article 36 of the Vienna Convention is inconsistent with the basic framework of the adversary system such as that of the United States. Furthermore, the Court held that *States* may subject claims under article 36 of the Vienna Convention to the same procedural default rules that apply generally to other *federal*-law claims.

Taking into consideration the jurisprudence of the International Court of Justice and the above described developments in US case law the question arises what means the Netherlands' government (and for that matter any other government) has at its disposal to intervene with the American authorities on behalf of its own nationals (including, in the case of the Netherlands, citizens of the Netherlands' Antilles and Aruba) who in the past have been arrested, detained and thereafter convicted without their rights under Article 36 of the Vienna Convention having been respected by US law enforcement officers (Article

---

37 *See* n. 9, *supra.*

38 On writ of certiorari to the Supreme Court of Michigan (No. 04-10566) and on writ of certiorari to the Supreme Court of Virginia (No. 05-51); decided 28 June 2006.

39 *See* n. 27, *supra.*

36(1)(b)) and US courts (Article 36(2)? Fortunately, at present there are no Dutch nationals at death row in the United States. However, there are a considerable number of Dutch citizens serving prison sentences.[40] At least one of them whose rights under the Vienna Convention may not have been respected, Harry Bout, is serving a life sentence.[41] Bearing in mind the statement of President Guillaume,[42] it may be argued that subparagraph 7 of the ICJ ruling in the *LaGrand* case is applicable to him. The Netherlands' government has made considerable efforts through diplomatic channels to draw the attention of the US authorities to a possible violation of the Vienna Convention vis-à-vis Bout and vis-à-vis the Netherlands in its own right. However, as yet this diplomatic action has not yielded any positive result. It seems to me that – apart from an *amicus curiae* brief – no other realistic means would be available for the Dutch authorities to intervene in this type of cases through other means than the usual diplomatic channels. Any action before the International Court of Justice and the US Supreme Court must be excluded. As of 7 March 2005 the United States has denounced the Optional Protocol Concerning Compulsory Settlement of Disputes to the Vienna Convention, which in Article I provides for the jurisdiction of the International Court of Justice. Action before the US Supreme Court against the United States and the constituent State concerned may fail in light of the earlier case law of the Court. In the motion of *Germany et al.* v. *the United States et al.*[43] The Supreme Court declined to exercise its original jurisdiction granted by Article III, section 2, clause 2 of the US Constitution ("In all cases affecting Ambassadors, other public Ministers and Consuls, and those in which a State shall be Party, the Supreme Court shall have original jurisdiction [...]"), in respect of Germany's action against both the United States and the State of Arizona. The Court considered *inter alia* that it is doubtful that the above-cited clause of the US Constitution provides an anchor to prevent execution of a German citizen who is not an ambassador or consul. With regard to Germany's action against the State of Arizona the Court held that a foreign government's ability here to assert a claim

---

40 The total number was 161 in 2004; *see Rapport Gedetineerdenbegeleiding Buitenland* (Report Support for Detainees Abroad) of the *Algemene Rekenkamer* (Government Audit-Office); TK 2004-2005, 30010, Nos. 1-2.

41 On several websites it is claimed that this person's rights under the Vienna Convention have been violated (http://www.patrickcrusade.org/HARRY_BOUT.html; http://www.injusticeline.com/bout.html).

42 *See* n. 27, *supra*.

43 *See* n. 18, *supra*.

against a State is without evident support in the Vienna Convention and in probable contravention of Eleventh Amendment principles.[44]

What remains is an *amicus curiae* brief in case a convicted Dutch national himself would start legal proceedings, *e.g.* by filing a motion for relief from judgment in view of new facts having occurred such as the rulings of the International Court of Justice in the *LaGrand* and *Avena* cases. It must, however, be admitted that the prospects for success of these legal proceedings may have been adversely affected by the recent Judgment of the Supreme Court in *Sanchez-Llamas* v. *Oregon* and *Bustillo* v. *Johnson*. As we have seen above,[45] submission of an *amicus curiae* occurs in all courts, both lower courts, namely State trial courts or federal district courts and – in particular – appeals courts. In the case of the above-mentioned Dutch national who is serving a life sentence several opportunities arose for the Netherlands to intervene by means of an *amicus curiae* brief. In October 2003 Bout filed a motion for relief from judgment before the 17th Circuit Court of the State of Michigan, *inter alia* on the basis of an alleged violation of the Vienna Convention.[46] After this State trial court dismissed his motion in June 2004, he started appeal procedures in June 2005 before the Appeals Court of the State of Michigan. After dismissal of his appeal on 10 February 2006 he appealed to the Supreme Court of the State of Michigan. As of 1 June 2006 this procedure was still pending.

Before the start of the proceedings in the State trial court the Netherlands' government had used and continued to use traditional means of diplomatic action on behalf of Bout. However, in view of the apparent ineffectiveness of these diplomatic steps it is remarkable that the government did not see fit to file an *amicus curiae* brief in the proceedings before the State trial court and that only in January 2006 the government submitted a brief to the State appeals court, *i.e.* six months after the start of the appeal procedures and one year and a half after Bout's attorney requested the Netherlands' government to intervene and suggested submission of an *amicus curiae* brief as one of the possible actions to assist his client.

In its statement of interest the Netherlands stressed that Article 36 of the Vienna Convention confers rights on both the individual and the country of which he is a citizen, and added that, as such, the Kingdom of the Netherlands

44 Eleventh Amendment: "The judicial power of the United States shall not be construed to extend to any suit in law or equity, commenced or prosecuted against one of the United States by [...] or by citizens or subjects of any foreign State".

45 *See* Section 2, *supra*.

46 The author does not express any view as to the legitimacy of this claim.

has an interest in securing compliance with rights guaranteed under Article 36. The Netherlands supported the position of the petitioner, Bout, that an effective review and reconsideration be conducted of both the conviction and the sentence, to fully ascertain the facts regarding the alleged treaty violation and the nature and degree of prejudice suffered by the petitioner as a consequence of any such violation. As the Appeals Court of the State of Michigan, while granting the motion of the Kingdom of the Netherlands to file an *amicus curiae* brief, failed to address the obligations of the United States as outlined in the brief and dismissed Bout's appeal, the Netherlands was obliged to submit on 7 April 2006 a second (virtually identical) brief to the Supreme Court of the State of Michigan. It seems to me that the Netherlands was right to persist in submitting these briefs.

Even though the action of the Netherlands must be welcomed, it must also be recognized that this action – at least at the level of the State appeals court – came at a late stage. Therefore, it is fair to conclude that – at least as far as intervention in a lack of consular notification case is concerned – the Netherlands' government seems to be hesitant to use submission of *amicus curiae* briefs as a tool for assisting its nationals. The reasons for this reluctance are set out in the final Section.

5 Situations Where the Netherlands Took Diplomatic Action but Refrained from Using the Instrument of an *Amicus Curiae* Brief

The US Alien Tort Statute is part of the 1789 US Judiciary Act[47] and provides that "[t]he district courts shall have original jurisdiction of any civil action by an alien for a tort only, committed in violation of the law of nations or a treaty of the United States". After having passed almost two centuries in obscurity, this Statute was brought to new life in 1980 when the Court of Appeals for the Second Circuit applied it in the *Filartiga* case.[48] In that case Filartiga, a Paraguayan national, living in the United States, brought legal action against two Paraguayan police officers who happened to be in the United States and whom Filartiga accused of having tortured his son to death in Paraguay. Since the mid nineties a number of civil lawsuits were brought under the Alien Tort Statute for violations of human rights in a number of foreign countries. One of these cases concerned the Dutch/British company Royal Dutch/Shell which

47 28 U.S.C. para. 1350.

48 Filartiga *v.* Peña-Irala; 630 F.2d 876 (2d Cir. 1980).

was accused by a number of private persons of complicity in human rights violations committed in Nigeria, in particular the execution on doubtful grounds of the Nigerian activist Ken Saro-Wiwa. After the Federal District Court for the Southern District of New York had dismissed the claim on *forum non conveniens* grounds the Federal Court of Appeals for the Second Circuit reversed, holding that the District Court had failed to give proper consideration to the choice of a US forum by US resident plaintiffs and to the interest of the United States in providing a forum for the adjudication of claims alleging international human rights abuses.[49] Another example of lawsuits under the US Alien Tort Statute that affected the interests of companies and raised concerns among the business community are the South African Apartheid Litigation cases which were filed in 2002 in a number of federal district courts. Complaints were filed against a considerable number of both US and non-US companies for vicarious liability for human rights violations committed by the former South African apartheid regime.

It is understandable that among the international business community concerns arose about the extraterritorial effect of application of the Alien Tort Statute. It was feared that the practice of suing companies in the United States, in particular foreign companies, for alleged events occurring in third countries would constitute an unacceptable extraterritorial extension of United States jurisdiction.

For the exercise of jurisdiction, both prescriptive or legislative and adjudicative or enforcement jurisdiction, international law makes a distinction between prohibitive rules and permissive rules. Permissive rules provide for the existence of a sufficiently close and genuine connection between the forum State on the one hand and the defendants and the incriminated conduct on the other. The seat of incorporation of the accused company and the place where the alleged wrongful act occurred constitute elements of such close and genuine connection.

It may have come as a relief for the business community that in 2004 the US Supreme Court had an opportunity to rule on the scope of applicability of the Alien Tort Statute in the case *Sosa* v. *Alvarez*.[50] Sosa is a Mexican national who in 1990 was used with the approval of the UN Drug Enforcement Administration (DEA) to assist in abducting Alvarez, also a Mexican national, from

49 United States Court of Appeals for the Second Circuit, 14 September 2000, Nos. 99-7223(L), 99-7245(XAP).

50 Sosa *v.* Alvarez, No. 03-339; United States *v.* Alvarez, No.03-485 on writs of certiorari to the United States Court of Appeals for the Ninth Circuit, 29 June 2004.

Mexico to stand trial in the United States for complicity in the torture and murder of a DEA agent. After his acquittal[51] and his return to Mexico Alvarez sued Sosa for violating the law of nations under the Alien Tort Statute.[52] The US District Court for the Central District of California awarded Alvarez summary judgment and damages on the claim under the Alien Tort Statute. The US Court of Appeals for the Ninth Circuit affirmed the Judgment.[53] After the Supreme Court had granted a petition by the US government (the US Solicitor General) for a writ of certiorari there followed a large number of *amicus curiae* briefs from different circles, both from governments and from non-governmental organizations.[54] Governments were aware that extraterritorial jurisdiction was not the main issue of the Alvarez case, but were hoping that this case would give the Supreme Court the opportunity to clarify the scope of applicability of the US Alien Tort Statute.

The Netherlands' government did not submit an *amicus curiae* brief on this issue, nor did it associate itself with either the brief of the European Commission[55] or the brief submitted by the governments of Australia, Switzerland and the United Kingdom.[56] It would seem that this lack of concrete action was not due to a lack of interest on the part of the Netherlands' government. The contrary is true. On several occasions the Netherlands' government had expressed, in direct contacts of cabinet ministers with their American counterparts, its concern at negative effects for the Dutch private sector of the application of the Alien Tort Statute to extraterritorial conduct. It seems to me that the Netherlands' government too would have welcomed a clarification by the Supreme Court of the scope of applicability of this Statute.

---

51 The acquittal of Alvarez by the District Court which was based on the grounds that the evidence adduced was insufficient to support a guilty verdict, came after the Supreme Court in 1992 had ruled that the forcible seizure and transfer of Alvarez to the United States, whether or not a violation of general international law principles, did not violate the U.S.-Mexico Extradition Treaty and therefore did not prohibit Alvarez' trial in a US court for violations of US criminal laws. *See* United States *v.* Alvarez-Machain, 504 U.S. 655 (1992).

52 Alvarez also sued the United States for false arrest under the Federal Tort Claims Act; *see* n. 50, *supra*.

53 The District Court dismissed the Federal Tort Claims Act claim (*see* previous note); the Appeals Court reversed the claim's dismissal.

54 *See* website http://www.nosafehaven.com.

55 Brief of *amicus curiae* the European Commission in Support of Neither Party.

56 Brief of the Governments of the Commonwealth of Australia, the Swiss Confederation and the United Kingdom of Great Britain and Northern Ireland as *amici curiae* in Support of the Petitioner.

One can only speculate on the grounds why the Netherlands' government saw fit to abstain from action, and in particular why it did not jump at the opportunity to join either of the two above-mentioned *amicus curiae* briefs.

Both the brief submitted by the European Commission and the one submitted by the three governments express concern at an interpretation of the Alien Tort Statute allowing the exercise of jurisdiction inconsistent with international law while at the same time recognizing the importance of respect for human rights: The brief of the three governments recognized the importance of human rights violations being dealt with fairly and promptly in the appropriate fora; the brief of the European Commission referred to the function of universal criminal jurisdiction in order to end impunity of the most fundamental norms of international law.

The fact that the brief of the three governments was in support of the petitioner and the brief of the European Commission in support of neither party does not seem to me to be decisive for the Netherlands' position. What matters is that both briefs focused on the need for the Supreme Court to recognize the limits to the exercise of jurisdiction imposed by international law and stressed the importance of respect for human rights. It would seem that this two-pronged approach is shared by the Netherlands.

As far as the *amicus curiae* brief of the European Commission is concerned, there may have been a formal reason preventing the Netherlands from associating itself with it. Although the European Commission is the executive body of the European Community[57] and although its *amicus curiae* brief explicitly states that it is the Community and its Member States who are entitled to express views on issues of extraterritorial jurisdiction in relation to their respective competencies,[58] the brief contains the view of the Commission itself. As it would have been inappropriate for the Commission to issue a statement together with one single Member State or even a few Member States, the Commission submitted the brief in its own right.

It would have been an alternative choice for the Netherlands to associate itself with the *amicus curiae* brief of the three governments. However, I note that this brief contains a statement which does not reflect Netherlands' policies. This may have been a reason for the Netherlands to refrain from joining the brief. I refer to the statement that "as a matter of international law, violations of customary international law do not give individuals the right to bring civil

57 The Commission is *not* the executive body of the European Union, but of the European Community, the so-called first pillar of the Union.

58 *See* n. 55, *supra*, at 1.

claims in respect of those violations".[59] The Netherlands may have adhered to the view that at least in this respect the European Commission takes a more balanced view. The Commission recognizes that – in addition to universal criminal jurisdiction under international law over most heinous crimes such as torture, genocide, war crimes and crimes against humanity – there may be some scope for universal civil jurisdiction as well. The Commission admits that universal civil jurisdiction has received less attention than universal criminal jurisdiction and that its existence and scope are not well established under international law.[60] In this context the Commission refers *inter alia* to the Restatement (Third) of the Foreign Relations Law of the United States,[61] the case law of the International Criminal Tribunal for the Former Yugoslavia,[62] the Separate Opinion of the Judges Higgins, Kooijmans and Buergenthal in the *Arrest Warrant* case in the International Court of Justice,[63] academic commentary[64] and certain practices in domestic legal systems which counsel in favour of recognizing universal civil jurisdiction for the offences that come within universal criminal jurisdiction such as the *action civile*.[65] The Commission also recognized that the exercise of universal civil jurisdiction, if justified by the international community's determination to end impunity for conduct that violates the most fundamental norms of international law, must comply with certain conditions such as the exhaustion of adequate and available remedies in the place in which the conduct giving rise to the claim occurred.[66]

The broader approach of the Commission as to the question of existence and scope of universal civil jurisdiction seems to me to be more in accordance with the position of the Netherlands. However, as already mentioned above, for reasons of institutional propriety it may have been inappropriate for the Netherlands formally to join the brief of the Commission.

Whatever the precise reasons for the Netherlands' government not to have submitted (or at least not to have joined in submitting) an *amicus curiae* brief,

59 *See* n. 56, *supra*, at 20.

60 *See* n. 55, *supra*, at 17.

61 *Id.*, at 17.

62 *Id.*, at 18; Prosecutor *v.* Furundzija, Case No. IT-95-17/1-T, Trial Chamber II, 10 December 1998, para. 155; 38 ILM (1999) at 317.

63 *See* n. 55, *supra*, at 18; Arrest Warrant of 11 April 2000 (Democratic Republic of the Congo *v.* Belgium), Merits, Judgment of 14 February 2002, 2002 ICJ Rep. 3, Joint Separate Opinion of Judges Higgins, Kooijmans and Buergenthal, paras. 48, 41.

64 *Id.* at 19.

65 *Id.*, at 21.

66 *Id.*, at 22-26.

it seems fair to conclude that – as we already have seen in Section 4 above – the Netherlands seems rather hesitant to use the instrument of an *amicus curiae* brief as a tool for diplomatic action on behalf of its nationals.

One may wonder whether and, if so, to what extent the briefs submitted have influenced the ultimate Judgment of the Supreme Court. In any case this Judgment must have been satisfactory for *amici* as well as for the Netherlands and the business community in holding that the respondent Alvarez was not entitled to recover damages from petitioner Sosa under the Alien Tort Statute. The Court, however, did not focus on the aspect of the extraterritorial application of the Alien Tort Statute, but rather gave a more restricted interpretation of the substantive scope of this Statute.[67]

6 CONCLUSION

It is difficult to draw an unequivocal conclusion with regard to the Netherlands' (limited) practice of submission of *amicus curiae* briefs. In particular, in regard of submission of briefs in cases involving lack of consular notification by US authorities the conclusion seems to be that the practice of the Netherlands – in spite of or rather because of the late submission of a brief concerning the Dutch national serving a life sentence – reveals a certain degree of restraint fully to exercise this tool for protecting its own nationals. Furthermore, the absence of action with regard to the issue of the scope of applicability of the Alien Tort Statute – even though one can only speculate on the reason thereof – indicates a similar restraint.

On the one hand this restraint or caution seems odd, as there are strong indications that there is no need to fear a counterproductive effect. As pointed out in Section 2, submission of *amicus curiae* briefs is an accepted practice in American court procedure and cannot be considered an unlawful intervention in the domestic affairs of the United States.

On the other hand the exercise of restraint in the submission of *amicus curiae* briefs is understandable. The use of the tool of an *amicus curiae* brief is only wise in proceedings which may lead to a judicial decision which would constitute a serious infringement of the international obligations of the United States. Since a court of justice, at State level as well as at the federal level, is an organ of the State (*i.e.* the United States), a judgment that might be

67 *See* n. 50, *supra*. I leave out of consideration the ruling of the Court in respect of petitioner's claim under the Federal Tort Claims Act.

considered a denial of justice engages the State responsibility of the State (the United States).[68]

Restraint is also understandable as to the level of the US court dealing with the matter that is subject of an *amicus curiae* brief. As pointed out above,[69] *amicus curiae* briefs may be submitted in all courts, both lower courts (State trial courts and federal district courts) and – in particular – appeals courts, but the Netherlands' government understandably is hesitant to use this tool in proceedings at these levels of jurisdiction and would seem to have – in general terms – a preference for restricting its use to proceedings before the Federal Supreme Court or – if need be – a supreme court at State level. This could explain why, as mentioned in Section 4, the Netherlands' government did not hesitate to submit an *amicus curiae* brief to the Supreme Court of the State of Michigan as soon as it became clear that the Appeals Court of the State of Michigan had dismissed the claim of the Dutch petitioner and had ignored the contents of the Netherlands' government's *amicus curiae* brief in support of the petitioner.

A final consideration for the Netherlands to show caution in the use of the *amicus curiae* brief as an instrument of diplomatic action on behalf of its nationals (or even diplomatic protection) is the perceived need to avoid concurrence with any action through diplomatic channels which in general terms is considered more effective, although in a situation where the latter approach does not seem to produce positive results a two-pronged approach may not be excluded.

My observation that the Netherlands' practice of submission of *amicus curiae* briefs reveals some degree of restraint is in my view not contradicted by the above-mentioned submission of a brief in a case involving antitrust law. We have seen in Section 4.2.1 that all the conditions for the Netherlands joining the common brief of the United Kingdom and Ireland in the case *Hoffmann-LaRoche Ltd. et al.* v. *Empagran S.A. et al.* and, thus, overcoming any possible reluctance, were met. The brief was filed in proceedings before the Federal Supreme Court. The main concern expressed in the brief related to the exercise by US courts of extraterritorial jurisdiction, which in the opinion of these States would have been a serious infringement of the international obligations of the

68 Art. 4(1) of the Articles on Responsibility of States for Internationally Wrongful Acts. This provision also contains the federal clause: "The conduct of any State organ shall be considered an act of that State under international law, [...] whatever its character as an organ of the central government or of a territorial unit of the State".

69 *See* Section 2, *supra*.

United States. Finally, there is no evidence in the public domain that a situation of concurrence with action through diplomatic channels has arisen.

11

DECLARATIONS OF IMMUNITY FROM SEIZURE OF FOREIGN ARTWORKS AND THE LEGAL POSITION OF SOVEREIGN ART LENDERS BEFORE US COURTS: THE *MALEWICZ* CASE

Nout van Woudenberg[*]

1 Introduction

On 9 January 2004, a group of thirty-five heirs of the world-renowned Russian artist Kazimir Malevich[1] filed suit in the US District Court for the District of Columbia in Washington D.C. against the City of Amsterdam.[2] The heirs' US

* Legal counsel at the International Law Division of the Ministry of Foreign Affairs of the Kingdom of the Netherlands. The opinions in this essay are solely the author's and do not necessarily represent those of the Kingdom of the Netherlands.

1 Kazimir Malevich was born on 11 March 1879 not far away from Kiev. In his development as a painter, he launched the Suprematist movement, which brought abstract art to a geometric simplicity more drastically than anyone had done previously. Malevich died in Leningrad (St. Petersburg) on 15 May 1935. When I refer in this analysis to the painter or his artworks, I use the name 'Malevich'. However, as the dispute before the US Court has been initiated by Leonard Malewicz c.s., I use the name 'Malewicz' when the case is concerned.

2 This is not the first time that the City of Amsterdam is before a US Court because of a dispute that involves artworks. The first time, in November 1993, the case had been initiated by the City itself, as the Stedelijk Museum brought action against conservator Daniel Goldreyer. The City claimed that Goldreyer failed to fulfil the conditions of a written agreement with the City of Amsterdam for the restoration of the painting 'Who's Afraid of Red, Yellow and Blue III' by the artist Barnett Newman. The painting was owned by the City and was located in the Stedelijk Museum. It was asserted that the method Goldreyer utilized resulted in substantial damage to the painting, as he allegedly over-painted the largest portion of the painting, instead of utilizing the 'pinpointing' method of restoring the damaged section of the painting. The City argued that it had

N. Blokker, R. Lefeber, L. Lijnzaad & I. van Bladel (eds.), *The Netherlands in Court. Essays in Honour of Johan G. Lammers*, © 2006 Koninklijke Brill NV. Printed in the Netherlands, pp. 223-245.

complaint is seeking the recovery of fourteen Malevich artworks,[3] loaned by the Stedelijk Museum Amsterdam for a special exhibition at the Solomon R. Guggenheim Museum in New York[4] and The Menil Collection in Houston.[5] The complaint was filed two days before the exhibition in Houston closed. The fourteen artworks are part of a larger collection of some eighty-four paintings, gouaches, drawings and theoretical cards that were purchased by the Stedelijk Museum Amsterdam (a museum owned by the City of Amsterdam) in 1958. The case raises a number of legal questions: Is the City of Amsterdam entitled to immunity from jurisdiction before the US Court? Does an Immunity from Seizure Declaration issued by the US Department of State not immunize the artworks, or its sovereign owner, against judicial procedure?

Given that the lawsuit between the Malevich heirs and the City of Amsterdam was *sub judice* as this publication went to press, and in light of the unpredictability of its outcome, this analysis will be confined to highlighting some elements concerning the international and US approaches regarding immunity of the cultural property of a state and to describing the practice of Immunity from Seizure Declarations regarding cultural property in the United States of America and the Netherlands in the light of the US lawsuit. In describing these elements and pertinent aspects of the US lawsuit, no position is taken on any of the arguments advanced by either party to that lawsuit.

Most of the contributions in this book deal with the State of the Netherlands as a party to a dispute before international or national courts. In this analysis, it is the City of Amsterdam which is the subject. While under both international and national law the City is a political subdivision of the State of the Netherlands, this fact results in a somewhat different approach to the analysis here undertaken.

In my analysis, I will start with highlighting some elements concerning the international and American approach on immunity of the property of a state and will continue by describing the practice of Immunity from Seizure Declarations regarding cultural property in the United States of America and the Nether-

suffered damages in the amount of 3.5 million dollars due to reduction in the value of the artwork. Goldreyer filed a motion to dismiss the claim, but this was denied in its entirety by the Court. The case ended with a settlement between the City and Goldreyer, and the City paid a sum of 100,000 dollars. Amsterdam *v.* Daniel Goldreyer, LTD., 882 F. Supp. 1273 (E.D.N.Y. 1995).

3 13 paintings and one drawing.

4 This exhibition took place from 22 May 2003 till 7 September 2003.

5 This exhibition took place from 2 October 2003 till 11 January 2004.

lands. These topics will then come together in my summary of (the initial phase of) the *Malewicz* case which follows.

2 International and US Rules on State Immunity

2.1 General; from Absolute to Restrictive Immunity

Until the twentieth century, it was believed that sovereign immunity from the jurisdiction of foreign courts left no room for exception. However, as governments became increasingly engaged in commercial activities, the view emerged that immunity of states engaged in such activities should not be supported by international law. After all, it deprived private parties that dealt with a state of their effective remedies and it gave states an unbalanced advantage in competition with private commercial enterprises. As a result of this shift in view, basically two differing views on the issue of state immunity began to emerge. On the one hand, there were those who believed in absolute state immunity. In other words, the state is under all circumstances immune from the interference of a foreign court and also from any measures of constraint that may be imposed by a foreign court, irrespective of whether the action of the state in question may be described as typical government action or as being tantamount to a private commercial transaction. This is the standpoint which has been taken by a number of developing countries. Western countries, on the other hand, generally took a more restrictive approach. This restrictive principle of immunity spread rapidly after the Second World War. Under the restrictive theory, a state is immune from any exercise of judicial jurisdiction by another state in respect of claims arising out of governmental activities (*acta de jure imperii*); it is not immune however from the exercise of such jurisdiction in respect of claims arising out of activities of a kind carried on by private persons (*acta de jure gestionis*).[6] Even in such a situation, however, the state in question is regarded as retaining a right to immunity from the enforcement of any judgment issued

---

6 The question whether and when an activity should be considered as *de jure imperii* or *de jure gestionis* must in the view of these countries, first and foremost be answered by assessing the nature of the activity, as opposed to its purpose. However, as we will see below in Section 2.2, according to the UN Convention the purpose should also be taken into account if the parties have so agreed, or if, in the practice of the state or the forum, that purpose is relevant to determine the non-commercial character of the contract or transaction.

against it, albeit that courts in a number of Western countries, including the Netherlands, accept that property that is not intended for use by a foreign state for government non-commercial purposes may be attached.

2.2 International Instruments on State Immunity

On 2 December 2004, the UN General Assembly adopted without a vote Resolution A/Res/59/38 regarding the UN Convention on Jurisdictional Immunities of States and Their Property.[7,8] It had come a long way, since the General Assembly invited the International Law Commission[9] to start work on the issue of jurisdictional immunities of states and their property in 1977.[10] The Convention consists of thirty-three articles. The text reflects a compromise between the advocates of the absolute theory of state immunity, and the supporters of the restrictive theory. The preamble expressly refers to state immunity as a principle of customary international law.[11] Article 5 expresses the basic principle of state immunity and declares that a state enjoys immunity, in respect of itself and its property, from the jurisdiction of the courts of another state subject to the provisions of the Convention.[12] Subsequently, in part III of the Convention (Articles 10-17),[13] the proceedings in which state immunity cannot be invoked are enumerated.

---

7 The text of the UN Convention is attached to this UNGA resolution.

8 For a comprehensive article on this issue, *see* G. Hafner & U. Köhler *The United Nations Convention on the Immunity of States and Their Property* 35 NYIL 3 (2005); *see also* D.P. Stewart, *Introductory note on the UN Convention on jurisdictional immunities of states and their property,* 44 ILM 801 (2005).

9 In 1947, the International Law Commission was established by the General Assembly to promote the progressive development of international law and its codification.

10 GA Res. 32/151 of 19 December 1977.

11 "Considering that the jurisdictional immunities of States and their property are generally accepted as a principle of customary international law".

12 The City of Amsterdam falls under the definition of "State" as used in this Convention, being a "political subdivision of the State" (Art. 2, para. 1(b)(ii)).

13 Art. 10: Commercial transactions; Art. 11: Contracts of employment; Art. 12: Personal injuries and damage to property; Art. 13: Ownership, possession and use of property; Art. 14: Intellectual and industrial property; Art. 15: Participation in companies or other collective bodies; Art. 16: Ships owned or operated by a State; Art. 17: Effect of an arbitration agreement.

Commercial transactions constitute one of the most important exceptions to immunity under the Convention.[14,15] Article 2, paragraph 2, states that in determining whether a contract or transaction is a 'commercial transaction' under the Convention, reference should be made primarily to the nature of the contract or transaction; but its purpose should also be taken into account if the parties to the contract or transaction have so agreed, or if, in the practice of the state or the forum, that purpose is relevant to determining the non-commercial character of the contract or transaction.

Cultural valuables play a special role under the Convention when it comes to immunity from measures of constraint. While the UN Convention proceeds from the principle that no measures of constraint may be taken against property of a state, it also provides for certain exceptions to that principle. The Convention makes a distinction between state immunity from pre-judgment measures of constraint[16] and state immunity from post-judgment measures of constraint.[17] Most exceptions to the principle that no measures of constraint may be taken against property of a state apply to both pre-judgment and post-judgment measures of constraint.[18] However, there is one exception that applies to post-judgment measures only. State property of which it has been established that it is specifically in use or intended for use by a state for other than government non-commercial purposes and that is in the territory of the state of the forum does not as such enjoy immunity from post-judgment measures of constraint, provided that post-judgment measures of constraint may only be taken against property that has a connection with the entity against which the proceeding was directed.[19] Article 21 of the Convention limits the foregoing by stating explicitly, amongst others, that property forming part of the cultural heritage of a state[20] or property of a state forming part of an exhibition of objects of scientific, cultural or historical interest[21] shall not be considered

14 Art. 10.
15 Art. 2, para. 1(c), defines the term 'commercial transaction'.
16 Art. 18.
17 Art. 19.
18 These exceptions lack relevance for discussion under this analysis.
19 *See* Art. 19(c).
20 Or part of its archives and not placed or intended to be placed on sale.
21 And not placed or intended to be placed on sale.

as property specifically in use or intended for use by a state for other than government non-commercial purposes;[22] therefore, this property is excluded from the exception of Article 19(c) and is immune also from post-judgment measures of constraint.

The Convention will be open for signature by all states until 17 January 2007.[23] On 23 August 18 countries had signed the Convention already. It was ratified by one state. The Convention will enter into force when thirty instruments of ratification, acceptance, approval or accession have been deposited with the Secretary-General of the United Nations.[24]

At the European level, the European Convention on State Immunity with its Additional Protocol was concluded on 16 May 1972.[25] On 11 June 1976, it entered into force. Currently it has eight European State Parties. On the basis of Article 15 of this Convention, a Contracting State shall be entitled to immunity from the jurisdiction of the courts of another Contracting State if the proceedings do not fall within the enumeration of Articles 1 to 14.

The Convention is based on the outline above, under 2.1, regarding the extensive competence of a foreign court to declare cases with or against foreign states regarding acts *de jure gestionis* of those states admissible. It has no specific provisions on cultural property. The Netherlands has been a party to the European Convention since 22 May 1985.

Finally, Article 27 is worth mentioning. In the UN Convention (see *supra* n. 12), and in US legislation (see *infra* 2.3), a political subdivision of a state, such as the City of Amsterdam, is considered as falling within the definition of a state under these instruments. However, the European Convention states in Article 27 that for the purposes of that Convention, a Contracting State does not include any legal entity of a Contracting State which is distinct therefrom and is capable of suing or being sued, even if that entity has been entrusted with public functions. Consequently, proceedings may be instituted against such entity before the courts of another Contracting State in the same manner as against a private person; however, the courts may not entertain proceedings in respect of acts performed by the entity in the exercise of sovereign authority (*acta jure imperii*).

---

22 Para. 1, paras. (d) and (e).

23 Art. 28.

24 Art. 30.

25 Trb. 1973, 43. *Also* on http://conventions.coe.int/Treaty/en/Treaties/Html/074.htm.

2.3 US Policy on State Immunity

Like the Netherlands, the United States of America adheres to a restrictive view on sovereign immunity. However, this has not always been the case. Until 1952, foreign states enjoyed absolute immunity from law suits in federal courts. In that year, in response to changing practices among states, Jack B. Tate, the Acting Legal Adviser for the Secretary of State, explained in a letter to the Attorney General that the State Department would from that moment on apply the 'restrictive theory' of sovereign immunity.[26]

This change had little impact on federal courts, as they continued to abide by the Department's specific immunity suggestions in individual cases. Furthermore, diplomatic pressure by other states became an instrument of importance: it sometimes prompted the State Department to file suggestions of immunity in cases in which immunity would not have been available under the restrictive theory. And when foreign nations were not asking the Department for immunity, the courts had to determine whether immunity existed. So, the conclusion can be drawn that the responsibility for immunity determinations was in practice a competence of both the Executive and Judicial Branch.

In view of these inconsistent standards in applying restrictive theories of sovereign immunity between those two Branches, on the 21 October 1976, the 94th Congress adopted the Foreign Sovereign Immunities Act (FSIA)[27] to codify the restrictive theory of sovereign immunity and to place the primary responsibility for immunity determinations with the Judicial Branch.[28] The FSIA

---

26 Letter from Jack B. Tate, Acting Legal Adviser, US Department of State, to Acting US Attorney General Philip B. Perlman (19 May 1952), reprinted *in* 26. Dept. State Bull. 984-985 (1952). Also known as the so-called Tate Letter. This letter states: "A study of the law of sovereign immunity reveals the existence of two conflicting concepts of sovereign immunity, each widely held and firmly established. According to the classical or absolute theory of sovereign immunity, a sovereign cannot, without his consent, be made a respondent in the courts of another sovereign. According to the newer or restrictive theory of sovereign immunity, the immunity of the sovereign is recognized with regard to sovereign or public acts (jure imperii) of a state, but not with respect to private acts (jure gestionis) [...] [I]t will thereafter be the Department's policy to follow the restrictive theory [...] in the consideration of requests of foreign governments for a grant of sovereign immunity".

27 Public Law 94-583, 90 Stat. 2891, 28 USC. Section 1330, 1332(a), 1391(f) and 1601-1611).

28 The Congress itself described the purpose as "to define the jurisdiction of the United States courts in suits against foreign states, the circumstances in which foreign states

grants federal courts jurisdiction over civil actions against foreign states and singles out expropriation and other exceptions to the general grant of immunity. At the same time, it seeks to limit the role of the Executive Branch in suits against foreign governments by precluding the State Department from making decisions on state immunity.[29]

The objectives of the FSIA are set out at 28 USC., paragraph 1602:

> "The Congress finds that the determination by United States courts of the claims of foreign states to immunity from the jurisdiction of such courts would serve the interests of justice and would protect the rights of both foreign states and litigants in United States courts. Under international law, states are not immune from the jurisdiction of foreign courts insofar as their commercial activities are concerned, and their commercial property may be levied upon for the satisfaction of judgments rendered against them in connection with their commercial activities. Claims of foreign states to immunity should henceforth be decided by courts of the United States and of the States in conformity with the principles set forth in this chapter".

The definitions of a foreign state under the FSIA can be found at 28 USC., paragraph 1603:

> "For purposes of this chapter
> (a) A "foreign state [...] includes a political subdivision of a foreign state or an agency or instrumentality of a foreign state as defined in subsection (b).
> (b) An "agency or instrumentality of a foreign state" means any entity
> (1) which is a separate legal person, corporate or otherwise, and
> (2) which is an organ of a foreign state or political subdivision[30] thereof, or a majority of whose shares or other ownership interest is owned by a foreign state or political subdivision thereof, and
> (3) which is neither a citizen of a State of the United States as defined in Section 1332(c) and (d) of this title, nor created under the laws of any third country".

This means that under the FSIA, as under the UN Convention, the City of Amsterdam is considered as falling within the definition of a "foreign state".

are immune from suit and in which execution may not be levied on their property, and for other purposes".

29 By a circular note dated 10 December 1976, the Department of State informed all foreign embassies in Washington of the enactment of the FSIA.

30 The term 'political subdivisions' includes all governmental units beneath the central government, including local governments, according to the Act's legislative history.

The same provision contains the following formulation of "commercial activity":

> "(d) A "commercial activity" means either a regular course of commercial conduct or a particular commercial transaction or act. The commercial character of an activity shall be determined by reference to the nature of the course of conduct or particular transaction or act, rather than by reference to its purpose.
> (e) A "commercial activity carried on in the United States by a foreign state" means commercial activity carried on by such state and having substantial contact with the United States".

Sovereign immunity of foreign states is provided in 28 USC., paragraph 1604:

> "Subject to existing international agreements to which the United States is a party at the time of enactment of this Act a foreign state shall be immune from the jurisdiction of the courts of the United States and of the States except as provided in Sections 1605 to 1607 of this chapter".

Relevant for this analysis is par. 1605(a)(3) which states that a foreign state shall not be immune from the jurisdiction of courts of the United States or of the States in any case

> "in which rights in property taken in violation of international law are in issue and that property or any property exchanged for such property is present in the United States in connection with a commercial activity carried on in the United States by the foreign state; or that property or any property exchanged for such property is owned or operated by an agency or instrumentality of the foreign state and that agency or instrumentality is engaged in a commercial activity in the United States".

On 7 June 2005, the US Supreme Court held in *Republic of Austria* v. *Altmann*[31] that the FSIA should be applied retroactively to acts that occurred prior to the FSIA's 1976 enactment and even prior to the United States' 1952

---

31 142 F. Supp. 2d 1187 (CD Cal. 2001), 317 F.3d 954 (9th Cir.2002), 327 F. 3d 1246 (9th Cir. 2003), and 124 S.Ct.2240 (2004). The *Altmann* case regarded a dispute over six Gustav Klimt paintings that belonged to plaintiff's uncle before being seized by the Germans after the 1938 'Anschluss' and allegedly expropriated by Austria following Second World War in 1948. Maria Altmann filed an action in a California federal court against Austria and its instrumentality, the Austrian Gallery, to recover the paintings, asserting jurisdiction under the FSIA. A central question in this case was whether Austria and its instrumentality would have immunity under the FSIA.

adoption of the so-called 'restrictive theory' of sovereign immunity. Prior to this precedent, there was a general presumption that foreign states and instrumentalities had absolute immunity regarding their pre-1952 acts.

3 Immunity from Seizure Declarations Regarding Cultural Property

3.1 Procedure in the Netherlands

Over the past years, Dutch museums increasingly demanded, often at the request of foreign museums, that the Dutch government grant an exemption from judicial seizure for the artworks they were planning to borrow from these other museums or institutions. In the Netherlands, the Ministry of Foreign Affairs is charged with issuing such Declarations.[32] The issuance of these Declarations serves the international collection mobility, as foreign museums are more willing to lend their artworks if a Declaration is issued. Besides, it seems to have a positive influence on the amount of the insurance premium. Therefore, museums attach great importance to these Declarations, and sometimes even consider them as a *conditio sine qua non* for loaning artwork.

From a legal point of view, those Declarations cannot as such be considered as 'hard' law. A Declaration merely states that the Netherlands' authorities, within their legal limits, will do their utmost to assure that the artworks can return to the institution or person of origin. When it concerns the property of a state, the Declaration refers to the rules in the UN Convention on Jurisdictional Immunities of States and Their Property (see also *supra* 2.2). Consequently, in the area of measures of constraint, state property can enjoy more protection than privately owned cultural valuables.

Overall, the Declaration has the following form and content:

> "On behalf of the Government of the Kingdom of the Netherlands, and with reference to Article [X] of the loan agreement between [name Dutch museum or institution] and the [name foreign museum or institution], concerning the loan of art objects for the purpose of [name and data of the exhibition], the Minister for European Affairs[33] herewith declares as follows.

32 Drafted by the Cultural Division and the International Law Division, signed by the Secretary General of the Ministry of Foreign Affairs on behalf of the Minister for European Affairs.

33 The Minister for European Affairs is responsible, together with the State Secretary for Culture, for the Dutch international cultural policy.

In accordance with international law and with the laws and regulations of the Netherlands, the Government of the Kingdom of the Netherlands will do everything that is legally within its power to ensure that the art objects loaned by [name foreign museum or institution] to the [name Dutch museum or institution] for the period [data] shall not be encumbered at any time while they are located on Dutch territory. In the event that the items concerned are the property of [name of the state concerned], the Government of the Kingdom of the Netherlands will follow the rule as currently reflected in the 2004 UN Convention on Jurisdictional Immunities of States and Their Property. In consequence, the Government of the Kingdom of the Netherlands will consider these items to be state property, which as such enjoy immunity from measures of constraint."

3.2 Procedure in the United States of America

The Netherlands is not the only country which issues these kinds of Declarations. The United States also has a procedure in place for handling this issue, although it operates in a somewhat different manner.

The US Department of State processes applications for exemption from seizure of loan exhibitions under the Federal Immunity from Seizure Act, 22 USC. 2459.[34] The full name of this Act is 'Exemption from Judicial Seizure of Cultural Objects Imported for Temporary Exhibition'. Its subtitle reads: 'an act to render immune from seizure under judicial process certain objects of cultural significance imported into the United States for temporary display or exhibition, and for other purposes'. The gist of this Act is that artwork brought into the United States from any foreign country for temporary non-profit exhibition is immune from measures of constraint or a US court process for the purpose or having the effect of depriving a US cultural institution or carrier of the custody or control of that artwork if, before the importation, "the President or his designee has determined that such object is of cultural significance and that the temporary exhibition or display thereof within the United States is in the national interest, and a notice to that effect has been published in the Federal Register".[35]

34 Public Law 89-259. (S.2273), 79 Stat. 985, approved 10/19/65 & #185.

35 22 USC. para 2459(a) reads: "Whenever any work of art or other object of cultural significance is imported into the United States from any foreign country, pursuant to an agreement entered into between the foreign owner of [sic] custodian thereof and the United States or one or more cultural or educational institutions within the United States providing for the temporary exhibition or display thereof within the United States at

So, a warranty of the US authorities actually consists of two steps, as paragraph (a) of the Act stipulates that in cases where concrete works of art are at stake the "President or his designee", which in practice will be the US Department of State, may direct in writing that these artworks are of "cultural significance" and are covered by the aforementioned Act.

In recent years, the US government has seen a rise in the number of immunity applications. American museums have increasingly availed themselves of the federal protection afforded by Section 2459 – sometimes on their own, and sometimes at the insistence of foreign lenders. In their Statement of Interest in the *Malewicz* case (see *infra* 4.2), the US authorities explained that in the years 1994-2004, as indicated by a search of the Westlaw Federal Register database, the United States Information Agency and Department of State have published immunity notices under Section 2459 for more than 600 exhibits. More than 900 such notices have been published since 1980.[36]

On 11 April 2003, prior to the loan of the Malevich artworks to the US institutions, the US Department of State issued Public Notice No. 4335, which notice was published in the Federal Register.[37] In this notice,[38] Patricia S. Harrison, Assistant Secretary for Educational and Cultural Affairs, Department

---

any cultural exhibition, assembly, activity, or festival administered, operated, or sponsored, without profit, by any such cultural or educational institution, no court of the United States, any State, the District of Columbia, or any territory or possession of the United States may issue or enforce any judicial process, or enter any judgment, decree, or order, for the purpose or having the effect of depriving such institution, or any carrier engaged in transporting such work or object within the United States of custody or control of such object if before the importation of such object the President or his designee has determined that such object is of cultural significance and that the temporary exhibition or display thereof within the United States is in the national interest, and a notice to that effect has been published in the Federal Register." The Act has a subdivision (b) and (c) as well. Subdivision (b) reads: "If in any judicial proceeding in any such court any such process, judgement, decree, or order is sought, issued or entered, the United States attorney for the judicial district which such proceeding is pending shall be entitled as of right to intervene as a party to that proceeding, and upon request made by either the institution adversely affected, or upon direction by the Attorney General if the United States is adversely affected, shall apply to such court for the denial, quashing or vacating thereof". Subdivision (c) concerns certain exemptions which for this analysis are of no relevance.

36 Malewicz *v.* City of Amsterdam, Statement of Interest of the United States, 22 December 2004, at 4.

37 Federal Register, 11 April 2003, Vol. 68, No. 70, at 17852-17853.

38 The notice carried the title Culturally Significant Objects Imported for Exhibition Determination: "Kazimir Malevich: Suprematism".

of State, declared that the objects to be included in the Malevich exhibitions at the Guggenheim Museum and The Menil Collection were of "cultural significance" and that the exhibitions were "in the national interest".[39] Through this Declaration, it was the evident intention of the US authorities to safeguard the artworks concerned against any measures of constraint or judicial process in the US, as also can be concluded from Section 4.2 *infra*.

4 THE *MALEWICZ* CASE

4.1 Arguments of the Parties

As mentioned in Section 1 *supra*, the heirs filed suit before the US District Court in Washington, D.C. on 9 January 2004. In this lawsuit, the principal question to be determined at the outset of the proceedings is of a procedural nature, namely, whether the US Court has jurisdiction to entertain the claim of the heirs. After all, the primary rule in international disputes is that legal disputes are to be instituted in the country of residence of the defendant. Furthermore, the case presents several immunity questions which must be resolved at the outset of any proceeding involving a sovereign defendant.

To summarize the claim with respect to content, the heirs are claiming that the City of Amsterdam wrongfully acquired the Malevich artworks that are in the Stedelijk Museum Amsterdam when the City purchased them from the German architect Hugo Häring, a friend of Malevich, in 1958.[40] Therefore, the heirs maintain that they are entitled to a rescission of the sale of the artworks as well as to recovery of the works from Amsterdam. They also claim to have been damaged by the conversion of their property and that they are entitled to either a recovery of the artworks or payment of their interest in the works, which interest they say should be valued in excess of USD 150 million. Finally, the heirs claim that the City of Amsterdam has unjustly enriched itself, and

39 "I hereby determine that the objects to be included in the exhibition "Kazimir Malevich: Suprematism" imported from abroad for temporary exhibition within the United States, are of cultural significance. These objects are imported pursuant to loan agreements with foreign lenders. I also determine that the exhibition or display of the exhibit objects at the Solomon R. Guggenheim Museum, New York, New York, from on or about May 22, 2003, to on or about September 7, 2003, the Menil Collection, Houston, Texas, from on or about October 2, 2003, to on or about January 11, 2004, and at possible additional venues yet to be determined, is in the national interest."

40 *See* Plaintiffs' Amended Complaint, 9 January 2004, at 3, 15.

that, as a result of Amsterdam's alleged repeated violations of international law, they have suffered damages entitling them to compensatory damages in an amount to be determined by the Court.[41]

I will not go into the afore mentioned acquisition of the artworks in 1958 by the City of Amsterdam, as the principal question is of a procedural nature; the heirs claim that the US Court has jurisdiction over the dispute under the FSIA, as in this case the City should not be entitled to immunity.[42]

Specifically, the heirs have invoked the FSIA's expropriation exception of 28 USC. Sections 1603(a) and 1605(a)(3), whereby a foreign state (including a political subdivision thereof) shall not be immune from suit in a case in which rights in property taken in violation of international law are in issue and that property is present in the United States in connection with a commercial activity carried on in the United States by a foreign state (or political subdivision). The heirs claim that the City of Amsterdam violated international law, and they rely on the recent presence of the fourteen artworks in the United States in connection with an alleged commercial activity.[43]

In the heirs' view, the exhibition of the artworks in the two US museums fulfilled the conditions of the FSIA, as the artworks were present in the United States at the time the heirs filed their complaint, and the heirs consider the loan by the Stedelijk Museum to constitute commercial activity.[44]

On 30 April 2004, the City of Amsterdam filed its motion for summary dismissal of the complaint.[45] The foundations of this motion are basically the following.

---

41 *Id.*, at 17-19.

42 *Id.*, at 3-4.

43 *Id.*, at 5.

44 The words "Present in the United States in connection with a commercial activity" are sometimes interpreted rather liberally. In *Republic of Austria* v. *Altmann* (*see supra* n. 31), Maria Altmann argued that by selling a catalogue in the United States containing photos of certain paintings, Austria had forfeited its immunity under the FSIA. The District Court and the Court of Appeals held that the Gallery's activities in the United States, such as publishing and advertising, satisfied the condition of the FSIA that the Gallery, as an 'agency or instrumentality of a foreign state' was engaged in commercial activity in the United States and that therefore the Courts could have competence in this case, even without those paintings being present in the US. The Supreme Court did not go into an analysis of this question. It should be pointed out that the *Malewicz* case has nothing to do with the restitution of Holocaust-related art – the Holocaust does not feature in this case.

45 The City of Amsterdam's motion to dismiss the amended complaint in its entirety ('Motion to dismiss'), 30 April 2004.

As a political subdivision of the Netherlands, the City of Amsterdam qualifies as a "foreign state" under the FSIA.[46] As such, the City of Amsterdam presumably is immune from jurisdiction and suit in the United States courts and claims against the City are barred unless the FSIA's pertinent exception to immunity applies.[47] The City of Amsterdam claimed that the heirs were not able to satisfy any of the required elements of the exception,[48] so that the court lacks subject-matter jurisdiction.[49] The City pointed out that the heirs cannot claim an expropriation in violation of international law, unless they first have exhausted all of their remedies in the Dutch courts.[50] The heirs refrained from doing so, even though the courts in the Netherlands are available to them and courts in the United States have acknowledged the adequacy of the legal system in the Netherlands.[51] The fourteen artworks at issue were temporarily present in the United States in connection with exhibitions in New York and Houston. After these exhibitions, the artworks returned to Amsterdam. The City of Amsterdam emphasized that this is insufficient to be considered "present in the United States" under the FSIA,[52] and that, in any event, the artworks were no longer "present in the United States" at the relevant time. An important reason why the City believes in this case the "present in the United States"-condition has not been fulfilled for legal purposes, is that the artworks were brought into the United States while enjoying immunity from judicial process under 22 USC., Section 2459 (see *supra* 3.2).[53] The City of Amsterdam stated furthermore that, in spite of what has been claimed by the heirs, the loan of the artworks by the Stedelijk Museum did not constitute any "commercial activity".[54] The loan was not the type of activity by which a private actor

46 This follows from 28 USC. para. 1603(a); *see supra* Section 2.3.

47 *See* Motion to dismiss, at 1.

48 These elements were: Rights in property taken in violation of international law are at issue, the property is present in the United States, in connection with a commercial activity carried on in the United States by a foreign state.

49 *See* Motion to dismiss, at 2, 10.

50 *Id.*, at 3.

51 *Id.*, at 4.

52 *Id.*, at 4.

53 *Id.*, at 4.

54 The City referred to the FSIA, which defines "commercial activity" as "either a regular course of commercial conduct or a particular commercial transaction or act", as well as to the judgement of the US Supreme Court in *Republic of Argentina* v. *Weltover, Inc*, 504 US 607 (1993), at 614, in which the Supreme Court explained that determining whether "commercial activity" exists requires an inquiry into "whether the particular

would engage in trade and traffic or commerce. In the view of the City, the loan and exhibition should be regarded as a non-commercial cultural exchange between non-profit educational institutions.[55]

So, as none of the required elements of the FSIA's expropriation exception could be fulfilled, the City maintained that it was immune from suit and that the complaint should be dismissed with prejudice.[56] The City submitted a number of additional arguments challenging the US Court's jurisdiction, which go beyond the scope of this analysis.

4.2 The Role of the US Authorities

On the basis of 28 USC., paragraph 517,[57] it is possible for the US Department of State to file a Statement of Interest with a US Court and thereby inform the Court of the US administration's view on certain legal issues presented by a particular case.

On 22 December 2004, the State Department and the Department of Justice filed such a Statement of Interest,[58] to inform the US District Court of the background and purpose of Section 2459 (see *supra* 3.2) and to present their concerns as to the potential effects of the heirs' lawsuit upon the interests that Section 2459 is designed to foster.[59] The US authorities pointed out that under 22 USC., Section 2459, the artworks concerned were considered to be immune from seizure and other forms of judicial process while in the United States and that until the present proceeding, 22 USC., Section 2459 has served as an effective and efficient means for protecting these kinds of artworks from litigation.[60] The US authorities recalled in their Statement of Interest that Congress' stated purpose in enacting Section 2459 was "to encourage the exhibition in

---

actions that the foreign sovereign performs are the type of actions by which a private party engages in trade and traffic or commerce".

55 *See* Motion to dismiss, at 5–7.

56 *Id.*, at 10.

57 "The Solicitor General, or any officer of the Department of Justice, may be sent by the Attorney General to any State or district in the United States to attend to the interests of the United States in a suit pending in a court of the United States, or in a court of a State, or to attend to any other interest of the United States."

58 Statement of Interest of the United States, dated 22 December 2004 ('Statement of Interest').

59 *Id.*, at 2.

60 *Id.*, at 1.

the United States of objects of cultural significance which, in the absence of assurances such as are contained in the legislation, would not be available". At the time Section 2459 was enacted, such objects had become more vulnerable to lawsuits as a result of the enactment of the Second Hickenlooper Amendment,[61] approximately one year prior to the promulgation of Section 2459.[62] That Amendment sharply restricted application of the Act of State doctrine as a barrier to jurisdiction over claims to property allegedly taken in violation of international law. The immunity provided by Section 2459 thus addressed the threat to cultural exchange posed by the increased vulnerability to lawsuits of foreign artwork on temporary loan to US cultural institutions.[63]

The US authorities expressed the fear that the 'unprecedented' approach of the heirs would introduce a great level of uncertainty as to whether sovereign lenders will be confronted with greater litigation risks, simply by means of an immunized exhibit into the United States.[64] They also feared that this can result in frictions in US relations with other countries.[65] The authorities called it undisputed that the heirs could not seek to seize the artworks while they were in the country under a grant of immunity. It also appeared to be undisputed to the United States that if the heirs had filed their lawsuit prior to the importation of these works, or following their departure, the court would have had no jurisdiction over their claims. The heirs were therefore using the window of opportunity afforded by the US exhibition as the jurisdictional hook for their claims.[66]

Regarding the condition in Section 1605(a)(3) of the FSIA that artworks at stake should be "present in the United States in connection with a commercial activity carried on in the United States by a foreign state", the US authorities emphasized that foreign states are unlikely to expect that this condition is satisfied by a loan of an artwork for a US government-immunized exhibit that must be carried out by a borrower on a non-profit basis. The possibility that such a minimal level of contact will necessarily suffice to provide jurisdiction threatens to chill the willingness of sovereign lenders to participate in the Section 2459 program. Just as a foreign lender will be less likely to send valuable artwork to the United States if the artwork is subject to seizure while

61 22 USC., para. 2370(e)(2).

62 *See* Statement of Interest, at 5.

63 *Id.*, at 6.

64 *Id.*, at 2.

65 *Id.*, at 6.

66 *Id.*, at 4.

it is there, such a lender will be discouraged from lending such works if the loan will provide the sole jurisdictional basis for an expropriation lawsuit that could not have occurred in the absence of the loan, the US authorities pointed out.[67] The authorities ended their Statement with an appeal to the District Court to consider the interest of the United States where appropriate in evaluating the City's motion to dismiss.[68]

On 17 March 2005, the US authorities filed a Supplemental Statement of Interest,[69] "to explain further their concerns that a finding of jurisdiction based solely on lending immunized artwork for a cultural exhibition will undermine the purposes of Section 2459".[70] The United States restated that if jurisdiction over a sovereign lender could be established solely by virtue of introduction into the United States of an exhibit immunized under Section 2459, foreign states would be far less likely to agree to share their artwork with the American public.[71] This would undermine the principal objective of Section 2459. A finding of no jurisdiction in this case would merely prevent claimants from transforming into a sword what was intended to be only a shield.[72]

4.3 The March 2005 Memorandum Opinion of the US District Court[73]

On 30 March 2005, Judge Rosemary M. Collyer of the US District Court for the District of Columbia issued an Order stating that "Defendant's motion to dismiss is DENIED." In the Memorandum Opinion accompanying the Order, the District Court stated that it intends to convene a status conference to determine whether the parties wish to proceed by way of affidavits or limited jurisdictional discovery to develop record evidence on whether, through its immunized loan of cultural and educational artworks, the City of Amsterdam had "substantial contacts with the United States" within the meaning of 28 USC., paragraph 1603(e).[74] The Court came to its conclusion on the basis of the following reasoning.

---

67 *Id.*, at 7.
68 *Id.*, at 8.
69 Supplemental Statement of Interest of the United States, 17 March 2005.
70 *See* Supplemental Statement of Interest, at 1–2,
71 *Id.*, at 2–3, 4.
72 *Id.*, at 7.
73 Malewicz *v.* City of Amsterdam, 362 F. Supp. 2d 298 (D.D.C. 2005).
74 At that time, the Court will also inquire of the City whether it will waive any potential statute-of-limitation defences otherwise available before the Dutch courts.

The Court tried to answer the question whether it had jurisdiction to hear the merits of the complaint. The Court acknowledged that the FSIA is the "sole basis for obtaining jurisdiction over a foreign state in our courts". The Court went on to point out that the City of Amsterdam is therefore immune from the jurisdiction of the courts of the United States, unless one of the FSIA statutory exceptions would apply.

The Court concluded that the heirs' filing of the complaint while the artworks were physically present in the United States was sufficient to meet the "present in the United States" factor. Whether the artworks were present in the United States also for purposes of legal process raised a different question. After all, the City argued that the fourteen Malevich works at issue were protected by the immunity from judicial process and therefore were not "present in the United States" for legal purposes. The Court emphasized that it was undisputed that the heirs could not seek to seize the artworks while they were in the US under a grant of 22 USC., Section 2459 (the Federal Immunity from Seizure Act). As the heirs did not contend that they could have filed this suit prior to the importation of the works or following the departure, the Court observed that the heirs were using the window of opportunity afforded by the Malevich exhibitions as the jurisdictional hook for their claims. The Court considered it beyond doubt that Section 2459 protects loaned artworks and cultural items from seizure or judicial process "for the purpose or having the effect of depriving such [US cultural] institution … of custody or control of such object". A litigant with a claim against a foreign sovereign may not seize that sovereign's property which is in the US on a cultural exchange, and the litigant may not serve the borrowing museum with judicial process to interfere in any way with its physical custody or control of the artworks. The Court noted that the Malevich heirs had tried to do neither. They have sued the City of Amsterdam, not the Guggenheim or The Menil Collection. Had this lawsuit begun and concluded before the Malevich collection left the US, no order of a US Court would have, or could have, affected the custody or control that the museums (and carriers) exercised over the artworks. The Federal Immunity from Seizure Act deprives all US Courts from taking any action to obtain physical custody of the Malevich collection or other cultural objects granted immunity while in the United States. The presence or absence of the property makes no difference during the litigation, as long as it was "present" when suit was filed, the Court explained. Because the Malevich heirs were not seeking judicial seizure of the artworks, the Court considered the City's reliance on Section 2459 misplaced, as immunity from seizure is not the same as immunity from suit for a declaration of rights or for damages arising from an alleged conversion if the other conditions for FSIA jurisdiction are satisfied. The Court therefore concluded that the fourteen artworks were "present in the United States" for the purposes of FSIA jurisdiction.

With reference to 28 USC., paragraph 1603(e), the Court held that "commercial activity carried out in the United States by a foreign state" means "commercial activity carried out by such state and having substantial contact with the United States". Regarding these commercial activities, the key question is whether the foreign sovereign's contract is "of the same character as a contract which might be made by a private person". The Court in this case referred to the judgement of the Supreme Court in *Republic of Argentina* v. *Weltover, Inc.*:[75] "Because the Act provides that the commercial character of an act is to be determined by reference to its "nature" rather than its "purpose", the question is not whether the foreign government is acting with a profit motive or instead with the aim of fulfilling uniquely sovereign objectives. Rather, the issue is whether the particular actions that the foreign state performs (whatever the motive behind them) are the type of actions by which a private party engages in "trade and traffic or commerce". And also 28 USC., paragraph 1603(d) states: "The commercial character of an activity shall be determined by reference to the nature of the course of conduct or particular transaction or act, rather than by reference to its purpose". With that understanding, the Court concluded that the City of Amsterdam had engaged in 'commercial activities' when it loaned the fourteen Malevich works to museums in the United States. Regarding the key element of "substantial contact with the United States", the City of Amsterdam argued that the City's contacts with the US were insubstantial and insufficient to expose it to FSIA jurisdiction. The Court concluded that it could not at this stage of the proceedings determine whether the City of Amsterdam's contacts with the United States in connection with the loan of the Malevich artworks were "substantial" within the meaning of the FSIA, 28 USC., paragraph 1603(e) to support jurisdiction. The extent and nature of the City of Amsterdam's contacts with the United States therefore had to be identified and addressed before it would be possible for the Court to determine its own jurisdiction, or lack thereof, over the heirs' complaint.

75 504 US 607 (1992).

4.4 Continuation after the Lower Court's Order

On 6 April 2005, the City of Amsterdam lodged an appeal with the United States Court of Appeals for the District of Columbia against the negative interlocutory order issued by the District Court on 30 March 2005.[76]

The fact that the motion of the City of Amsterdam was dismissed in March 2005 does not mean that the proceeding has reached its substantive phase; the Memorandum Opinion of the District Court did not consider all the jurisdictional arguments that had been put forward by the City. The City of Amsterdam nonetheless appeared to consider that the filing of an appeal was appropriate in the circumstances. After all, by its Order of 30 March 2005, the City's motion to dismiss had been 'denied' by the District Court.

The heirs disagreed and argued that the District Court did not issue a definite opinion on the immunity question, pointing out that the Court suggested that more information would be necessary to reach a final conclusion on the element of the substantiality of US contacts in connection with the loan to the US museums. Therefore, the Court of Appeals was called upon to rule whether the appeal of the City of Amsterdam was ripe.

To support the views expressed by the City of Amsterdam, and earlier by the US Department of State, the Association of Art Museum Directors (AAMD) and nearly forty American and foreign museums filed a motion for leave to file a brief as *amici curiae*, which is possible on the basis of US procedural law.[77] In such a motion, the court is asked to take into account the views of the AAMD and the museums.

---

76 In *Beecham* v. *Socialist People's Libyan Arab Jamahiriya*, 424 F.3d 1109 (D.C. Cir. 2005) the US Court of Appeals for the District of Columbia stated: "In cases arising under the Foreign Sovereign Immunities Act, we have recognized our jurisdiction to review a district court's order denying a foreign state's motion to dismiss on the ground of sovereign immunity. The theory is that under the collateral order doctrine, *see Cohen* v. *Benficial Indus. Loan Corp.*, 337 US 541 (1949), such orders finally determine the foreign state's right to be immune from burdens of a lawsuit altogether. *See, e.g.*, Jungquist *v.* Sheikh Sultan Bin Khalifa al Nahyan, 115 F.3d 1020, 1025-26 (D.C. Cir. 1997)". Under US law, sovereign defendants have the right to immediately appeal against a negative decision regarding immunity questions with the US Court. This appeal will be given preferential treatment in relation to the other aspects of the case, and will freeze the procedure before the lower court for the duration of the appeal. If the higher court comes to the conclusion that the lower court unjustly rejected the immunity defence, the whole case will be terminated because of lack of jurisdiction.

77 *See* for more on the issue of *amici curiae* briefs the contribution of W. van Reenen in this book.

On 10 January 2006, the US Court of Appeals for the District of Columbia Circuit ruled that it did not have appellate jurisdiction to review the District Court's interlocutory order issued on 30 March 2005.[78,79] Also, for these reasons, the Court of Appeals dismissed the motion to file an *amici curiae* brief as moot. Therefore, the case was referred back to the District Court for a determination on the issue of the substantiality of US contacts in the context of the question of immunity from jurisdiction.

5 Concluding Remarks

As a result of the March 2005 Memorandum Opinion of the US District Court, especially its interpretation of the Federal Immunity from Seizure Act, it is unclear whether foreign museums and institutions now must fear being brought within the jurisdiction of a US Court notwithstanding the issuance of an Immunity from Seizure Declaration by the US Department of State. From the Statements of Interest of the US State Department and the Department of Justice, it can be concluded that it was their intention to safeguard the artworks against any measures of constraint or judicial process, whereas the lower court gave a more limited interpretation. If such a Declaration does not shield the foreign lending museum from the jurisdiction of a US Court, this interpretation, if allowed to stand, could have a 'chilling effect' on the cultural exchange between the United States and the rest of the world. It could lead to foreign museums, especially those that otherwise might enjoy sovereign immunity, becoming hesitant to provide works of art on loan to US museums and institutions. This presumably was the reason why the US government filed its two Statements of Interest, and why US museums filed their *amici curiae* motion.

In the end, it might turn out to be necessary for the United States Congress to amend the Federal Immunity from Seizure Act to reflect more appropriately the purpose of the US government in issuing Immunity from Seizure Declarations so as to provide foreign institutions and museums with the full protection they desire. This, however, would probably be a rather time-consuming process.

---

78 Malewicz *v.* City of Amsterdam, 2006 US App. LEXIS 615 (D.C. Cir., Jan. 10, 2006).

79 The Court of Appeals stated: "[…] the district court properly moved beyond the pleadings to resolve its jurisdiction. […] At this point, however, the district court has not ordered jurisdictional discovery. Any decision by this court now would be premature". *See* Beecham *v.* Socialist People's Libyan Arab Jamahiriya, 424 F.3d 1109 (D.C. Cir. 2005).

In the meantime, interested parties will have to await the final outcome of the US lawsuit initiated by the Malevich heirs.

12

SENDING DUTCH TROOPS ABROAD, SOME DOMESTIC LEGAL ASPECTS

Liesbeth Lijnzaad[*]

1 INTRODUCTION

People everywhere, the Netherlands included, disagree with their governments. One of the issues that tends to lead to considerable debate is the way in which the government decides on issues of peace and security, ranging from strategical issues, such as whether to accept the stationing of nuclear weapons on one's territory, or the choice to deploy troops abroad. With straight-forward situations of self-defence against an attack on the territory being rare in Western Europe, attention focuses on situations where there may be no imminent need for a government to deploy troops abroad, but such deployment would rather be a policy choice. People may want to question the wisdom of such decisions, discuss the reasons for sending troops and consider whether alternatives to military action, such as negotiations, are still available. It has thus become a matter for public debate whether military participation in a certain conflict is indeed the best possible choice. Such choices, while clearly being political decisions, have legal aspects in the Netherlands legal order.

* Deputy head of the International Law Division of the Ministry of Foreign Affairs of the Kingdom of the Netherlands. Thanks are due to J.F.R.Boddens Hosang and J.J.P. Nijssen, who were so kind to read my draft and made useful comments. The opinions in this essay are solely the author's and do not necessarily represent those of the Kingdom of the Netherlands.

N. Blokker, R. Lefeber, L. Lijnzaad & I. van Bladel (eds.), *The Netherlands in Court. Essays in Honour of Johan G. Lammers*, © 2006 Koninklijke Brill NV. Printed in the Netherlands, pp. 247-264.

The legal framework for sending troops abroad lies at the crossroads of constitutional law and international law, and it has occupied the Ministry of Foreign Affairs in recent years. During the tenure as Legal Adviser of Johan Lammers, the number of court cases relating to the deployment of Dutch troops abroad has risen significantly. Also, Article 100 of the Netherlands constitution came into force providing a procedure on informing parliament about sending Dutch troops abroad. In the following, I will focus on the specific parliamentary procedure developed in the 1990s with respect to foreign military missions, as well as the frequently used step of trying to obtain an injunction against a government decision to participate in foreign missions. Both are ways to discuss the legal aspects of foreign military missions, and merit a comparative analysis. It would appear that both approaches, of either taking the government to court or a parliamentary debate, have more connections than one would expect at first sight.

2 Article 100 of the Netherlands Constitution

With the increased willingness of the government to contribute troops to military missions abroad, in particular to peace-keeping activities under the aegis of the Security Council, the Dutch parliament has in the 1990s become increasingly concerned about its ability to monitor such decisions, and indeed its role in the decision-making with respect to such missions.

Some see this concern as directly related to the presence of Dutch troops in Srebrenica in Bosnia and Herzegovina, where in July 1995 a massacre took place in the presence of Dutch peacekeepers. Senator Van Middelkoop, the intellectual father of the constitutional framework for the involvement of parliament in decisions on sending troops abroad that was to develop, has however asserted that the origins of the idea of constitutional rules on parliamentary involvement with sending Dutch troops abroad lies some years earlier. Whilst still a member of parliament, Van Middelkoop raised the issue in a parliamentary session in May 1993, expressing a wish to develop a formal basis for the existing constitutional practice of the government sharing its intention to send troops with parliament.[1] The government, however, had no intention of complying with this suggestion.

1 TK, 1992-1993, Handelingen 28, at 4968.

Early discussions about parliamentary involvement with foreign missions of the Netherlands military led to the development of a so-called "Assessment Framework" (*Toetsingskader*)[2] which the government first shared with parliament in 1995. This policy instrument sets out the conditions and criteria that are relevant to deciding on the participation of Dutch troops in foreign operations. While this has been described as a "rather loose set of points of attention which play a role in deciding whether or not to place Dutch troops at the disposition of international missions"[3], in practice it provides guidance for the preparation of missions. The framework is within the public domain and it is understood to be a set of policy rules that are not legally binding. It has become an important part of the discussions on foreign missions between government and parliament.

Since the inclusion of Article 100 in the Constitution in 2000, a parliamentary committee reported on the practice of foreign military missions and the role of the Assessment Framework in the preceding period, which lead to a revised Assessment Framework in 2001.[4] By 2006, a parliamentary commission headed by member of parliament Van Baalen produced a Report on the parliamentary involvement with decision-making about participation in the NATO response force and the EU battle groups.[5] This report also focuses on the constitutional rules on sending troops abroad.

Article 100 and the Assessment Framework may appear to be two sides of the same coin. In practice, the framework is a policy tool that has helped to structure the information that needs to be contained in an Article 100 letter, which will be discussed further below.

Van Middelkoop's motion held that a formal right of consent must be granted to parliament with respect to the deployment of military units abroad.[6] He later indicated that the reasons for this proposal were threefold: it is necessary that parliament consider the requests for military support made to the government by international organizations, that parliament takes its responsibility vis-à-vis the families of the military, and finally that it is hard to understand why parliament should have a constitutional role with respect to the ratification

2 TK, 1994-1995, 23 591 No. 5.

3 L.F.M. Besselink, *The constitutional duty to promote the development of the international legal order: the significance and meaning of article 90 of the Netherlands Constitution*, 34 NYIL 89 (2003) (hereafter: Besselink, *Article 90*), at 122.

4 TK, 2000-2001, 23 591 No. 7.

5 TK, 2005-2006, 30 162 No. 3 (hereafter: Van Baalen report). The report is under consideration at the time of writing.

6 TK, 1994-1995, 23 591 No. 2.

of treaties[7] but no analogous role with respect to the military arrangements with international organisations that underpin the deployment of troops abroad.[8]

The government's view has been that it was unconstitutional and undesirable for parliament to be involved in taking the actual decision. It is a policy decision of the government to contribute troops, which will come under parliamentary scrutiny once the decision had been taken. Also, it was felt that if parliament would be formally involved in taking the actual decision, this would limit its possibility to control the actions of the troops and to hold the cabinet responsible if necessary, as missions would then take place on the basis of the joint authority of the government and of parliament. Parliament would thus have lost its possibility to formulate an independent opinion on the success, or lack thereof, of a particular mission. In that view co-decisional authority of parliament would limit the political responsibility for such decisions.

However, Van Middelkoop's motion had been widely supported in parliament and the government considered that the formulation of a specific obligation for it to provide information on the intended contribution of troops could be an acceptable alternative. There was hesitation to formulate a specific right to information with respect to foreign military missions, as the constitution already contained a general right to information for parliament in Article 68.[9] In the end, with great reluctance, the government submitted a proposal for the future Article 100 to parliament in May 1997.

It should be mentioned that there are noticeable differences between Article 68 and what was to become Article 100. The first provision contains the traditional obligation for members of the cabinet to provide any information requested by parliament, unless this would be contrary to the interests of the State. This implies that the initiative lies with parliament, and that information may be requested both about future steps (such as policy decisions yet to be formalized) and about past events, the latter being probably the usual case. Hypothetically, Article 68 could also still apply to the deployment of troops abroad, even if it may be doubted that this will be necessary now that Article 100 has been included in the Constitution. Article 100 on the other hand puts the obligation on the government – it is for the cabinet to inform parliament

---

7 Art. 91 Constitution.

8 E. van Middelkoop, *De inzet van strijdkrachten zonder toestemming van de Staten-Generaal, reactie*, 44 NJB (1998) at 2022-2023.

9 Art. 68 reads: "Ministers and State Secretaries shall provide, orally or in writing, the Houses either separately or in joint session with any information requested by one or more members, provided that the provision of such information does not conflict with the interests of the State".

once a decision has been taken, irrespective of whether there is an interest in that information. The provision opens the possibility to control prior to the troops actively operating abroad.

Commentators have remarked that the provision does not specify exactly what type of information needs to be provided.[10] While this is true, it may be noted that constitutional provisions are rarely that detailed, and also that over the years a practice has developed and will continue to develop on the kind of information to provide. Clearly, this is an aspect where parliament may be able to exert its influence by indicating the kind of things it wishes to see in the Article 100 letters.

Article 100 reads:

> 1. The Government shall inform the States General in advance if the armed forces are to be deployed or made available to maintain or promote the international legal order. This shall include the provision of humanitarian aid in the event of armed conflict.
> 2. The provisions of paragraph 1 shall not apply if compelling reasons exist to prevent the provision of information in advance. In this event, information shall be supplied as soon as possible.[11]

Eventually the text of Article 100 was adopted, yet some parliamentarians continue to hold the view that even if it is not a formal right of consent, it substantively is.[12] In their view, parliament had gained a substantive right of consent with respect to foreign missions. This view must be understood as meaning that the information provided prior to the mission might lead to debate followed by the expression by parliament of its disapproval of a particular mission. The importance of a broad acceptance of such missions by parliament and indeed by the Dutch society at large is stressed, and it is suggested that

---

10 L.F.M. Besselink & R. de Lange, *Kroniek Staatsrecht*, 77 Ars Aequi katern, at 3994; L.F.M. Besselink, *Militaire acties en de rol van het parlement*, 39 NJB (2001) at 1883-1887 (hereafter: Besselink, *Militaire acties*).

11 Art. 100 was adopted as part of the revision of the constitutional provision on international relations and defence; Stb. 2000, 294, of 18 July 2000. During the discussions on the formulation of the provision, one of the issues looked at was its location in the Constitution. It has been a deliberate choice to put this provision as Art. 100, in the sense that this numbering would make this obligation more visible, even if that was merely a psychological consideration.

12 *See* Van Baalen report, *supra* n. 5, at 18-19, for a discussion of this reading of Art.100; and J. van Schooten-van der Meer, *Inleiding artikelen 96-103: veiligheid, in* A.K. Koekkoek (ed.), De Grondwet 492 (2000) at 492-493.

in case such support is missing, the cabinet would in all likelihood not persist in sending troops. A negative reception of the plan to deploy troops cannot be ignored.[13]

This view of Article 100 as providing a substantive right of consent to parliament has been criticized by constitutional lawyers, who stress that the government may ignore disapproval from parliament.[14] There is no formal prohibition on acting contrary to the political views of parliament, unless of course the political situation would be such as to cause the government to fall.

The process of sending troops abroad tends to be initiated with a simple letter, the so-called "notification letter", indicating that the government is considering sending troops abroad.[15] At that time no decision has yet been taken, and the letter tends to contain barely any information, as substantive information will be put in the formal Article 100 letter which will provide the motivation for participation as well as information on operational and legal aspects. Article 100 provides that the government shall provide information after a decision has been taken and before troops are formally committed at international level and actions take place, unless time constraints make this impossible.[16] The government will take an autonomous decision on the deployment of troops, and a discussion with parliament on the basis of the information provided may follow after that decision and on the basis of the information provided to parliament, though this is by no means necessary. It is for parliament to initiate a debate.[17]

At the end of 2005, considerable discussion took place in parliament as to the question of whether Article 100 also applied to a *possible* decision to send troops abroad. The government had sent a letter to parliament that had all the characteristics of an Article 100 letter except for the fact that the word 'decision' was not mentioned. The letter concerned considering participation in ISAF[18] in Uruzgan, Afghanistan,[19] and was followed by another message that indicated that the government would decide about the mission, or possibly amend the mission, after discussion with parliament.[20] These communications

13 *See* Van Middelkoop, *supra* n. 8, at 2023, and P.P.T. Bovend'eert, *De inzet van strijdkrachten zonder toestemming van de Staten-Generaal*, 35 NJB 1594 (1998) at 1598.
14 *See* Bovend'eert, *supra* n. 13, at 1595-1597; and Besselink, *Militaire acties*, *supra* n. 10.
15 *See* TK, 2000-2001, 23 591, No. 7 at 4-5 for a description of the agreed procedure.
16 Besselink & de Lange, *supra* n. 10, at 3994; Bovend'eert, *supra* n. 13, at 1596.
17 C.A.J.M. Kortmann, Constitutioneel Recht (2001) at 184-185.
18 International Security Assistance Force.
19 TK, 2005-2006, 27 925, No. 193.
20 *Id.*, No. 194.

caused confusion, to say the least. Then the government stated it had "the intention to participate in ISAF",[21] creating a situation in which parliament refused to accept the communications as the start of the Article 100 procedure. Later, the government stated its "willingness" to participate in Uruzgan, adding "that this had been so decided at an earlier stage".[22] Parliament was not particularly happy with the way this developed, and was particularly concerned about the lack of clarity on what had been decided, a confusion caused by the different positions expressed by the government.[23]

Without wanting to discuss the party political aspects of this discussion, it must be noted that the implication of understanding Article 100 as covering a *possible* decision to deploy troops would seem to shift the obligation to provide prior information towards a right of prior consent for parliament, which had in earlier stages clearly not been the intention.[24] Article 100 would then become a procedure for testing the waters, for sounding out parliamentary views on a possible mission. In case of a negative parliamentary reaction to a *proposed, potential* or *possible* decision it is very likely that such a decision would not be taken in the end. This would in fact truly be substantive decision-making by parliament.

3 Article 100 within the Netherlands Constitution

The formulation of the rule on parliamentary information prior to foreign missions must be seen in the perspective of the constitutional provisions dealing with international relations and defence, Articles 90 to 100.[25] This part of the Constitution begins with Article 90 providing the framework for the Netherlands' actions in foreign relations.[26] Article 90 states: "The government shall promote the development of the international legal order". This formula was put in the constitution in 1983 to underline the broadly shared view of the Dutch role in international relations – the emphasis on contributing to the development

21 *Id.*, No. 195.

22 *Id.*, No. 197.

23 A motion was adopted stressing the need for clear decision-making with respect to Art. 100: *id.*, No. 203.

24 *See* TK, 1997-1998, 25 367, No. 5; EK, 1997-1998, 25 367, No. 226 b.

25 Chapter 5, Legislation and Administration, para. 2: Miscellaneous Provisions. The provisions on defence were amended in the 2000 review of the constitution. *See* Besselink, *Article 90, supra* n. 3, at 120-123, for the genesis of the provision.

26 *See* Besselink, *Article 90, supra* n. 3.

of the international legal order. As a constitutional provision it does not create specific obligations for the government nor does it create specific rights for parliament or for citizens, but it expresses a widely held view of a crucial component of Dutch foreign policy.

This reference to the promotion of the international legal order can similarly be found in Article 97 of the Constitution describing the two roles of the Netherlands' armed forces: the protection of the interests of the State as well as the maintenance and promotion of the international legal order. Here the scope is broader: the armed forces have a role not just with respect to the development of the international legal order, but also its maintenance. The notion of the maintenance and promotion of the international legal order returns in Article 100, and thus ties providing information to parliament about the deployment of troops abroad to the Netherlands' concern with the development of the international legal order. Article 100 picks up constitutional language on the traditional view of the Netherlands as supporting the legal character of the international system.

The situation in which Article 100 is applicable implies a voluntary and autonomous decision to contribute troops to military actions abroad in support of the international legal order. This must be distinguished from participation in an armed conflict that directly affects the interests of the Netherlands as a State, such as situations of self-defence.[27] Fortunately such situations have not arisen in the recent past, yet if they did they would not fall under Article 100 but rather under the ordinary provision concerning defence in the constitution, Articles 96 to 99.[28] Article 96 establishes the general rule that a state

27 Van Baalen report, *supra* n. 5, at 21-23; *see also*: *Nederland en crisisbeheersing – drie actuele aspecten*, 34 Report Adviesraad Internationale Vraagstukken (Advisory Council on International Affairs), March 2004, at 35 (http://www.aiv-advies.nl).

28 Art. 96:

1. A declaration that the Kingdom is in a state of war shall not be made without the prior approval of the States General.

2. Such approval shall not be required in cases where consultation with Parliament proves to be impossible as a consequence of the actual existence of a state of war.

3. The two Houses of the States General shall consider and decide upon the matter in joint session.

4. The provisions of the first and third paragraphs shall apply *mutates mutandis* to a declaration that a state of war has ceased.

Art. 97:

1. There shall be armed forces for the defence and protection of the interests of the Kingdom, and in order to maintain and promote the international legal order.

2. The Government shall have supreme authority over the armed forces.

of war may only be declared with prior approval of the States General. This is a clear case of prior parliamentary consent, not a mere obligation to inform. Yet, declarations of war have slipped into oblivion since the establishment of the UN Charter and it is doubtful what the contemporary role of this provision really is.

The question of the relevance of Article 100 to situations of self-defence became prominent at the time of the attack on the Twin Towers and the ensuing military reactions.[29] Post 9/11, some authors have expressed the view that actions taken in collective self-defence in which the Netherlands would participate, such as the NATO decision to invoke Article 5 of the North Atlantic treaty, ought to be notified to parliament on the basis of Article 100.[30] Remarkably the attention seems to have focused primarily on the North Atlantic treaty, but it would seem that the more general direct link to the international legal order would in fact be Article 51 of the UN Charter which specifically caters for situations of self-defence.

There are two possibilities as to why this issue was raised at the time – the commentators may have felt that in general it would have been politically desirable to discuss this particular issue with parliament based on information provided under a constitutional obligation. Also under Article 5 of the North Atlantic treaty there is no prescribed way of contributing to the collective self-defence, participating States have the possibility to determine how they will react (albeit that this is coordinated and negotiated).[31] One could thus argue that the government had a choice as to whether and how to participate in the collective self-defence similar to the choices with respect to the maintenance and development of the international legal order. The attacks had a fundamental impact on international relations, and so did the decision to contribute to the ensuing collective self-defence.

Arts. 98 and 99 omitted.

29 TK, 2000-2001, 27 925, No. 1. This is the letter of the Ministers of Foreign Affairs and Defence informing parliament of actions taken by the European Union and NATO. No reference is made to Art. 100.

30 A. Koekkoek, *Voorzichtig met oorlogsverklaring*, NRC Handelsblad, 19 September 2001; N.Schrijver, *De aanslagen op de Verenigde Staten en het Volkenrecht*, 33 NJB (2001) at 1613-1614; Besselink, *Militaire acties*, *supra* n. 10.

31 Art. 5 of the North Atlantic Treaty reads: "[...] each of them, in exercise of the right of individual or collective self-defence recognised by Article 51 of the Charter of the United Nations, will assist the Party or Parties so attacked by taking forthwith, individually and in concert with the other Parties, such action as it deems necessary, [...]"

The other argument may be that action taken in collective self-defence is understood as action to "maintain or promote the international legal order" as stated in Article 100. The emphasis would then probably be on the maintenance of the international legal order rather than its promotion, as self-defence generally aims at the preservation of the *status quo*, or a rapid return to a prior situation. To a certain extent, it is a philosophical question what the connection between self-defence and the international legal order really is. Is the maintenance of international peace and security as the UN Charter puts it in Article 51, the same as the maintenance and promotion of the international legal order as mentioned in the Netherlands Constitution? If "international legal order" is understood as the absence of conflict, then self-defence may be seen as contributing to it in the long term. Others would feel that it is doubtful whether self-defence necessarily contributes to the international legal order as a moral notion. There are no clear answers to this issue, most of all because of the moral and ethical elements encompassed in the concept of the international legal order.

From the point of view of the constitutional law of the Netherlands, the issue of self-defence is a different one. Article 97 is a down-to-earth description of the military reality. The defence and protection of the interests of the Kingdom is the original role of the Netherlands military, quite apart from its relatively new role in the maintenance and promotion the international legal order. The second role of the armed force has a clear connection to Article 100, but the first role of defending and protecting the State does not. Participation in collective self-defence is clearly a form of defence of the interests of the State. So it is understandable that the government never considered itself to be under a formal obligation to provide information about its participation in the self-defence actions following 9/11 under Article 100 of the constitution.

In recent times, the discussion has developed towards the issue of whether the two notions can indeed be kept completely apart, or whether there is a grey zone in which self-defence may gradually become action in support of the maintenance and development of the international legal order. This view, also expressed by the government advisory council on international relations[32] has been understood by government, who have indicated that also in situations where Article 100 would not be applicable, they would be willing to provide information along the lines of the Assessment Framework.[33]

32 *See* AIV report, *supra* n. 27.

33 TK, 2001-2002, Handelingen 24, at 1767. *See also* TK, 2004-2005, Handelingen 56, at 3661.

4 The Article 100 Letters

Article 100 has since the year 2000 led to the practice of sending "Article 100 letters" to parliament. These have developed into an important practice, and have contributed to standardizing the political debate about the foreign missions. There is no prescribed format for such a letter, but it will always refer to the constitutional obligation to provide this information, identifying the letter as an Article 100 letter. Also there will be a passing reference to the fact that the Assessment Framework has been followed when drafting the letter. Frequently it will be sent to parliament within a very short timeframe – such as the day after a resolution was passed, which means that the drafting of the letter has taken place in conjunction with the negotiating of a resolution. The letter is sent by the Ministers of Foreign Affairs and Defence jointly.

These letters will contain a description of the local situation in the operations area, of the nature of the request for a Dutch military contribution, information about the types of materiel and armaments that will be deployed, about the local security situation, and most important from our perspective: the legal underpinning of the mission. While most of the content is thus geared towards a systematic discussion of the elements of the Assessment Framework mentioned earlier, the letters will also contain specific information on the legal basis for a particular mission. Parliament will be interested in the legality of the operation, as the deployment of Dutch troops abroad needs to be properly motivated. Thus the letter will explicitly refer to relevant Security Council decisions with respect to peacekeeping.[34] In general this will relate to the legitimacy of military actions on foreign soil, as the troops would not participate as parties to an armed conflict. Increasingly information is provided on the applicable rules of engagement, which is a subject that has attracted more and more interest in the past years.[35] The information contained in the letter has rarely led to a specific discussion of the legal aspects of a mission in parliament.[36] However, in June 2003, parliament took the initiative to organize a hearing with legal

34 Thus letter TK 2005-2006, 27 925, No. 193, on participation in the ISAF mission in South Afghanistan cites SC Res. 1623.

35 *Id.* This letter explicitly mentions the rules of engagement, and describes how these will be disseminated to the troops during the mission.

36 An exception would be the discussion that led to TK 27 925, 2004-2005, No. 166, describing the legal basis for the participation of Dutch Special Forces in Operation Enduring Freedom in Afghanistan. This is however beyond the scope of this contribution, as this operation took place as collective self-defence, a situation not covered by Art. 100.

experts to discuss the legal underpinning of the Netherlands' participation in actions in Iraq.[37] The discussion specifically dealt with the question whether Security Council Resolution 1483 was indeed a sufficient legal basis for sending troops. This is the only case to date in which parliament specifically discussed the legal aspects of a mission.

Surprisingly, the inclusion of specific legal information in the Article 100 letters has so far received little attention in the constitutional debate, as the discussion has specifically focused on the question whether or not parliament had co-decisional authority. Yet the information on the mandate and its legal underpinning imply that this aspect of the mission may be discussed in parliament, and will form part of the parliamentary debate. As we will see, this has been useful for the government in dealing with court cases in which the legitimacy of the mission is at stake.

In sum, Article 100 of the Netherlands constitution has sought to find a balance between the executive's role of deciding on defence related matters and the desire of parliament to be fully involved in taking such decisions of great importance. The letter has become refined over the years and now includes a specific reference to the mandate and discusses other legal issues surrounding the particular mission, such as the relevant rules of engagement. The constitutional obligation to provide this information has given parliament ample opportunity to consider and, if desired, discuss all aspects of a mission in order to satisfy possible concerns. At the same time some issues related to the scope of the obligation remain, more specifically whether Article 100 would also apply to missions taking part under agreements concerning collective self-defence. The current view of the government is that this is not the case, but this view may come under pressure in future.

5 Taking the Government to the District Court of The Hague

Concern about sending troops abroad is not only an issue for parliament in the Netherlands. In the recent past the government has been taken to court over foreign missions on various occasions.

Foreign missions in the Kosovo conflict, in Afghanistan and in Iraq have led to a number of injunction actions brought against the State. NGOs and

37 On 16 June 2003 a discussion with legal scholars took place. The issue whether the Netherlands would become an occupying power as a consequence of participation in Iraq was one of the matters discussed.

concerned citizens will be able to bring an injunction action on the basis of tort law against a policy decision by the government, provided that they will be able to prove an interest in the issue – in terms of the mandate and statutory aim of their association – as well as demonstrating the urgency required for an injunction action. NGOs with a specific mandate related to the promotion of peace and stability may have a relevant interest, and thus *locus standi* in a domestic court. Once a decision to send troops has been taken, there will normally also be a certain urgency. Thus the option is open to bring an injunction action against the government under civil law rules on tort.

In the Dutch legal system it is relatively easy to take the State to court. There is no immunity for the government on account of the matter being of a military nature, and no so-called "political questions doctrine" would apply in the Dutch judicial system. Under the rule of law, the government needs to reply to cases brought against it, even if on paper such cases may be *prima facie* inadmissible. Consequently the government will have to argue issues of admissibility as well as issues of substance.

In the relevant injunction actions, the plaintiffs have mainly argued that a decision to send troops abroad would be in violation of rules of *ius ad bellum*, or alternatively that a violation of the rules of *ius in bello* (international humanitarian law) was to be foreseen. While the first may be something to discuss prior to the arrival of the troops at their destination, the latter would be an assumption for which there would normally be no factual basis. It is hard to imagine that the Netherlands would send troops abroad with the clear intention to violate international humanitarian law.[38] Frequently complaints before court suffer from a common error, that of mistaking possible violations of the *ius ad bellum* with a prediction of violations of the *ius in bello*. It is a beginner's mistake, mostly made by students, yet all too often repeated before the District Court of The Hague. The analysis of whether the political decision to contribute troops to a particular mission has been taken in violation of the existing rules of *ius ad bellum* is understandably an important one. This may sometimes be a matter for debate, and it is an aspect that is of concern to parliament, in light of the constitutional role of the government to promote the development of the international legal order as laid down in Article 90 of the Netherlands constitution.

An additional argument frequently presented in court is that a particular mission would be contrary to the obligation to develop the international legal

38 Leaving aside the obvious legal question as to whether international humanitarian law would apply in such situations to troops who are not technically a party to the conflict.

order as laid down in Article 90 of the Netherlands constitution. This line of reasoning would seem to assume that a possible violation of international law necessarily leads to a direct violation of constitutional law. In general the Netherlands Constitution is non-justiciable: it is not possible to test the constitutionality of laws.[39] Relying on Article 90 seems to suggest that it would be clear for everyone, the District Court of the Hague included, that a particular mission would be contrary to international law. In giving a thorough analysis of the meaning and content of Article 90 of the Netherlands constitution, Besselink has noted that a reference to this provision is frequently used as referring to desired international law (*lege ferenda*) as opposed to existing international law (*lex lata*).[40]

Over the past few years several cases have been brought against the government of the Netherlands. These concern participation of Dutch troops in the conflict in Serbia and Kosovo, as well as the conflicts in Afghanistan and in Iraq.[41] Four requests for injunctions were brought with respect to the Kosovo conflict,[42] one of them being a rare case concerning the personal responsibility of the individual ministers concerned.[43] The intervention in Afghanistan was and is partially an action of collective self-defence under Article 51 of the UN Charter (Operation Enduring Freedom), and partially an action under the aegis of the Security Council (ISAF). As indicated above, the obligation of providing information to parliament does not formally apply to actions in self-defence.

39 Art. 120 of the Netherlands Constitution reads: "The constitutionality of Acts of Parliament and treaties shall not be reviewed by the Courts".

40 Besselink, *Article 90*, *supra* n. 3, at 131, writes that court cases are "about the international legal order as it should be, not about the legal order as it is".

41 It is important to qualify this list – the Kosovo conflict took place in 1999 when Art. 100 had not yet been adopted.

42 *Vereniging van Juristen voor de Vrede* et al. v. *the Netherlands*, District Court of The Hague, KG 99/69, 18 March 1999; *Danikovic* et al. v. *the Netherlands*, District Court of The Hague, KG 99/339, 7 April 1999; The Hague Court of Appeal, KG 99/0451, 23 November 2000; Supreme Court, C01/027H, 29 November 2002, *published in* 35 NJ (2003) and 35 NYIL 522 (2004); *Tijsterman* et al. v. *the Netherlands*, District Court of The Hague, KG 99/523, 28 May 1999; The Hague Court of Appeal, KG 99/735, 25 March 2004; *Dedovic* et al. v. *Wim Kok, Frank de Grave and Josephus J. van Aartsen* (respectively the Prime Minister, the Minister of Defence and the Minister of Foreign Affairs during the Kosovo conflict), District Court of Amsterdam, KG 99/1222, 3 June 1999; Amsterdam Court of Appeal, 759/99 SKG, 6 July 2000, *reproduced in* 26 NJCM Bull. 208 (2001).

43 *See* W. Ferdinandusse & A. Nollkaemper, *NAVO-Bombardementen op Joegoslavie onrechtmatige daad?*, 26 NJCM Bull. 208-221 (2001) discussing the decision of the Amsterdam Appeals Court in the *Dedovic* case.

One case was brought against the State concerning the conflict in Afghanistan.[44] And finally, the participation of the Netherlands in the conflict in Iraq after the occupation led to two injunction actions.[45]

Consultations in preparation for a court case will take place between the ministries most concerned, normally the Ministry of Foreign Affairs and the Ministry of Defence, and the State Advocate who will be conducting the case before the District Court of The Hague.[46] These consultations will serve to elaborate on the international legal issues related to governmental policy choices. In that respect, the legal basis for sending the troops abroad will be addressed, and this will often directly focus on questions related to the mandate for a particular mission and the political agreements underlying that mission. In its reply to the plaintiffs, the State will – after the admissibility stage – normally refer to the legal basis. Thus the fact that decisions have been taken in the Security Council will be noted, but there will also be attention for the fact that the legal basis has been mentioned in the Article 100 letter and has been discussed in parliament. This amounts to saying that the whole issue of the legitimacy of the mission, though relevant, has already been discussed. As the matter has been the subject of debate with parliament, the argument is that there is no remaining reason to discuss this question before court. Or – to put it differently – the executive has already taken its responsibility of dealing with the matter of the legitimacy, and there is no residual role for the courts.

In terms of the division of power within the State, as the government will take the political responsibility for sending troops abroad, the judiciary is merely called upon to check whether the formalities surrounding such decisions have been fulfilled. The court will frequently take the view that, once the international legal aspects have been or could have been discussed in parliament there is no reason for a court to re-evaluate the political desirability of a mission. This amounts to saying that the plaintiffs are raising their issue in the wrong forum – the debate has already taken place in parliament and there is no room for another discussion in court. This is in a way a classical *trias politica* argument.

44 *Vereniging van Juristen voor de Vrede* et al. v. *the Netherlands*, District Court of The Hague, KG 01/1219, 26 October 2001; The Hague Court of Appeal, KG 01/1216, 16 May 2002; Supreme Court, C02/217HR, 6 February 2004.

45 *Mubarek* et al. v. *the Netherlands*, District Court of The Hague, KG 03/284, 28 February 2003; *Lafteh* et al. v. *the Netherlands*, District Court of The Hague, KG 03/331, 31 March 2003.

46 There is a legal obligation to bring all cases against the State before the District Court of The Hague, as this is the seat of government: Art.1:10(2) Burgerlijk Wetboek *juncto* Art. 99(1) Wetboek van Burgerlijke Rechtsvordering.

From the limited case law on sending troops abroad a number of common threads can be deduced. In particular, four aspects frequently reappear in the decisions in the injunction actions, and following appeals and possible decisions in cassation.

First of all, there is a distinct reticence within the judiciary to pronounce on the legality of foreign missions, since the decisions that underlie the mission are seen as mostly political.[47] Whether or not the law of peace and security has been violated by the government is a matter for which a domestic court may be ill equipped, not only because the civil law division of a domestic court may not be suspected of an extensive knowledge of the law on peace and security, but also because the political judgement and indeed the political responsibility lies with the executive, not with the judiciary. It is rare for a judge to fully review the legality of a policy decision on sending troops abroad, though it sometimes happens.[48] There may be room for a judicial testing of the quality of decision-making, in the sense of establishing whether all relevant aspects have been included in the decision-making process. Some may see this as an approach that is not sufficiently critical of the government, but at times the judiciary have formulated their limited role vis-à-vis international policy decisions very eloquently. What is required is a careful and thorough process that has led to the governmental decision. It is submitted that the adoption of the Article 100 procedure has significantly strengthened the decision-making process and consequently limited the potential role of the judiciary.

A second aspect in the case law is that it confirms that the rules on peace and security are essentially addressed to States, and can not be invoked by individuals. The clearest thread in the court judgments, whether at the level of an injunction action before the District Court of The Hague or before the Supreme Court is that the court will indicate, in one form or another, that Article 2(4) of the UN Charter, frequently mentioned by the plaintiffs, is not the kind of provision that individuals can rely upon as it is clearly addressed to States.[49] This may be obvious to many readers, yet the possibility in Article 93 of the

---

47 *See Danikovic* Supreme Court Judgement, para. 3.3; *Tijsterman* Appeal Judgment, para. 3.2 citing *Danikovic* case; *Mubarek* Judgment, para.7; *Lafteh* Judgment, paras. 4.3-4.4.

48 In the decision in the case of *Vereniging Juristen voor de Vrede* et al. v. *the Netherlands* on the collective self-defence actions in Afghanistan, the judge did fully review the legality.

49 *See Danikovic* Supreme Court Judgment, paras. 8-16; *Juristen voor de Vrede* (Afghanistan) Supreme Court Judgement, para. 3.4; *Dedovic* Appeal Judgment, paras. 5.3.5-5.3.7; *Juristen voor de Vrede* (Kosovo) Injunction Judgment, para. 4; *Lafteh* Judgment, para. 46; *Tijsterman*, Appeal Judgment, para. 2.

Dutch Constitution to invoke provisions of treaties as directly applicable made it necessary to determine whether the obligation to abstain from the use or threat of use of force in international relations belonged to that category.[50] Similarly, judges have indicated that Articles 42 and 51 of the UN Charter do not create individual rights in the Netherlands legal order. This view is so consistent that is may now be understood as standard case law on the issue of the direct applicability of Article 2(4) of the Charter.

A further issue is that the judiciary has not been sympathetic to cases in which the plaintiffs have pointed to the obligation contained in Article 90 of the Constitution, and to the fact that a particular deployment of Dutch troops would in their view be contrary to the aim of promoting the development of the international legal order. The argument based on Article 90 has mostly been received with the comment that one cannot rely on this provision in court.[51]

And finally, the numerous claims that specific rules of international humanitarian law will be violated by Dutch troops, or that Dutch troops will become complicit in violation of the *ius in bello* by others have not been taken up by the courts on account of such complaints frequently not being substantiated. Plaintiffs would tend to refer to Article 52 of Additional Protocol I, the provision on the protection of civilian objects, as well as the issue of collateral damage.[52] With respect to the later issue, courts tend to be satisfied with assurances by the government that all efforts have been taken to prevent such damage, and often note that the plaintiffs have not credibly elaborated on the potential risk they would be facing.

The question may be raised whether these court cases are indeed a genuine threat to government decisions to send troops abroad. While these cases tend to be surrounded by lots of publicity, particularly if a mission is controversial, they have so far not been won. Though there is a significant number of injunction actions being brought against the State, these are rarely reported in law journals but rather in the daily press.[53] Little attention has been given to them in academia. It may well be that the importance of such cases lies in their value

50 Art. 93 of the Netherlands Constitution reads: "Provisions of treaties and of resolutions by international institutions which may be binding on all persons by virtue of their contents shall become binding after they have been published".

51 *Juristen voor de Vrede (*Afghanistan*)* Supreme Court Judgment, para. 3.4; *Tijsterman* Appeal Judgment, para. 45; *Mubarek* Judgment, para. 9.

52 *Dedovic* Appeal Judgment, paras. 5.3.19-5.3.24; *Tijsterman* Injunction Judgment, paras. 3.2-3.3.

53 Currently only the *Dedovic* case and *Danikovic* case seem to have been reported, some of the other cases mentioned may be retrieved on http://www.rechtspraak.nl.

in terms of attracting publicity, rather than having the concrete aim of seriously influencing the government. For the government, however, they continue to be a source of concern as it remains essential to indicate that legal considerations have been given due attention in the process leading to the decision to participate in a particular mission.

6 Conclusions

In general, there are different ways to express discontent with a decision of the Netherlands government to send Dutch troops abroad to participate in peacekeeping or peace-enforcement operations. In the foregoing, I have specifically looked at the steps that can be taken within the domestic legal framework, that is either taking the government to court with the aim of obtaining an injunction against the intended participation of Dutch troops in a military operation abroad, or the path leading to a full parliamentary debate on the basis of Article 100 of the Netherlands constitution.

The road towards the creation of Article 100 has not been easy, the government and parliament have had different views on the role of parliament with respect to sending Dutch troops abroad. And even when the provision had been finalized, it turned out that it unexpectedly caused problems towards the end of 2005. This must be related to the fact that issues of peace and security tend to stir up emotions, and at times lead to very politicized debates.

It would appear that even if the possibility exists to bring the matter of sending troops before court, the development of both the Assessment Framework and in particular the so-called Article 100 letters have largely reduced the chances of success for the initiators of such court cases. The judiciary would tend to think that, as the possibility for parliamentary debate on intended participation of Dutch troops had existed, there is but limited possibility for the involvement of the judiciary in such issues. The court cases seem to primarily have a role in publicity.

In the final analysis it would appear that the thoroughness of the information on the legal basis for the operations, as provided in the Article 100 letter, and the way in which this has been debated in parliament are relevant to protecting any government decision against interference by the judiciary. This is an unintended benefit of the establishment in 2000 of the Article 100 procedure, which seems to have put the debate about foreign missions back into the perspective of the *trias politica*: there is no role for the judiciary when the executive has taken a decision and the legislative has had the opportunity to control the actions of the executive. This aspect is certainly not one anticipated by the drafters of Article 100, but it seems to reinforce the views held by the government at the very start of the debate.

www.ingramcontent.com/pod-product-compliance
Lightning Source LLC
LaVergne TN
LVHW080848300926
849162LV00003B/371